A00454532001

W9-CAB-113

PHILOSOPHY OF SOCRATES

GULLEY, NORMAN R

B317.G778 1968

NE

The Philosophy of Socrates

By the same author

PLATO'S THEORY OF KNOWLEDGE

The Philosophy of
Socrates

NORMAN GULLEY

Reader in Classics and Ancient Philosophy
University of Bristol

Macmillan
London · Melbourne · Toronto
St Martin's Press
New York
1 9 6 8

© Norman Gulley 1968

Published by
MACMILLAN AND CO LTD
Little Essex Street London W C2
and also at Bombay Calcutta and Madras
Macmillan South Africa (Publishers) Pty Ltd Johannesburg
The Macmillan Company of Australia Pty Ltd Melbourne
The Macmillan Company of Canada Ltd Toronto
St Martin's Press Inc New York

Library of Congress catalog card no. 68–27596

Printed in Great Britain by
ROBERT MACLEHOSE AND CO LTD
The University Press, Glasgow

Contents

vi

Preface

I have tried in this book to deal comprehensively with the philosophy of Socrates. The book is not concerned with questions of Socratic biography. Nor is it designed to be a contribution to the so-called Socratic problem. It gives reasons for ascribing this or that doctrine to Socrates. But historical questions are not its real business. It is a philosophical study. Those who cannot agree with its conclusions about what is genuinely Socratic thought and what is not will still, I hope, find it a useful study of an important stage in the development of Greek philosophy.

I think there is room for a study of this kind. In recent years there has been a marked increase in the attention given by scholars to problems in the interpretation of Socrates' moral paradoxes and in the assessment of the scope and aims of his method. But there has been no comprehensive study of these problems. In attempting such a study I have given special attention to Aristotle's criticism of Socrates' method and of his moral paradoxes. And I have emphasised the significance of the paradoxes as an illuminating analysis of the Greeks' moral language.

In a final chapter, I have examined Socrates' conception of the good. The moral paradoxes are in this respect uninformative. It is from Socrates' political and religious views and from what it is not too pretentious to call his philosophy of mind that a picture of his moral ideals has to be constructed. Primarily because we have no guidance at all here from Aristotle, the arguments of this chapter are more speculative than those of the earlier chapters. But a study of Socrates' philosophy would be incomplete without some consideration of his conception of the good and of the kind of theoretical framework he used to support it.

I am grateful to the University of Bristol for granting me the term's leave which enabled me to complete this study. I am grateful also to Miss Anne Savery and Miss Rosalind Edwards for preparing the typescript.

Bristol   N. G.
September 1967

Acknowledgments

The author and publishers thank the following for permission to use extracts: Cambridge University Press, for the extract from *Plato's Phaedo*, translated by R. Hackforth; the Clarendon Press, Oxford, for the extract from *The Dialogues of Plato*, vol. 1, translated by Benjamin Jowett.

I

Socratic Method

IF we wish to understand the nature of Socrates' contributions to philosophical thought we must turn initially to the testimony of Aristotle. It is unfortunate that this testimony is rather scanty.[1] The philosophically significant part of it consists principally of (a) a few passages in the *Metaphysics* describing Socrates' influence on the formation of Plato's metaphysical theory, and (b) a few passages in the ethical works discussing Socrates' moral doctrines. Moreover, these passages present the thought of Socrates from Aristotle's own philosophical standpoint. Aristotle selects what appears from that standpoint to be philosophically interesting and worthy of appraisal.

Despite these disadvantages of scantiness and philosophical bias, Aristotle's testimony is of great value. For it is free from the dramatic or apologetic purposes which belong to the portraits of Socrates by Aristophanes, Xenophon and Plato. Aristotle is concerned to give a critical assessment, as a philosopher, of Socrates' thought, to distinguish it from that of other philosophers, and to place it in some kind of historical perspective. And it cannot reasonably be doubted that his basis for this assessment is a knowledge of Socratic thought which is not simply dependent on previous literary presentations of it.

An indication that Aristotle possessed such independent knowledge is that in the *Metaphysics* (1078b, 1086b) he firmly distinguishes Socrates' views from views which we find ascribed to

Socrates in the most impressive of earlier presentations of Socratic thought, the dialogues of Plato. In his long membership of Plato's Academy Aristotle would have had good opportunity to gain that knowledge. He would surely have learned there, from Plato and other members, both about the nature and extent of Socrates' influence on Plato's theory of Forms and about Socrates' positive moral doctrines.

For these reasons Aristotle's testimony is the best starting-point for an assessment of Socrates' thought. Although scanty, it is enough to indicate the originality of Socrates' contributions both to philosophical method and to ethics. And we are able to illustrate and to amplify what Aristotle tells us by reference to Xenophon and Plato. For if we turn from Aristotle's testimony to the Socratic writings of Xenophon and Plato we find in Xenophon's *Memorabilia* and Plato's early dialogues a Socrates whose views, in most philosophically significant respects, agree with those ascribed to him by Aristotle.

We will begin by examining Aristotle's testimony on Socrates' method. There are two passages in the *Metaphysics* (987b1–6, 1078b17–32; cf. 1086a37–b5) which indicate its main features. Aristotle is here giving a historical sketch of the origins of Plato's metaphysical theory and he is assessing Socrates' influence on that theory. This influence, he says, belonged to a time when Socrates was concentrating his interests on moral questions and not at all on natural science. Both Xenophon (*Mem* I i 11–16; cf. IV vii 2–8) and Plato (*Apology* 19c, 29d–30c) similarly represent Socrates as specialising in ethics and turning his back on physical speculations. According to Xenophon, Socrates' reason for rejecting scientific study was that speculation on the nature of the physical universe served no useful purpose and could yield no definite knowledge.[2]

Aristotle goes on to say (i) that Socrates' inquiries were directed to the establishing of general definitions of the virtues, (ii) that Socrates was the first philosopher to concentrate on definition, and (iii) that his search for definitions prompted Plato to find in the problem of general definition a pointer to the metaphysical theory of Forms. Aristotle is not saying here that Socrates was the first to attempt to define anything. He mentions Democritus[3] as an earlier thinker who offered definitions of a superficial kind within his physical theories. What he is saying is that Socrates was the first to make general definition a necessary and important feature in philosophical speculation.

He adds that it was with good reason that Socrates attempted through definition to establish 'what a thing is', since 'he was attempting to syllogise, and the essence is the starting-point in syllogisms'.

This concentration on general definitions is, then, one of the features of Socrates' inquiries which Aristotle singles out as an original contribution to philosophical method. As a second original contribution he mentions 'inductive arguments'. Here again he is not assuming that before Socrates no one made use of inductive arguments. He means that Socrates was the first to make the systematic use of such arguments an essential feature of his philosophical method.

Aristotle concludes his assessment by saying that Socrates, unlike Plato, did not assign independent existence to the universals or definitions.

In examining this assessment it will be necessary to look at Socrates' practice in argument as Xenophon and Plato present it, and to look too, in considering Socrates' originality in this field, at the kind of philosophical argument which would be familiar to Socrates from his contact with other thinkers. But there are certain points in Aristotle's assessment which must first be considered in more detail.

As we have seen, Aristotle thinks that Socrates had good reason to search for general definitions since 'he was attempting to syllogise, and the essence is the starting-point in syllogisms'. Thus he presents Socrates' method as one which aimed to establish general definitions as principles from which other truths were deducible. Elsewhere Aristotle states his own view that the starting-point of all demonstration is a definition of what a thing is, more particularly that it is from the definition of a thing that its essential properties are deducible.[4] Thus it is 'in syllogisms' that a property is shown to belong to a thing by virtue of the thing's 'essence' or definition.

So far it would appear that Aristotle is commending Socrates not only for giving to general definition a central place in his method but also for aiming to use definitions as principles of demon.tration. However, Aristotle now adds (1078b25 ff.), as an explanation for Socrates' adoption of this method, that at this time such 'dialectical power' did not exist as would enable men 'to study contraries independently of the essence and to consider whether contraries are the objects of a single science'.

Aristotle seems to imply by this that, if Socrates had possessed such 'dialectical power', his inquiries in ethics would have benefited from it. Thus he seems to imply that Socrates' method was in some respects unsatisfactory. But what exactly is the nature of his criticism? He is not, of course, denying that Socrates used a dialectical method in the general sense of a conversational method, one which proceeds by question and answer and elicits admissions from an interlocutor. Aristotle elsewhere ascribes to Socrates a dialectical method in this sense.[5] His criticism in the *Metaphysics* is based essentially, I think, on his own conception of the distinction between dialectic and demonstrative science. Alexander, in his commentary on the *Metaphysics*,[6] construed Aristotle's remarks in that way. He assumed that Aristotle is here implicitly contrasting the method used by Socrates with the method of dialectic. He assumed further that the contrast reflects Aristotle's opposition of demonstrative science to dialectic.[7]

This is an opposition between (*a*) a method of *proving* that certain general propositions are true, by showing that they are deducible from premises which are necessary truths, expressing 'what cannot be otherwise', and (*b*) a method described by Aristotle (*Top.* 100a) as one 'by which we shall be able to argue about any proposed problem from probable premises, and shall ourselves under examination avoid self-contradiction'. The aim in dialectic is not to *prove* anything, but to acquire facility in argument and to secure logical consistency. Aristotle does not think, however, that dialectic has an exclusively gymnastic purpose. It can, by its critical analysis, serve as an aid in the discovery of the first principles of the different sciences. Moreover, there are subjects in which the demonstrative syllogism, the method of the demonstrative sciences, is inapplicable and in which dialectic is the only proper method to use. These are subjects in which there are no necessary or invariable truths, in which only what is true 'for the most part' can be established. They lack the 'exactness' of the genuine sciences. Ethics, in Aristotle's view, is one such subject. Method (*b*) rather than method (*a*) is the method appropriate to it. And Aristotle's criticism of Socratic method in ethics would therefore seem to be that Socrates wrongly chose method (*a*).

Now it is in terms of this opposition between demonstrative science and dialectic that Alexander explains Aristotle's remarks. He says that Socrates concentrated on definition, seeking 'definitions of everything', because lack of dialectical power at that time made it impossible to employ syllogisms independently of definition, such as dialectical syllogisms, i.e. syllogisms employing merely probable premisses; hence Socrates chose the method used by 'geometers and the rest', i.e. the method of scientific demonstration from first principles, those principles being definitions.

These comments by Alexander are a valuable guide in interpreting Aristotle's assessment of Socrates. They suggest that Aristotle is assessing Socrates' aim and method in ethics in terms of the aim and method which he himself thinks proper only to scientific demonstration. And Aristotle is criticising Socrates for this scientific conception of ethics, while admitting that at that time the dialectical techniques which were proper to ethical inquiry had not been developed. It would seem too that when Aristotle ascribes to Socrates the use of 'inductive arguments' he is thinking of this feature as part of Socrates' conception of a science of ethics. For when he specifies universal definition and inductive arguments as the two things which may fairly be ascribed to Socrates, he adds that both these 'are concerned with the starting-point of science (*epistēmē*)'. His association of them in this way with the 'starting-point of science' suggests that he is thinking in terms of his own conception of induction as a means of coming to know first principles in science. This is a method of generalisation from particulars which 'leads on' the mind to an intuitive recognition of first principles.[8] Thus Aristotle seems to be ascribing to Socrates the use of inductive arguments as a means to definition and as part of a scientific method in ethics.

Aristotle's implicit criticism of Socrates' method in ethics is a reflection of the views which he expresses at several points in his *Nicomachean Ethics* about the proper method of ethics.[9] He shows there that the first principles of ethics cannot be known with certainty to be true, and that to assume the possibility of demonstrative certainty in its conclusions is wrongly to assimilate knowledge in ethics to scientific knowledge.

Once we recognise the sort of distinctions Aristotle has in mind when he assesses Socratic method we can appreciate better the significance of his remarks about the lack of 'dialectical power' in Socrates' time. It is from the standpoint of his own conception of dialectical method that Aristotle makes these remarks. And since he claims (*Soph. El.* 183b ff.) that he was entirely original in establishing and ordering, in the *Topics* and *Sophistici Elenchi*, the methods of dialectical argument, it becomes understandable that he finds Socrates' ethical inquiries lacking in 'dialectical power'.

Even so, there seems to be some exaggeration in denying to Socrates the dialectical ability to 'study contraries independently of the essence and to consider whether contraries are the objects of a single science'. At least it appears exaggerated if we take Plato's early dialogues to be at all reliable as a presentation of the sort of arguments which Socrates used. Thus the argument of the *Hippias Minor* (366a ff.) can be construed as a consideration of whether contraries are the objects of a single science. It argues that in professional skills knowledge of how to do well implies knowledge of how to do badly. It also explores some of the possible implications of applying the notion of knowledge of contraries to moral knowledge. As for 'studying contraries independently of the essence', Alexander gives as an example the study of the theses that pleasure is good and that it is bad. If we look at such Platonic dialogues as the *Protagoras* and Socrates' examination there of the question whether virtue is teachable or not, it is difficult to deny to Plato's Socrates some ability 'to study contraries independently of the essence'. Admittedly in the *Meno*(86c–e) Socrates protests that such questions should not be discussed 'independently of the essence'. But that he has some skill in argument for dealing with them is quite clear.

In more general respects the method of Socrates as portrayed by Xenophon and Plato is of a kind which makes Aristotle's denial to him of dialectical power appear exaggeratedly partisan. Xenophon, who does not usually show much of a nose for points of significance in philosophical method, singles out for special mention (*Mem.* IV vi 15) Socrates' habit of starting from premisses which were commonly accepted truths, as a good basis for developing his arguments. This, for Aristotle, would be good dialectical practice. There are other important general features of Socratic method portrayed by Xenophon and Plato about which Aristotle is completely silent and yet which reflect a sophisticated level of question-and-answer technique in argument. The most important of these, which we will examine later, are the *elenchus* and the use of hypothesis. Moreover this question-and-answer method ascribed to Socrates seems to have played an important part in the development of the exercises in dialectic which Aristotle tries to systematise in the *Topics*.[10] In view of this, it appears almost churlish of Aristotle to speak of the lack of dialectical power in Socrates' time.[11]

The most probable explanation of this apparent churlishness lies, I think, in Aristotle's radical disagreement with Socrates' method as a method of ethical inquiry. Aristotle viewed Socratic method as one which recognised no distinction between a method of scientific demonstration and a properly dialectical method. He considered that, for lack of such a distinction, Socrates wrongly assumed the possibility of making ethics a demonstrative science. From that point of view Aristotle would find Socrates' inquiries in ethics lacking in properly dialectical method, and would tend to minimise his 'dialectical power'. This criticism of the scientific nature of Socrates' ethics is found, as we shall see in the next chapter, in Aristotle's ethical works as well as in the *Metaphysics*.

As for Aristotle's silence about the features of the Platonic Socrates' method which we mentioned above, we have to remember that Aristotle is not pretending to give a complete account of Socratic method. His primary concern is with those original features of the method relevant to his present subject – the development of Plato's theory of Forms. Thus the explanation of his silence may be that he considered those features irrelevant or unimportant to his thesis. Another possible explanation is that he did not consider them original contributions by Socrates to philosophical method. This is one of the questions about Aristotle's assessment we will discuss later when examining, in the light of other testimony, the originality of the method practised by Socrates. We will have to discuss too the more general question of whether Aristotle is giving a fair picture of Socratic method in presenting it as a scientific rather than a dialectical method. But first it is important to look at the way in which Xenophon and Plato present the two features of Socratic method specifically mentioned by Aristotle – the search for general definitions and the use of inductive arguments.

B. DEFINITION

Aristotle's point that Socrates directed his inquiries in ethics to the establishing of general definitions of the virtues is amply illustrated in Xenophon's *Memorabilia* and Plato's early dialogues. Several of the early Platonic dialogues – *Euthyphro, Laches, Charmides* and

Hippias Major – are directly devoted to this end. Others – *Lysis* and *Protagoras* – are indirectly devoted to it.[12] Xenophon too represents the search for definitions as a constant feature of Socrates' discussions (*Mem.* I i; III ix; IV vi).

The great importance attached here by Socrates to the search for definitions is closely tied to his convictions (i) that moral knowledge is knowledge *through definition* of what goodness or virtue is and of what the particular virtues are, and (ii) that possessing this moral knowledge is a necessary and sufficient condition of being good and hence of doing what is good. In the *Eudemian Ethics* and *Nicomachean Ethics* Aristotle, like Plato, ascribes these convictions to Socrates.

An assumption of the first conviction is that to define the good is to formulate a moral ideal. Socrates' concern is with real definitions, in the sense that he assumes that each moral term which he seeks to define designates a form (*eidos*) or universal which is analysed through definition. Thus in Plato Socrates' attempt to define piety is represented as an attempt to define a single form possessed by all particular instances which are properly described as pious (*Euthyphro* 5d, 6e). It is assumed that there are certain general characteristics which constitute the real nature or 'essence' (*ousia*) of this form; these are its defining characteristics and are to be distinguished from merely accidental characteristics (*Euthyphro* 11a). The unity of the form and its status as a universal are emphasised by a contrast between 'the one' and 'the many'. For example, the many particular instances of what is pious are contrasted with the single form 'by which all particular instances of piety are constituted as instances of piety' (*Euthyphro* 6d). Similarly, in asking for a definition of courage, Socrates asks what the common quality is which is the same in all instances of courage (*Laches* 191e, 192b).

Further emphasis is given to the distinction between the form and its particular instances by Socrates' insistence that a mere enumeration of instances is never sufficient to establish the definition of the form. 'Prosecuting one who is guilty of murder, sacrilege and such offences' (*Euthyphro* 5c) is not a definition of piety, nor is 'remaining at one's post and fighting against the enemy' (*Laches* 191a) a definition of courage. For there are many other kinds of action which have the common quality of being pious or of being courageous. What Socrates demands is a universal definition, one which takes the form or universal as the *definiendum* and explicates its structure in general terms in such a way that its 'essence' (*ousia*) is revealed.

Both Xenophon and Plato indicate also the practical moral importance attached by Socrates to definitions of this kind. Their practical importance is that they may be used as general principles or premisses from which to draw conclusions offering practical guidance in moral behaviour. To know the form of piety is to possess a standard by which to measure whether or not particular actions or types of action are properly designated as pious (*Euthyphro* 6e). Again, in order to discover what form of training and exercise is best for a young man, it is necessary to go back to a first principle (*Laches* 189e) in the form of a definition of virtue. To attain this will be to know what virtue is. And this knowledge will enable its possessor to specify the best means of acquiring virtue (*Laches* 190b; cf. Xen. *Mem.* iv vi 1). Similarly a definition of virtue will resolve the problem of whether virtue can be taught (*Protagoras* 360e–361a).

All this serves to emphasise Socrates' view of definitions as *descriptive* analyses of the form (*eidos*) of the virtues. According to Socrates correct analyses are true specifications of a moral ideal and imply the falsity of other specifications in whatever form. That is why he feels able to express such confidence in the practical moral value of establishing general definitions of the virtues. It is this conception of the nature and purpose of definition which explains also why Socrates gives absolute priority in discussion to the question of 'what a thing is'. It is true that in the *Meno*, in a passage (86c ff.) which we noticed in discussing Aristotle's testimony, Plato represents Socrates as agreeing to discuss whether virtue can be taught before it has been established what it is. But

Socrates emphasises that the question of what it is has priority. Only with reluctance does he agree to his interlocutor's demand that the secondary question should be discussed. And it is significant that his method of dealing with this secondary question is a method of analysis which starts from the hypothesis that virtue can be taught and works back to a first principle in the form of a definition. From this principle Socrates aims to demonstrate syllogistically that virtue can be taught.[13]

It is clear that this general picture we get from Plato's earlier dialogues, and from Xenophon too, of the fundamental part played by definition in Socrates' method is one which is in close agreement with what Aristotle tells us about it. There is little to be said for the argument that the reason for this close agreement is that Aristotle, without any independent authority, is simply using Plato's dialogues as the basis of his testimony. Aristotle explicitly rejects as non-Socratic an important part of what Plato puts into Socrates' mouth. By implication he rejects a good deal more. He does indeed sometimes rely on Plato's early dialogues for the form of his presentation of a Socratic doctrine, as we shall see in discussing Socrates' moral paradoxes. But this is natural enough. Why should he not turn to Plato's presentation of a doctrine which he had independent grounds for ascribing to Socrates?

From Xenophon, Plato and Aristotle we have, then, a clear and consistent picture of the role of general definition in Socrates' method. No doubt it is easy to criticise Socrates' conception of definition. We do not nowadays think of definition in ethics in terms of the descriptive specification of a moral ideal, nor do we associate it in the way that Socrates did with the solution of practical moral problems. Yet we should not for that reason overlook the importance of Socrates' concern with general definition as an original contribution to philosophical method. Aristotle was right to emphasise Socrates' originality in this respect. He recognised in the problems of general definition raised by Socrates an important influence in the development of Plato's metaphysical theory of Forms. And his own interest in the logical aspects of Socrates' search for general definition was of fundamental importance in the development of his own theory.

There is one final point to be made about Socratic definition. Although the notion of *knowledge* of 'what a thing is' is prominent in his discussions, Socrates does not seem to have concerned himself with problems in the theory of knowledge. Certainly he considered that in ethics knowledge of the virtues through definition was fundamental. This represents a positive doctrine about the nature of moral knowledge. But the doctrine is not associated with the sort of distinctions which would suggest a clear awareness of, or interest in, epistemological questions. For example, Socrates does not ask to what extent, if any, the source of knowledge of the virtues is empirical. And although we readily, and no doubt rightly, think of Socrates' exercises in definition as exercises in the analysis of concepts, we should not assume that the notion of concept was present in Socrates' mind. Plato appears to have been the first thinker to show awareness of the conceptual nature of thinking as a level of abstraction distinguishable from perception of particulars. He marks this in the *Phaedo* (73c, 74b, 75b) by a distinction between conceiving and perceiving, when he first introduces his theory of Forms. And that theory, as Aristotle tells us, goes beyond what can be ascribed to Socrates.

Just as Socrates does not think of his search for definitions in epistemological terms, so he does not think of it in metaphysical terms. It is clear that Socrates' search is for real definitions, in the sense we have noted, and not for nominal definitions. His assumption is, as Richard Robinson has put it, 'that the form or essence or one in the many is not a word in the mouth, nor a concept in the head, but something existing in the Xes independently of man'. Yet, although Socrates makes a realist rather than a nominalist assumption about the status of the 'what-a-thing-is', this distinction 'is nothing that enters his head, but only one of the logical consequences of what does enter his head'.[14]

Thus we must not look for metaphysical or epistemological distinctions as part of Socrates' concern in his attempt to establish general definitions. His concern is primarily with practical moral problems. He considers that his method of establishing general definitions is not merely a method which clarifies and makes precise men's opinions about commonly accepted virtues but a method of establishing principles of supreme practical value in determining what it is morally right to do.

C. INDUCTION

'Inductive arguments' is the second original feature of Socrates' method which Aristotle specifies, in a context which suggests, as we have seen, that it was as a means to definition that Socrates used these arguments. By 'inductive arguments' Aristotle means arguments which 'lead on' the mind to grasp a general truth by pointing out particular cases of it. This notion of 'leading on' seems to have been the primary meaning of the Greek term for 'induction' (*epagōgē*), at least in Aristotle's use of it.[15]

Again there is ample illustration in Xenophon and Plato of Aristotle's point. We find that Socrates' habit of appealing to a wide variety of cases to drive home some general truth is represented as a pervasive element in his method, one which some of his contemporaries regarded with a mixture of amusement and irritation; they were puzzled by the apparent triviality or irrelevance to the argument of the cases to which Socrates appealed. 'You never stop talking about cobblers, dyers, butchers and doctors', says Callicles to Socrates in Plato's *Gorgias* (491a), 'as though the argument had something to do with people of that kind'.

In a similar vein Xenophon relates (*Mem.* I ii 33–7) how Socrates was interviewed by Critias and Charicles and forbidden to have conversation with the young men of Athens. Suppose, says Socrates, a young man has something to sell which I want. May I ask him what the price is? Or suppose I am asked where

Charicles lives. May I answer? Yes, says Charicles. 'But you must stop talking', Critias adds, 'about your cobblers and carpenters and smiths. I think they must be quite worn out now with all your talk about them.' In that case, Socrates says, I must presumably stop talking about matters which are bound up with them – justice, piety, and other such subjects.

In his use of cases to lead on his respondent to a universal truth, Socrates generalises either from a number of particular instances to a general proposition, or from a number of general propositions to another, more general proposition. Sometimes the generalisation is explicitly made. Sometimes it is merely implicit in an argument from one case to another. Socrates puts the method to a wide variety of uses. He uses it to correct or refute a proposed definition or other proposition (e.g. Plato, *Euthyphro* 10a–11a, *Charmides* 167b–168a), to reveal ambiguities in meaning (*Euthyphro* 13a–d), to support a definition (Xenophon, *Mem.* III ix 10), to elucidate practical moral problems (Plato, *Crito* 47a–48a), to reveal absurdities or anomalies (*Hippias Minor* 373c–376c). In general the method is used to clarify and give precision to the argument at any step by calling to mind relevant instances and principles from a wide and varied field of experience.

Aristotle himself gives an illustration in his *Rhetoric* (1393b) of a typically Socratic 'inductive argument'. In this passage he is dealing with 'example' (*paradeigma*). He describes this elsewhere (*Posterior Analytics* 71a 10) as a kind of induction. He distinguishes it from perfect induction in that (i) it does not generalise from all instances, and (ii) it finishes by applying the generalisation to a new particular (*Prior Analytics*, II 24). Here is his illustration of it, described as characteristically Socratic. Suppose one wished to argue that magistrates should not be chosen by lot. One could show by examples – that of an athlete or a pilot – the absurdity of choice by lot instead of by the criterion of skilled knowledge. The general principle can then be applied to the case of choice of magistrates.

Xenophon (*Mem.* I ii 9) appears to confirm that this is a

genuinely Socratic argument. Xenophon is speaking here of criticisms of Socrates for his bad influence on young people, in particular of the charge that he caused his associates to despise the established laws. Socrates' opposition to the choice of magistrates by lot is mentioned as one of the grounds of this criticism. He is said to have argued that it was 'foolish to elect the magistrates of the state by beans; no one would be willing to employ a pilot elected by beans, or an architect or a flute player, or a person in any other such profession, where in fact errors cause far less harm than errors in the administration of a state'. Socrates' use of this kind of induction is illustrated again by Aristotle in the *Eudemian Ethics* (1235a–b). This illustration too has its parallel in Xenophon (*Mem.* 1 ii 54). There are many other illustrations in Plato's early dialogues (e.g. *Laches*, 185b–d).

An important part of Socrates' skill in his use of inductive arguments is a skill in picking out what seemed to him to be the significant points of analogy between various particular cases. It is also a skill in distinguishing between cases which are in some respects analogous but in others are not. For he makes frequent use of arguments from negative as well as positive resemblances between cases. His skill in these respects is perhaps best illustrated by considering the use he makes of one of his favourite analogies, the analogy between moral behaviour and the practice of professional skills.

Let us look first at his arguments to show the positive resemblances between the two. In Plato's *Euthydemus* Socrates appeals to various professional skills as examples of knowledgeable and successful practice. He uses them to suggest that, just as knowledge is a condition of successful practice in this sphere, so it is a condition of success or 'good fortune' in the broader sphere of moral behaviour. Here is his argument (279d ff.). Success in navigation, warfare, medicine and music belongs to those with expert knowledge in those fields – expert sailors, soldiers, physicians and musicians. In general, knowledge leads to success or 'good fortune'. More specifically the expert knowledge of the carpenter or other craftsman enables him to use his materials and implements advantageously, i.e. to further the end of his craft. Similarly in moral behaviour it is knowledge which enables a person to use his resources – his material possessions, his physical capacities, his gifts of temperament – advantageously or beneficially, i.e. to promote the end of his moral behaviour, 'good fortune' or happiness (*eudaimonia*). Socrates concludes that knowledge is the one good (281e).

Socrates recognises, however, that there is a negative analogy between the two types of activity. In the *Hippias Minor* (365d ff.) he establishes, after reviewing various examples of professional skills and sciences, that in that sphere ability implies knowledge, and that it is the able man who is properly described as a *good* craftsman or scientist. He suggests further that it is only the *good* craftsman or scientist who is able to do either what is right or what is wrong in his particular field. This idea can, however, be refined in a way which takes into account accidental or unintentional wrong actions. If we look at skills such as running, wrestling, singing, archery and so on, we can see that it is universally true of these skills that the *good* man is the man who is able deliberately or intentionally to do what is wrong or right. For example, the good runner is able to win or to lose a race deliberately. The bad runner is not simply the one who loses a race. He is the one who loses it when he wants to win it; he loses against his will (373d–e).

This association of goodness with deliberately doing wrong prompts the generalisation that it is 'better' to do wrong deliberately than to do it involuntarily. But is the principle universally valid? Can it be extended from the field of professional skills to that of moral behaviour? If it is so extended, it follows that the moral agent who deliberately does wrong is better than the one who does wrong against his will. The former is the morally good man, the latter the morally bad. Socrates makes clear his unwillingness to accept this consequence (376b). The analogy does not in this respect hold good.

As a final illustration of Socrates' inductive arguments a

passage in Xenophon's *Memorabilia* deserves notice. Xenophon, as we noted earlier, does not have much of a nose for points of general significance in philosophical method. He is a practical man, able to appreciate properly only the practical side of Socrates' thought. Yet he appears to have been much impressed by Socrates' skill in picking out examples to refute or to modify an interlocutor's proposals. In one passage he illustrates admirably how effectively Socrates uses the appeal to negative instances in a discussion about the nature of justice and injustice.

In this passage (*Mem.* IV ii 13–19) Socrates and Euthydemus are trying to define justice. Socrates continually criticises Euthydemus' proposals by pointing to actions which conform to what is proposed and yet obviously do not constitute instances of the *definiendum*. Thus Euthydemus thinks it is unjust to lie, to deceive, to injure or to enslave a person. Yet, Socrates says, it is surely not unjust for an army commander to deceive, injure or enslave a hostile people. Euthydemus replies that it is actions of that kind against friends which he classifies as unjust. But suppose, Socrates says, a general saves his troops from despondency by falsely pretending that reinforcements are on the way. Or suppose a father whose son is sick and yet refuses to take medicine, tricks him into taking it by presenting it as ordinary food and thus restores him to health. Euthydemus agrees that these are instances of just actions. In this way he is continually prompted to modify his views and to gain a clearer understanding of the general principle which it is Socrates' aim to elicit.

These various illustrations show that Socrates had developed a fairly elaborate and sophisticated technique in his use of 'inductive arguments'. Nor have we any reason to doubt Aristotle when he ascribes originality to Socrates for his use of such arguments. The implication of Aristotle's remarks is that Socrates was the first to make the systematic use of these arguments an essential feature of his philosophical method. That this is so is confirmed by such evidence as we have about the method of earlier thinkers. It is true that in Socrates' time Greek medicine was developing methods of diagnosis which can be fairly described as inductive in procedure. At least it is true that in the Hippocratic collection of medical writings, some of which may belong to the fifth century, we have many examples of acute analogical reasoning, as well as examples of generalisation from the detailed observation of similarities and differences in cases.[16] Hippocrates himself was a contemporary of Socrates. Yet even if we referred any of the Hippocratic collection to the fifth century, there is nothing to suggest that such work had any influence in the development of Socrates' techniques. Scholars have rightly noted the similarities between Socrates' inductive method and the method described in the Hippocratic corpus.[17] But we cannot seriously assume an influence of the one on the other.

We may, then, accept that Socrates was the first to make systematic use of inductive argument an essential part of philosophical method. But how systematic was his use of it? It is as easy to criticise Socratic induction, especially isolated examples of it, as it is to criticise the assumptions of his views on definition. For example, Professor Vlastos[18] argues that 'when it comes to assessing the support which this or that premise can get from observed or observable facts, Socrates seems quite satisfied with acrobatic jumps to reckless conclusions from remote, shaky and dubiously relevant data'. There is undoubtedly some ground for this sort of criticism. Some of Socrates' generalisations and some of his analogical reasoning are based on a very narrow range of examples or on imprecise analysis. Occasionally his selection of examples seems so unfair that he gives the impression that he is trying to hoodwink his interlocutor rather than to make a serious contribution to the argument. But does Professor Vlastos base his own highly critical generalisation about Socratic induction on fair samples? I do not think that he does.

The sample which he takes is an argument in Plato's *Protagoras*. Socrates' concern in this argument (349e–350c) is to show the unity of the virtues of courage and wisdom. He suggests that courageous men are 'confident' men, ready to face what most men are afraid to face. He suggests further that it is knowledge or wisdom which is the basis of this confidence. He uses an inductive argument to support this. He takes the cases of three classes of people with particular specialised skills or knowledge – divers, cavalrymen, and light-armed foot soldiers (peltasts). He argues that in the field of operation of his particular skill it is true in each case that the man with specialist knowledge is more confident than the man without. And Protagoras accepts the generalisation that 'this is true of all other cases. Those who have knowledge are more confident than those who have no knowledge.'

No one would deny that this is a hasty generalisation and that a condition of its validity is that all cases of possessing knowledge should be 'homogeneous with the odd samples in the premise'. Vlastos asks whether Socrates has established this. 'Has he shown that, when we talk of my 'knowledge' that it is wrong to harm my enemy and the peltast's 'knowledge' of the right way to use a shield we are talking about the same thing and may thus extrapolate statements about the former from statements about the latter?' He argues that 'Socrates does not seem to realise that such questions affect the substance of his reasoning, else he would not have ignored them. The reason he disappoints us is that his *method* does not recognize the importance of such queries'.[19]

This criticism is a criticism not only of a particular generalisation but of the whole Socratic method of induction. Let us look first at the particular generalisation. It occurs in a part of the *Protagoras* in which Socrates is using a variety of logical arguments to show Protagoras that, if he takes any two particular virtues, then one is equivalent to the other. Now this part of the *Protagoras* is notorious for its dubious logic. Protagoras himself is allowed to protest at one of its fallacies. This is just one of the indications that these initial arguments in the *Protagoras* for the equivalence of the virtues are merely preliminary skirmishes, designed to weaken Protagoras' resistance to the idea of the equivalence of the virtues rather than to offer a positive and serious interpretation. The basis for such an interpretation is provided with the introduction (at

351b) of the thesis that knowledge of what is good is a necessary and sufficient condition of doing what is good. This general thesis is immediately applied to the analysis of courage (358d ff.), in a manner which we will be examining in detail when considering Socrates' moral doctrine. This final analysis, in terms of knowledge of the good, implicitly rejects the sort of analogy between the knowledge of specialised skills and all other kinds of knowledge which the earlier generalisation had assumed. And other early dialogues confirm that this analysis is more properly representative of Socrates' views than the initial argumentative skirmishes of the *Protagoras*.

One such early Platonic dialogue is the *Laches*, which *explicitly* rejects the analogy. In the *Laches* (192d ff.) the initial attempt to define courage clearly recalls the initial attempt in the *Protagoras* to identify courage with wisdom or knowledge. Laches suggests that courage is a sort of endurance. But he agrees that endurance without wisdom is not sufficient to constitute courage, since folly is incompatible with the 'nobility' of courage. In the *Protagoras* (349e–350c) it is agreed, for just the same reason, that confidence without wisdom is not sufficient to constitute courage.

Unlike the *Protagoras*, however, the *Laches immediately* and *explicitly* raises the problem of what kind of knowledge constitutes 'wisdom' (*sophia*). And while the *Protagoras* appeals to particular cases of professional skills to support the generalisation that 'those who have knowledge are more confident than those who have no knowledge', the *Laches* appeals to precisely the same cases – the diver, the cavalryman, the expert foot-soldier – as *negative* instances to rule out any suggestion that the 'wisdom' to be associated with courage is professional knowledge of this kind. Subsequently the *Laches* offers essentially the same analysis of courage as the *Protagoras* later does, in terms of knowledge of the good. It shows, with appeal to many particular examples, that 'knowledge of what is to be feared and what is not' (195a) is knowledge of a kind which does not fall within the province of professional skills. For it shows that judgments as to what is a proper object of fear are judgments of value which depend for their soundness on a knowledge of what is good and what is bad.

Thus the *Protagoras* implicitly, and the *Laches* explicitly, reject the sort of 'reckless' generalisation which Socrates had suggested at an early stage of the *Protagoras*' argument. Moreover, the *Laches* rejects it on the basis of precisely the sort of distinction which Vlastos criticises Socrates' method for failing to recognize. And it uses an inductive argument to point to that distinction. Socrates' inductive arguments are not above criticism. But critics of the method's sampling should themselves use fair samples as a basis for their general criticisms. This is especially important in the case of criticism of the analogy which is more important than any other in Socrates' ethical analysis – the analogy between the practice of professional skills and moral behaviour. This analogy, explored with great care and insight in respect of both its positive and negative resemblances, is the basis of much of the analysis which yields Socrates' familiar moral paradoxes.

It must be added that there is no defect *in principle* in the method to justify the criticism that it is 'a method which does not recognise the importance'[20] of such questions as whether all the cases embraced in a generalisation have the relevant homogeneity to justify the generalisation. Indeed, the method seems to be designed *in principle* to ensure the highest degree of probability for its generalisations and analogies. The technique of *elenchus* or refutation, which we will examine shortly, is designed to reveal short-comings and contradictions in any thesis advanced in the discussions. And a characteristic feature of the method is that it treats any thesis as provisional only, as subject always to revision and modification.

A tentative and exploratory method of this kind demands, of course, as a condition of its fruitfulness, that those who practice it should bring to it some gift for careful analysis and observation. If in principle the method is satisfactory, criticism of Socrates' 'inductive arguments' becomes the criticism that he did not bring to it adequate gifts of careful analysis and observation. How then should we determine what is adequate in this respect? There is little doubt, as we have seen, that Socrates was *original* in his use of this type of argument. He was well known among his contemporaries for the variety and range of his examples and analogies. And it is a mark of his originality that his arguments aroused irritation or amusement in those who found his favourite analogies either trivial or irrelevent.

But were his inductive arguments good arguments? If we look at isolated examples of Socrates' generalisations and analogies there are few which we would think completely justified by the evidence used to support them. But if the test of their adequacy is whether or not they yielded new insights into the Greeks' moral language and into problems of moral psychology, then they are good arguments. To appreciate their value it is necessary in the first place to see them within the broad context of Socrates' exploratory question-and-answer method. The rest of this chapter will try to outline that context. In the second place they have to be assessed for their positive contribution to the main tenets of Socrates' ethics. The detailed examination of Socrates' moral paradoxes in the next chapter will indicate, I hope, that at least some of Socrates' inductive arguments are more perceptive and more philosophically significant than some of his critics suppose.

D. ERISTIC AND DIALECTIC

We have now considered two important features of Socratic method. We have seen that the method aims to establish universal definitions in ethics, and that what Aristotle calls 'inductive arguments' were persistently used by Socrates to further that aim.

In his *Sophistici Elenchi* Aristotle mentions another important feature of the method. At 187b he characterises the method as one which asks questions but does not give answers, and associates this feature of the method with Socrates' confession that he 'does not know' anything. What is well illustrated by Socrates' method, he says, is the difference between the art of interrogating and the art of establishing and defending a thesis in response to questions. The latter assumes a knowledge of the subject under discussion. The former does not.

We see from this aspect of Socratic method that it is conversational or 'dialectical' in form. Socrates practises it with one or more interlocutors, his own role being primarily that of questioner while his interlocutors provide the answers. This is the aspect of the method which yields the familiar picture of Socrates, presented by Plato and Xenophon, as a person who persistently questions his fellow-citizens, reduces them to perplexity by revealing inconsistencies in their moral thinking, and rids them of the conceit of believing that they know what they are talking about. It is also an aspect of the method which Plato considered to be an essential feature of any good philosophical method and hence, in his opinion, essential for establishing the truth of any proposition.

One reason why Socrates himself valued so highly a question-and-answer technique of analysis is to be found in his conception of his mission in life as a kind of intellectual gad-fly (Plato, *Apol.* 29d–31b). If you are fired with the altruistic aim of doing moral and intellectual good to others by exposing the inadequacies of their opinions and rousing their intellectual curiosity, then you will value a method which directly confronts them in debate and allows them to see, by their own answers and admissions, the shortcomings of their views. It is this directness of the method, coupled with its application to the analysis of the views of the *individual*, which recommends it to Socrates for furthering his altruistic aim.

An important influence on Socrates in this respect was the atmosphere of intellectual debate, of pitting one thesis against another, which prevailed in Athens in the latter half of the fifth century. The emergence in Greece at this time of professional teachers of rhetoric, the Sophists, did much to create this atmos-

c   G.P.S.

phere. It will be useful to survey the nature of the argumentative techniques used by the Sophists, especially since the question of their influence on Socrates embraces the question of Socrates' originality in his use of a particular form of question-and-answer method.

One important method of argument, developed independently of sophistic influences but subsequently used for their own purposes by both the Sophists and Socrates, is the method of *reductio ad absurdum*. The originality in developing this belongs to Parmenides' pupil, Zeno of Elea, born thirty years or more before Socrates. His aim was to defend Parmenides' theory by revealing contradictions in the theories of his opponents. And his method was to take an opponent's postulate and work out from it a pair of contradictory conclusions. There is no good evidence that he used a question-and-answer form for his method.[21] But the method played an understandably important part in later question-and-answer techniques.

The Sophists quickly appreciated its value in rhetorical argument, both as an indirect method of defending a particular thesis and a direct method of refuting it. Plato pays a good deal of attention to the methods of argument used by the Sophists. A general term which he sometimes uses to characterise their mode of argument is 'eristic'.[22] Although he uses it almost as a term of abuse, since he is anxious to dissociate it from his own art of dialectic, we should not infer that this tone always belonged to it. One piece of evidence to show that the Sophists themselves used it to describe their own methods of argument is the mention in Diogenes Laertius (IX, 55) of an *Art of Eristics* as the title of one of Protagoras' works. It is unlikely that Diogenes has got this wrong. We may accept it as correct.[23]

What, then, is 'eristic'? It is a win-at-any-price type of argument which aims not at truth but at victory. Aristotle (*Soph. El.* 183b) indicates the two different forms it might take. It might take the form of a series of rhetorical arguments for or against a standard theme. Or it might take the form of question-and-answer exchanges in which the questioner tries to reduce his respondent to self-contradiction.

The *Dissoi Logoi* (*Twofold Arguments*)[24] an essay written at the end of the fifth century B.C., may be taken as representative of the rhetorical type of eristical argument, i.e. giving sets of arguments for or against a particular thesis. In the *Dissoi Logoi* arguments are presented on two opposite sides of a series of standard themes – e.g. that good and bad are 'the same' (inasmuch as they are merely relative terms) and that they are 'different'; that wisdom and virtue can be taught and that they cannot be taught; and so on. Where one thesis has an obviously greater plausibility than its opposite, the defence of the less plausible thesis becomes an example of 'making the worse cause appear the better', a sophistic practice caricatured in Aristophanes' *Clouds* (882 ff.) in 423 B.C. The *Encomium on Helen* by Gorgias[25] is a rhetorical exercise of that kind. It is essentially a defence of Helen's conduct in going to Troy, consisting of a series of arguments designed to show her innocence of charges commonly brought against her.

A second type of eristical argument, recognised by both Plato and Aristotle, employs a question-and-answer technique. In his *Sophist* (225b–c) Plato associates with the Sophists a skilled type of disputation, 'eristic', which is cut up into questions and answers and disputes about 'justice and injustice and things in general'. It is the type of disputation illustrated in his *Euthydemus*, where again it is associated with the Sophists and called 'eristic' (272b). One has to allow, of course, for some caricature in Plato's presentation of it, but that it presents a generally fair picture of the aims and methods of eristical argument is confirmed by Aristotle's presentation of these in his *Sophistici Elenchi* and his use of examples there from the *Euthydemus*.

In the *Euthydemus* the method used by the Sophists Euthydemus and Dionysodorus is a method of questioning aimed at reducing a respondent to self-contradiction, mainly by playing on ambiguities in the meaning of words. It demands short answers to questions framed in such a way that the respondent must accept one or other of two propositions (e.g. do you know something or nothing?) or must simply answer 'yes' or 'no'.[26] It is a rule of the game that the respondent does not attempt to qualify his answer in any way or to ask questions himself (295–6). And the aim of the game is simply that of winning the argument by trapping the respondent into contradiction. The aim is not to establish something as true.

Here is an example from the *Euthydemus* (283 ff.). Ctesippus says that it is possible to say what is false. Euthydemus proceeds to refute this, gaining from Ctesippus a string of admissions which lead to the contradiction of his thesis. Thus to say what is false is to say something. So what is said *is* something. So to say something is to 'say what is'. And 'he who says what is says the truth'.

Ctesippus attempts to counter this by maintaining that to say what is false is to 'say what is not'. The answer to this is that 'what is not' is nothing at all. And no one can speak and yet say nothing. So 'no one says what is not'. So no one says what is false. If a person says anything 'he says what is true and what is'. Thus all statements are true.

Socrates notes that this has for long been part of the repertoire of sophistic arguments (286). He considers it to be a destructive and suicidal argument. Yet, though it is presented in the *Euthydemus* as a contentious, win-at-any-price type of argument, it raises a philosophical puzzle to which Plato pays a considerable amount of attention.[27] Protagoras, the originator of the argument, possibly used it as a logical support for his subjectivist views. It is a good example of the philosophical stimulus provided by the destructive techniques of the Sophists' eristic.

These, then, were the two main types of eristical argument. One took the form of a series of arguments for and/or against a particular thesis, the other the form of a rapid series of questions designed to reduce a respondent to self-contradiction. Both these forms of eristic were being practised by the Sophists in the latter half of the fifth century. Moreover it seems fairly certain that some form of eristic was being practised by the earliest of the Sophists before Socrates began to use his own method of cross-examination in ethics. Protagoras, the first avowed professional Sophist, and much older than Socrates,[29] was the first, according to Diogenes Laërtius (IX 51), to maintain that on every subject there are two opposite positions which can be defended, and the first to institute contests in argumentative debate (*logōn agonas*). Diogenes tells us also that Protagoras wrote, in addition to his *Art of Eristics*, a work on *Contradictory Arguments* (III 37).

This makes it very probable that Protagoras, as a pioneer in the Sophists' techniques of argumentative debate, had some influence on Socrates in the development of his method. For, as we shall presently see, an essential part of Socrates' art of cross-examination is the art of convicting others of inconsistencies in their views. In the general shape of Socrates' arguments, at least of his negative contradiction-finding arguments, the influence of Protagoras' method can, I think, fairly clearly be detected.

It will be worthwhile to examine the extent of this influence in more detail. One point to be considered is whether Protagoras preceded Socrates in developing a question-and-answer form of argument and prompted Socrates to adopt this form of argument for his own purposes. Or were Protagoras' *Art of Eristics* and *Contradictory Arguments* concerned only with the long-speech form of eristical argument, suited to rhetorical debate, and was Protagoras a pioneer only in that kind of eristic and not in the question-and-answer kind?

If we look at Plato's dialogues, we find some indication that the question-and-answer form of eristic was developed by the Sophists a good deal later than the other form. In the *Euthydemus* Plato says that the two Sophists, although long skilled in rhetoric, have only a year or two ago acquired the art of question-and-answer eristic (272a–c).[30] The dramatic date of the *Euthydemus* is about 420 B.C.[31] Socrates is 'quite elderly' (272b, 293b) and yet anxious to learn something of this new eristic technique. The implication is that the earliest Sophists did not practice the question-and-answer kind of eristic, or at least came to it only late in their career. A further implication is that this kind of eristic was first practised by the Sophists at a time when Socrates himself had been practising his own dialectical method for some time.

I see no good reason for not accepting these implications. But it is relevant to note that the comparatively new eristical technique exemplified in the *Euthydemus* is obviously a fairly elaborate procedure with fixed rules and objectives. If we accept that it was developed later than Socrates' own question-and-answer method, this does not imply that Protagoras and the earlier Sophists were not practising *any* sort of question-and-answer method of argument. Is there anything, then, in Plato's portrait of them to suggest that they were accustomed to a question-and-answer mode of argument, albeit a much less rigid and less systematised method than the eristic of the *Euthydemus*?

Plato's portrait of Protagoras in the *Protagoras* presents him as much more thoroughly versed in the long-speech type of argument than in any short question-and-answer exchanges. His natural inclination is to state his case in a 'fine long speech'; he is ill at ease with a question-and-answer method. Though he accepts an invitation to act as questioner, he does so with reluctance and soon hands over the task to Socrates. And in the role of answerer he finds himself quite unable to defend his position against Socrates' arguments.

Sidgwick[32] considered it 'quite incredible' that 'if Protagoras had really not only practised but actually invented Eristic, as described in the *Sophistes* – methodical disputation by short question and answers – he could ever have been represented as Plato represents him in the dialogue which bears his name'. His conclusion about Protagoras' work was that his *Art of Eristics* was concerned only with the earlier, non-dialectical form of eristic, and that it 'contained instructions how to make speeches on both sides of a case, no doubt with the aid of logical fallacies'.[33] He was further 'disposed to think' that 'the Art of Disputation which is ascribed to Sophists in the *Euthydemus* and the *Sophistes* ... originated entirely with Socrates, and that he is altogether responsible *for the form at least* of this second species of Sophistic'.[34]

My own view is that Sidgwick is probably right about the general content of Protagoras' *Art of Eristics*. I also think it probable, from the suggestions of the *Euthydemus*, that the Sophists' own eristical brand of question-and-answer argument, a fairly late development, was influenced in its formulation by Socrates' question-and-answer method of cross-examination. But it is going too far to suggest that Socrates was 'altogether responsible' for its form, and that it 'originated entirely' with Socrates. In the *Protagoras* Plato includes Protagoras among the admittedly few people at this time (the dramatic date of the *Protagoras* is about 431 B.C.) who are practised not only in making fine long speeches but also in giving answers to questions and acting as questioners themselves (329b).[35] Nor is it difficult to imagine a professional debater such as Protagoras introducing some element of questioning into his technique. We can see from the *Dissoi Logoi* how easy and natural it was in the continuous development of a particular thesis to express possible objections to the thesis in the form of questions put by some imagined interlocutor.[36] Thus it is reasonable to suppose that the 'argumentative debates' first instituted, according to Diogenes, by Protagoras incorporated such devices. Indeed, Diogenes tells us that Protagoras, besides being the first to maintain that on every subject there are two opposite positions which can be defended, was also the first to use a method of questioning in his arguments to establish such opposite positions. Diogenes claims, in view of this, that Protagoras was the first to introduce the 'Socratic form' of argument.

Diogenes is not, of course, claiming here that all the characteristic features of Socrates' method were first introduced by Protagoras. We have already looked at Socrates' originality in philosophical method in respect of his use of inductive arguments and his quest for general definitions. Aristotle's testimony about this is clear and convincing. It is not these features of Socrates' arguments that Diogenes has in mind. The context in which he attributes to Protagoras the first introduction of the 'Socratic form' of argument indicates that he is thinking in the first place of the question-and-answer form of Socrates' method. He is probably thinking also of Socrates' *elenchus*, his art of refuting another's thesis, which characteristically takes the form of convicting an interlocutor of inconsistency by deducing from premisses which the interlocutor accepts the contrary of his original thesis.

In both these respects Diogenes is probably right in claiming that Protagoras influenced Socrates. His testimony accords well enough with what Plato says about Protagoras and with the association of Protagoras' name in antiquity with the argumentative techniques of 'making the worse cause appear the better' and of showing that two contradictory positions can be defended with equal plausibility.[37] As for the comparative weight of these two points of influence, I think that Protagoras is likely to have stimulated Socrates' thinking much more as an expert in 'contradictory arguments' than as an early experimenter in techniques of questioning. The importance of these 'contradictory arguments' is that they revealed, in the most striking way possible, puzzles and inconsistencies which immediately prompted questions about the validity of hitherto accepted views in a wide range of subjects.

For his 'contradictory arguments' Protagoras was certainly indebted to Zeno's method of *reductio ad impossibile*. But his own technique is not to draw from a single thesis self-contradictory consequences. It is to find sets of arguments of which one set will yield a conclusion contradicting the conclusion yielded by another set. Naturally his skill and ingenuity in this was exercised more strikingly in demonstrating the truth of the less plausible of two opposite theses. Hence his fame in 'making the worse appear the better'. But his concern is not to reduce one or other of the two theses to impossibility or absurdity, but to show the possibility of making both theses acceptable on equally plausible grounds. In Aristophanes' *Clouds* we have, in the contest between Just and Unjust Causes (882 ff.), a caricature of Protagoras' method of

presenting 'contradictory arguments'. The arguments of the
Unjust Cause provide an example of 'making the worse cause
appear the better' (1036–1104; note especially the language of
1038–1042). Later the *Dissoi Logoi*, which by its title seems to
proclaim its Protagorean ancestry, provides further example of
'contradictory arguments'.

This method of revealing inconsistencies was, in my view, the
most important influence in shaping the form of the Socratic
elenchus. It is true, as we shall see, that the Socratic art of revealing
inconsistencies serves far different purposes than Protagoras' art.
It is part of a progressive method of reaching definitions which
aims to resolve finally any inconsistencies found on the way. But
Protagoras' influence is still an important one.

Nor should we overlook the more general influence of
Protagoras and the earlier Sophists on Socrates' method. In the
first place they directed attention to ethics as a field of inquiry in
which, perhaps pre-eminently, inconsistencies of thought could
be revealed. Secondly, they emphasised the importance for precise
and effective argument of the right use of words. We know from
Plato and Aristotle of Protagoras' considerable interest in this.[38]
Prodicus of Ceos, who was frequently in Athens, was especially
noted, as Plato's many references to him make clear, for his work
on correct terminology.[39] In particular, he tried to give precision
to the use of words by carefully distinguishing the meanings of
apparent synonyms. Though Socrates sometimes treats him as a
hair-splitting pedant, he properly recognises the importance and
influence of his work. As we shall see in the next chapter, the
Socratic paradoxes in ethics are based on much searching linguistic
analysis of the relations in meaning between the most familiar
Greek moral concepts and of the relations between their usage in
ethical and non-ethical contexts. There is little doubt, I think, that
the early Sophists played some part in stimulating this interest of
Socrates in linguistic analysis as a fruitful approach to the elucidation of philosophical problems.

The influence of Protagoras in prompting Socrates' adoption

of a question-and-answer method is more difficult to estimate. The evidence suggests, as we saw, that the element of questioning in direct debate was only a small part of Protagoras' method and did not belong to his special skills. Judging from the specialised form of question-and-answer eristic later developed by the Sophists, and from the possible value of question-and-answer to Protagoras' aims in debate, I would guess that questioning was introduced as an almost incidental element, its purpose being to lend the appearance of added plausibility to the arguments in favour of a particular thesis. The added plausibility would come from the willing acceptance by a partner of the steps in the argument, put to him in the form of rhetorical questions inviting a string of admissions.

Thus it is probable that any element of questioning in the method of Protagoras had a dramatic rather than a philosophical significance. There is no suggestion in the testimony on Protagoras, or indeed on any other Sophist, that the question-and-answer technique had any more significance for them than this.

It would seem, therefore, that it was this philosophically insignificant use of a question-and-answer form which, with the other features of Protagoras' method we have considered, was familiar to Socrates when he was beginning to reflect on problems in ethics, and which was subsequently taken up by him to serve the aims of his own method. What philosophical significance does it acquire, then, as part of Socrates' method? And, more generally, what characteristics of the Socratic method of cross-examination distinguish it from the eristic of the Sophists and justify Plato's claim that it is of greater philosophical value than eristic?

Let us follow Plato and call the Socratic method 'dialectic' in contrast to the 'eristic' of the Sophists. Dialectic[40] is Plato's name for the method, question-and-answer in form, which he claims to be the ideal philosophical method of analysis. Developments in his conception of dialectic take him, certainly, well beyond the

Socratic notion of what is a good philosophical method. For example, the formal dress and metaphysical significance given to dialectic in the *Republic* (511, 522–3) are Platonic, not Socratic. But Plato's distinction between dialectic and eristic is already explicit before he associates dialectic with his own metaphysical theory and recommends it as his own ideal method. When he first makes the distinction at *Meno* 75c–d he does so in the course of a typically Socratic piece of cross-examination. It would seem to be a reasonable inference that Plato considered that *Socrates'* method was properly to be called dialectical and not eristical.

Now from the beginning Plato thinks of the question-and-answer method of dialectic as a method having two essential aims. Firstly, its aim is to discover the truth, most especially the truth expressed in the form of definition. Secondly, it aims to educate others to discover the truth. It is considered by Plato to be the best possible method for achieving these aims. And Plato considers these to be philosophically laudable aims. In each case the aim is to satisfy the desire for knowledge. Eristic, on the other hand, is severely condemned by Plato, principally for its indifference to the truth. This robbed it, he thought, of any genuine scientific aim, and made its avowed educational aims valueless. So he concluded that it was of virtually no philosophical value.

Here is the way in which he marks this contrast in the dialogues. In the question-and-answer form of eristic the questioner's aim is to trap his respondent into contradiction, the respondent's is to avoid this trap at all costs without consideration of whether his answers express what he believes to be true. At *Theaetetus* 154c–d Theaetetus is tempted to play the eristic game of avoiding contradiction, but acknowledges that this would involve answers contrary to his genuine belief. In contrast to eristic Socrates emphasises as essential to the purposes of his own method that the respondent must not give assent to any proposition unless he seriously believes it to be true (e.g. *Crito* 49d, *Lach.* 193c, *Prot.* 331b–d). A good example is *Gorgias* 495a–b. Here Socrates insists that to assent to a proposition contrary to what one believes to be true, merely in order to avoid inconsistency (cf. *Laches* 196b), is to ruin the attempt to establish what is true.[41]

Elsewhere eristic or 'antilogic' is condemned for its concern with merely verbal consistency, for its contentious and aggressive bullying of a respondent into contradiction, and for its indifference to truth in its desire to win the argument (*Meno* 75c–d; *Ph.* 89d ff.; *Rep.* 454a, 499a, 539b; *Soph.* 225a–d). The *Euthydemus*, with its extensive illustration of the eristical arguments of the Sophists Euthydemus and Dionysodorus, shows how important Plato felt it to be to emphasise the dangers and shortcomings of eristic and to emphasise by contrast the value of a method which was concerned to establish the truth.

It is important to note that this eristical or 'antilogical' spirit is presented by Plato as characteristic of all forms of argument and debate used by the Sophists. Although his particular references to eristic or antilogic are normally to question-and-answer eristic, he makes clear in the *Sophist* (232b–233c) that the same kind of contentious spirit and purpose belongs to all the Sophists' argumentative techniques, including the long-speech forms pioneered by Protagoras.

Thus the method of the Sophists lacks, in Plato's view, the scientific aim of dialectic. It is not concerned to establish the truth. Nor does Plato think that it has any other acceptable aim. As professional teachers the Sophists did, of course, claim for their activities an educational aim. Some of them specified this aim as an aim to teach 'virtue' (*aretē*) or moral excellence. But it was difficult to get from them any precise specification of the excellence they claimed to teach except in terms of skill in persuasive argument. In Plato's *Protagoras* (312d) Hippocrates, asked what knowledge or skill a Sophist imparts, gives the ready and acceptable answer that it is skill in speaking. But he is unable to specify any particular subject in which a Sophist can be said to be skilled in speaking, or any further aim to which a Sophist can be said to direct his teaching in that skill.

It is left to Protagoras to specify for himself a social and political aim. He claims to teach others to be good citizens, equipped with 'good counsel' to order their own affairs and the affairs of the state (318e). Yet no clear specification of 'good counsel' is given. If we accept as genuinely Protagorean what is said in the *Theaetetus* on Protagoras' behalf, then the good counsel which Protagoras claims to impart is reducible to persuasive advocacy of whatever one wishes to convince others is right (166d ff.)

Other Sophists are similarly represented by Plato as teachers lacking any acceptable aim. Gorgias does not profess to teach 'virtue'. He claims only to be a teacher of rhetoric (*Gorgias* 449a). Yet he implicitly assumes that his teaching does some good, without having given any precise thought as to what good it does. His reluctant admission, under questioning, that his persuasive skills are designed to impart moral knowledge (460a) is part of Plato's attempt to indicate that as a professional teacher Gorgias should have some regard for the truth and for the specifically moral effects of his teaching. Later experts in question-and-answer eristic like Euthydemus and Dionysodorus claimed that they were teachers of virtue (*Euthydemus* 273d). But Plato clearly treats their claims as bogus if they are claims to teach anything more than skill in verbal trickery.

These are the grounds, then, – the lack of any scientific or serious moral and educational aim – on which Plato condemns the method of the Sophists as philosophically barren. The condemnation in some respects is not convincing, and is hardly consistent with the amount of serious philosophical attention which Plato himself gives to particular philosophical arguments and doctrines of the Sophists, especially those of Protagoras. Certainly there can be little sympathy with the condemnation in so far as it is a condemnation of a particular conception of moral excellence with which Plato happens to disagree. Nor can we sympathise entirely with the dismissal as philosophically barren of a method which seeks out contradictions and puzzles and thereby sometimes raises problems of much philosophical interest.

Yet it remains true that the essentially rhetorical purposes and moral aims to which the argumentative techniques of the Sophists were geared were prejudicial to the fruitful development of those techniques by the Sophists as methods of philosophical analysis. Inconsistencies and contradictions are revealed, but there is no desire or attempt to resolve them. For the method which reveals them is indifferent to the problem of their possible resolution since it is indifferent to establishing the truth.

Admittedly some of the Sophists had positive philosophical theories which might appear to be general theoretical answers to that problem and hence to constitute a refutation of the charge of indifference. Such theories are the subjectivism of Protagoras and the scepticism of Gorgias.[42] But we lack satisfactory evidence to show what connexion, if any, existed between these theories and the general aims and methods of the Sophists who proposed them. Were the theories in fact serious philosophical attempts to justify the aims and methods? I very much doubt it. In his *Theaetetus* (166d ff.). Plato suggests what sort of connexion existed between Protagoras' subjectivism and his sophistic aims. His suggestion may or may not represent Protagoras' own views. If it does, it constitutes a surprising exception to the Sophists' lack of interest in the strictly philosophical value of, and justification for, their aims and methods. As for Gorgias' scepticism, it appears to have had no connexion at all with the rest of his views and aims as a Sophist. The exposition of his sceptical position has the air of a display of metaphysical fireworks rather than of a serious contribution to philosophy.

This review of the Sophists' aims, in contrast to those ascribed by Plato to Socrates' dialectic, will help us in our assessment of the originality and philosophical value of Socrates' method. We saw earlier that the Sophists' art of constructing contradictory arguments and of 'making the worse cause appear the better' was an important influence on Socrates' art of *elenchus*. We saw too that the art of questioning introduced by the early Sophists was probably the source of Socrates' interest in the possible value of a question-and-answer technique as a feature of his method. We now see in what way the Sophists' techniques were limited in their fruitfulness and in the possibilities of developing them further by the aims to which they were linked. And in the light of this we can go on to ask in what way the important difference in the aims of Socrates' method allowed him to develop what he inherited from the Sophists into a philosophically more valuable method.

Thus the element of questioning in the Sophists' methods is philosophically insignificant. This is true not only of its part in the early Sophists' method, but also of its part in later question-and-answer eristic. The rigid restrictions on the kind of answers possible rob the interlocutor of all effective choice of what he answers. And the questions are essentially rhetorical. Whatever value the method has as a means of sharpening the questioner's wits does not derive from its question-and-answer form. Nor does the respondent gain anything from being a respondent rather than a listener to a continuous argument. We have to consider then what significance the question-and-answer form gains when it is linked to the aims of Socrates' dialectic.

Again, the arguments of the Sophists are unconcerned with establishing a positive conclusion as true; this is in conformity with their essentially rhetorical aims. So we must ask, in considering Socrates' *elenchus*, what significance it gains through its relation to the scientific and educational aims of dialectic.

Finally we must compare Plato's portrayal of the spirit and aims of Socrates' dialectic with Xenophon's and Aristotle's, and consider how faithful Plato's portrayal is likely to be.

E. *Elenchus* AND HYPOTHESIS

Let us look first at the formal character of the *elenchus*. Richard Robinson has said that the art of *elenchus* 'is to find premisses believed by the answerer and yet entailing the contrary of his thesis'.[43] A typical *elenchus* has the following form.[44] Socrates' respondent proposes a definition of some moral term. Socrates shows that this proposition (*A*) implies other propositions (*B*, *C*, *D*). He then gets the respondent to admit the truth of some further proposition (*W*) and hence of what is implied by that further proposition (*X*, *Y*, *Z*). His aim is to reveal, in what is implied by *W*, a proposition (*Z*) which contradicts what is implied by *A*(*D*). He is then able to argue that so long as the respondent believes *Z* to be true he must believe *D* to be false, and hence, since *D* follows from *A*, he must believe *A* to be false. So the respondent, if he is to be consistent in his views, must abandon *A*.

Within this general pattern the *elenchus* varies greatly in complexity and length. The chain of inferences from *A* and *W* may be short or long. Sometimes, without deduction from *A* or *W*, the respondent may be led on inductively to generalise to *W*, which contradicts his thesis *A*. A good example of this is Plato, *Charmides* 167b ff.[45] Another is *Laches* 192d ff., where a review of cases leads to the generalisation that courage is foolish endurance, a result which contradicts the earlier proposal that courage is wise endurance.

Plato, *Apology* 26–7, is a simple instance of the usual form of Socrates' *elenchus*. Meletus has accused Socrates of belief in spiritual powers. In court he declares Socrates to be an atheist. But, says Socrates, *A* (to be an atheist) is equivalent to *B* (to deny that there are gods). And *X* (belief in spiritual powers) implies *Y* (belief in spirits (*daimones*)). Here Socrates, with his characteristic resort to cases, supports the inference by pointing out that belief in specifically equestrian matters implies belief in horses, belief in flute-playing matters implies belief in flute-players. Further, *Y* (belief in spirits) implies *Z* (belief in Gods). And *Z* is inconsistent with *B* and hence with *A*.

Gorgias 497d ff. is a more characteristic example. It illustrates admirably Socrates' habit of oblique approach to the contradictory of his respondent's thesis. Callicles has put forward the thesis that the good should be identified with pleasure. He has also maintained (491) that the good man is both brave and wise, and hence superior to the coward and the fool. Socrates reminds him of this (497e). And have you ever seen a foolish child rejoicing, he asks Callicles. Yes, Callicles answers. And a foolish man too? Yes, says Callicles, but what of that? He has not yet caught the drift of the argument. Socrates goes on to the case of the coward. Callicles agrees that cowards are more pained than brave men at the approach of the enemy, more pleased when the enemy withdraw. But he still has to confess ignorance of the point of the argument, even when Socrates asserts, on the implicit basis of Callicles' equation of the good with pleasure, that the case just considered makes the bad man, the coward, even better on occasion than the good (498c).

So Socrates has to spell it out for him and reveal the contradiction in his views. If Callicles' admissions are now reckoned up (498e), it can be seen from the cases Socrates has used that the coward or fool has as much pleasure and pain as the brave or wise man, and perhaps more of both. And on the basis of Callicles' hedonism, this is equivalent to asserting that the coward or fool is equally as good and as bad as the brave or wise man, and perhaps even better (499a–b). But this contradicts Callicles earlier admission that the good man is both brave and wise and hence that the brave or wise man is a better man than the coward or fool.

Finally, let us look at the argument, in slightly abridged form, of *Laches* 192cff. Here Socrates is asking Laches for a definition of courage:

Laches. If I have to state that essential nature of courage which belongs to all instances of it, I should say that it is a sort of endurance of the soul.

Socrates. But you do not mean, I imagine, that *all* endurance is courage. My ground for saying so is this. I am pretty sure that you think that courage is a very fine thing.

L. Yes, one of the finest.

S. And endurance combined with wisdom is fine and good.

L. Certainly.

S. And what of endurance combined with foolishness? Is it not harmful and bad?

D   G.P.S.

L. Yes.

S. And would you say that what is harmful and bad is a fine thing?

L. It would be quite wrong to say that.

S. Then I take it that you will not agree that endurance of that kind is courage. For such endurance is not a fine thing, but courage is.

L. True.

S. Then wise endurance, according to what you say, would be courage.

L. It would seem so.

S. But what do we mean by 'wise'? Wise in what? In everything and anything? Suppose a man shows endurance in spending his money wisely, knowing that his spending will bring him more in the end, would you call him courageous?

L. Certainly not.

S. Or suppose a physician steadfastly refuses to yield to requests for food and drink when his son, or some other patient, is suffering from inflammation of the lungs?

L. That would not be courage either.

S. Then take a man who shows endurance in war, and is willing to fight, a man who is wise in his calculations, knowing that others will come to his aid, that he will be fighting against men inferior to those on his own side and fewer in number, and that he has more advantageous positions – would you say that this man, whose endurance is based on such wise calculation and preparation, is more courageous than the man in the enemy camp who is willing to endure and stay at his post?

L. I should say the latter was braver.

S. But surely his is a more foolish sort of endurance than the other man's?

L. True.

S. Presumably, then, you would say that a skilled horseman who shows endurance in a cavalry engagement is less courageous than one who is unskilled?

L. Yes.

S. And you would say the same of the expert in slinging or archery or other skill?

L. Certainly.

S. And those willing to go down a well and dive, and to show endurance in this or any other similar activity without being skilled in it – you will admit that they are more courageous than the experts in these activities?

L. What else can a man say, Socrates?

S. Nothing, if that is what he really thinks.

L. I do think that.

S. Well then, men like that are more foolish in facing danger and showing endurance than the professional expert who does so.

L. Obviously.

S. Then did we not previously find foolish daring and endurance to be disgraceful and harmful?

L. Yes.

S. But courage was admitted to be a fine thing.

L. Yes, it was.

S. Yet we are now saying that a disgraceful thing – foolish endurance – is courage.

L. It seems so.

S. Then do you think we are right to say this?

L. No, I do not think we are.

Here again are the characteristic features of Socrates' *elenchus* – its application to the proposed definition of a moral term, its use of inductive argument, its gradual eliciting of admissions from the respondent until the contradictory of his thesis is reached, and its insistence that the respondent should say what he really thinks.

The initial logical aim of the *elenchus* is to reveal a contradiction in the views of the respondent. Thus the respondent, if the contradiction is to be resolved, must abandon his belief in the truth of one of the contradictory propositions. It need not be his original thesis which is given up. For, as we can now clearly see, the typical *elenchus* does not take the form of a reduction to impossibility of a particular thesis by deducing from it, in the manner of Zeno, self-contradictory consequences. It takes the form of sophistic 'contradictory arguments', in the manner of the *Dissoi Logoi*. It shows that the consequences drawn from a particular thesis are incompatible with the consequences of an independent proposition which is held at the same time to be true.

The respondent, then, in order to resolve the contradiction, must choose between alternatives. Socrates, however, is never explicit about what sort of criteria might be appealed to in order to determine the choice. He recognises that in the field of ethics, where he is trying to establish definitions, no ready criterion appears to be available to resolve differences of opinion. Thus he recognises that problems in ethics are unlike arithmetical problems or problems where there is an accepted standard of measurement, e.g. problems of size and weight (*Euthyphro* 7b–c). At the same time he assumes that the contradictions which his *elenchus* reveals can be resolved. What awareness does he show, then, of the kind of criteria which are implicitly employed in his acceptance of one alternative and rejection of the other?

All that he explicitly emphasises is that the respondent must himself be sincerely convinced of the truth of one of the alternatives, and hence be ready to accept it at the expense of the other. It is *his* assent alone which is important; an appeal to popular opinion is not admissible (*Gorgias* 472b–c, 474a–b, 475e–476a; cf. *Laches* 184e). Yet, while in this way he appears to make the assent of the respondent the final authority (see *Gorgias* 486e, 487e), Socrates evidently thinks that one of the alternatives will almost invariably present itself as much more obviously true than the other. Thus he often assumes that his inductive arguments establish the truth of one of the alternatives. At *Euthyphro* 10a ff. his review of cases of the distinction between the active and passive uses of verbs leads to a generalisation which is then applied to show that 'being loved by the Gods' is a merely consequential characteristic and not a defining characteristic of piety. Euthyphro's assent to the steps in the argument is implicitly assumed to be an assent which he cannot, without repudiating the usages of Greek language, withhold. He therefore abandons his thesis that piety is 'what is loved by the Gods'.

Again at *Euthyphro* 12e ff., after Euthyphro has suggested that piety is definable as the part of justice which attends to the gods, Socrates reviews a variety of cases to show that one sense of attention is attention designed for the good or benefit of that to which the attention is given. Euthyphro accepts without question that this conclusion is sound, and that a definition of piety in terms of attention to the gods must be given up if that sense of attention is assumed in it. As at *Euthyphro* 10a–11b, Socrates assumes, without needing to make the point explicit, that the facts of linguistic usage are a sufficient criterion for the truth of his generalisation.

Sometimes he assumes that one of the alternatives is unquestionably true because it expresses some very common Greek conviction about the nature of human excellence. In the argument in the *Gorgias* (497d ff.) which we recently looked at, Callicles is convicted of inconsistency because he combines with his hedonistic views the view that the good man is both courageous and wise. As Dodds notes,[46] 'it was difficult for a Greek not to admit' this, since 'in common speech' a good man 'so often meant simply "a brave man" or "an able man" '. So Socrates, feeling that Callicles cannot fail to admit it, uses his argument not merely to reveal an inconsistency but to show that Callicles' hedonism is an untenable doctrine. A similar appeal to the generally accepted 'fineness' of courage is used in the *Laches* passage we recently quoted (at 193d) to refute the view that courage is definable as foolhardiness.

At *Protagoras* 332a–333b there is a further example of Socrates' presentation of his respondent's inconsistency as an inconsistency between the respondent's initial thesis and a proposition which Socrates takes to be self-evidently true. Protagoras has argued that wisdom and self-control are distinct. Socrates, on the basis of the principle that if a term has an opposite it has only one opposite, shows that they are identical. He then asks Protagoras which of the two propositions is to be given up, the proposition that everything has only one opposite or the proposition that wisdom is distinct from self-control. One of them, he says, must be given up, since the second cannot be true unless the first is false. Protagoras, implicitly acknowledging the self-evident truth of the first, reluctantly abandons his initial thesis.

Thus, while the initial logical aim of the Socratic *elenchus* is to reveal a contradiction in a respondent's views, its further aim is to establish as the contradictory of the respondent's initial thesis a proposition presented as so obviously true that the respondent is driven to abandon his thesis. In principle the method is a good one. Where concealed inconsistencies exist, it is a good thing to bring them to light and to point the way to resolving them. In practice the method can, obviously, be abused or mishandled. Does Socrates, then, abuse or mishandle it? Often he appears to be both honest in intention and logically accurate in his use of it. Sometimes, however, his logic is at fault when deducing consequences from one or other of the premises in the argument. And sometimes he seems to push the respondent too quickly and too uncritically to accept one of two alternative conclusions as true and reject the other as false. In the latter case the accepted alternative is usually one which furthers Socrates' aim of leading the argument towards one of his favourite positive doctrines.

For example, in the argument of *Euthyphro* 10a ff., we feel that Euthyphro is trapped into admitting, rather incautiously, that piety 'is loved by Gods simply because it is pious', and that Socrates unfairly reduces his thesis that piety is 'what is loved by the Gods' to the statement of a consequential, not a defining characteristic. Socrates, we feel, should have presented Euthyphro with two possible alternatives – *either* an action is pious because it possesses certain intrinsic characteristics which constitute its piety independently of the approval of the Gods, *or* an action is pious simply because the Gods approve of it.

Again, at *Gorgias* 497d ff., Callicles could have retracted his admission that the good man is both courageous and wise. For this is not *necessarily* so. He would then have been able, without contradicting his hedonistic thesis, to admit the truth of Socrates' statements about the amounts of pleasure and pain experienced in battle by brave men and cowards. In the *Protagoras* the logic of Socrates' argument at 332a ff., highly suspect though it is, is left uncriticised by Protagoras. He does not protest that Socrates is using the ambiguity of the Greek *aphrosunē* (folly) to force the conclusion he desires. The protest would have been justified. So that Protagoras could have accepted without contradiction *both* the proposition that if a term has an opposite it has only one opposite *and* the proposition that wisdom and self-control are distinct.

It is not difficult, then, to find flaws in Socrates' arguments. And, quite apart from his dubious logic, he sometimes presents as obviously true a proposition which we recognise to be open to question. Nor does he show himself aware of the different grounds on which it can be claimed that a proposition is true. Examples of propositions which Socrates takes to be obviously true are necessarily true propositions (e.g. *Prot.* 333a), propositions which express some common Greek conviction in ethics (*Gorg.* 497e), and propositions which there are apparently good empirical grounds for believing to be true (*Men.* 89e ff.). But Socrates shows no awareness of a distinction between these.

Yet the general impression given by both Plato and Xenophon of Socrates' *elenchus* is that it is convincingly used in practice to aid precise and consistent thinking on moral matters. It reveals many genuine contradictions in the views of others, it clarifies the meaning of common Greek moral terms, and it prompts distinctions which are valuable for the understanding of moral problems. Socrates himself emphatically asserts the value of his persistent use of the *elenchus*. He argues that, if knowledge is to be achieved, an essential first step is the realisation that one does not know what one claims to know. In Xenophon's account (*Mem.* IV ii) the practical moral value of the *elenchus* is emphasised. It is a step on the road to self-knowledge, for it prompts a person to examine himself, to find out what sort of character he is (24), and to realise his abilities (25). The practical-minded Xenophon naturally stresses this aspect of the value of the *elenchus*. There is no doubt that Socrates felt that in using his *elenchus* he was providing for others the initial stimulus to a desire for moral knowledge. But Xenophon construes this moral knowledge in terms of the practical well-being in society which it brings, the life of honour and public esteem (26–30).

In Plato too Socrates stresses the moral value of his *elenchus*, though in less practical terms than in Xenophon. In the *Apology* he expresses his conviction that it is better to realise one's ignorance than to think that one knows what in fact one does not know. Coupled with this is his conviction, based on long experience, that he himself is unique in having realised this, and that, since his *elenchus* can bring others to realise it, it can make others better than they were (21-3). He makes clear later in his defence (29-30) that it is mistaken moral notions which his *elenchus* is designed to eradicate, and that the ultimate aim of his persistent questioning is to lead others to know for themselves what the good is.

Thus it is as an instrument of moral education that Socrates values the *elenchus*. And its educational aim includes a genuinely scientific aim. Its application is claimed to be essential as an initial negative method of eradicating false views and stimulating intellectual curiosity and desire to reach the truth. In his dialogue with the slave in Plato's *Meno* (84a–c)[47], Socrates brings the slave to realise that what he initially proposed as the solution of a geometrical problem was wrong. 'He thought he knew what it was, and answered confidently as though he knew, without thinking he was in any difficulty. But now he realises he is in difficulty, and, conformably with his lack of knowledge, does not imagine at all that he does know.' Because of this Socrates thinks the slave is 'better off', for the *elenchus* has made a useful contribution 'towards finding out the truth'. It has made the slave eager to search out the truth. He would not have 'tried to search out the truth or to learn what he thought, despite his ignorance, he did know, if he had not fallen into difficulties through realising that he did not know and had not in this way gained the desire to know'.

This justification of the *elenchus* as a stimulus to intellectual curiosity seems to us much more convincing than its justification as a means of specifically moral education. This latter justification is bound up with Socrates' doctrine that virtue is knowledge, and this link explains why Socrates, in Xenophon and in Plato's *Apology*, feels able to attach such important practical significance to the *elenchus* as a means of leading a man to a life of goodness and of transforming his 'soul'. But without accepting that doctrine we are still able to grant the rightness of Socrates' assessment of his *elenchus* as a valuable stimulus to philosophical thought and a valuable method of educating others in habits of precise and consistent thinking.

As a final point about Socrates' *elenchus* we should note an important difference between Xenophon's presentation of it and Plato's. There is not much illustration of the *elenchus* in Xenophon's *Memorabilia*. It is, however, mentioned as a characteristic feature of Socrates' method. Hippias refers to Socrates' habit of 'questioning and refuting everybody' (IV iv 9; cf. III viii 1). And in Socrates' conversations with Euthydemus (IV ii) there are several good examples of this. But for the most part Xenophon is concerned to answer the charge that Socrates corrupted the young men of Athens. He therefore concentrates his attention on showing the practical moral benefit which others gained from conversation with Socrates. And in thus concentrating on the positive and practical side of Socrates' teaching he tends to leave in the background the negative and critical method of the *elenchus*.

Plato presents the other side of the coin. He does more than present Socrates throughout the earlier dialogues as a persistent user of the *elenchus*. He presents the *elenchus* as such a dominant feature of Socratic method that it triumphs over all attempts to reach a positive conclusion. Admittedly Socrates is shown, as we have seen, using the *elenchus* not merely to reveal contradictions but also to reveal one of the contradictory propositions as true and the other as false. The respondent is prompted by this to try to make such modifications in his thesis as will free it from inconsistencies already revealed. Yet, when a final consistent result appears to be achieved or to be within close reach of achievement, Plato presents Socrates as taking an almost perverse delight in directing the argument to a conclusion which contradicts that apparently consistent result. For example, when it has been argued and agreed in the *Meno* that virtue is knowledge, Socrates draws from this thesis consequences which he asserts, on empirical grounds, to be false. He argues, therefore, that virtue is not know-ledge. In the *Euthyphro* it is argued and agreed that piety cannot be defined as what is loved by the gods since this states a merely con-sequential characteristic, and not one which belongs to the 'essence' of piety. Yet when a positive and promising suggestion is made as to what are the essential characteristics of piety, Socrates reduces it to the statement that piety is what is loved by the gods.

The formal pattern here is the pattern of the Sophists' 'contra-dictory arguments', of the *Dissoi Logoi*. We may readily admit that some of the arguments and topics of the *Dissoi Logoi* most probably come from Plato's early dialogues. But the basic pattern itself is a Sophists' pattern, not an original Socratic or Platonic one. Several early Platonic dialogues stick closely to this pattern, presenting arguments for each of two theses which at the end of the dialogue stand in unresolved contradiction to one another. Thus in the *Euthyphro* the thesis that piety is not definable as 'what is loved by the Gods' is set against the thesis that it is so definable. In the *Meno* the contradictory theses are that virtue is knowledge and that it is not knowledge. In the *Protagoras* the contradiction between the theses that virtue can be taught and that it cannot be taught is left at the end as one which Socrates 'would like to clear up' some time. And at the end of the *Laches* Socrates confesses that he has failed to discover what courage is because the result of the discussion is an unresolved contradiction between the thesis that courage is a distinct part of virtue as a whole and the thesis that courage is equivalent by definition to virtue as a whole. The other early dialogues do not follow this pattern so closely. But they all end inconclusively.

Thus we see that the portraits of Socrates by Xenophon and Plato are opposed to one another in the important respect that in Xenophon Socrates' positive doctrine is in the foreground and his *elenchus* in the background, while in Plato the Socratic *elenchus* dominates the discussions so pervasively that no positive conclus-ions at all are reached. Whether Plato faithfully presents the spirit and the aim of Socrates' method as a whole by giving such dominance to the *elenchus* is a question we will have to discuss later, in relation especially to Aristotle's testimony. But at least we may safely assume, on the basis of the joint testimony of Xenophon and Plato, that the *elenchus* was an essential feature of Socrates' method. And the formal pattern which Plato imposes on so many of his early dialogues serves at least as an admirable illustration of the affinities we have noted between the Sophists' technique of presenting 'contradictory arguments' and Socrates' *elenchus*.

However, even if we accepted Plato's portrayal of Socrates' method as an essentially faithful one, this formal pattern should not mislead us into thinking that the method is limited in its procedures to the construction of 'contradictory arguments'. Within this pattern there are features of the method which are not found in any of the testimony we have about the Sophists' method. We have already noticed how the *elenchus* aims not only to reveal a contradiction but to point to its resolution. We must now consider the way in which these aims of the *elenchus* are linked to a progressive method of hypothesis.

The notion of 'hypothesis' is fairly prominent in Plato's early dialogues. In its relation to the *elenchus* it is used to describe both the respondent's thesis and the premisses from which the contradictory of that thesis is deduced.[48] Robinson, after a careful survey of Plato's use of the notion, concluded that 'the modern notion of hypothesizing as 'positing p in order to ascertain the truth of p' is to be found in Plato, but only subordinately to the original notion of 'positing p in order to infer q', from which it arose owing to Plato's conception of the Socratic elenchus'.[49] Xenophon (*Mem.* IV vi 13) mentions Socrates' use of a method of hypothesis, using the term in what Robinson argues to be the original sense. It is significant, I think, that Xenophon, whose lack of interest in methodology is marked by the scantiness of his remarks on Socrates' method, should have singled out the use of hypothesis as a feature of the method. It suggests that 'hypothesis' was a genuinely Socratic notion. It is important to consider how original Socrates was in his use of it.

There is no evidence that the pre-Socratic natural philosophers used the word 'hypothesis'. But the way in which their thought developed until its culmination in Democritus's atomic theory shows quite clearly that there were critical thinkers before Socrates accustomed to treating the theories of their predecessors and contemporaries as subject to criticism and open to modification. Professor Popper[50] has persuasively championed the pre-Socratic natural philosophers of the sixth and fifth centuries B.C. as founders of 'the rationalist tradition, the tradition of critical discussion'. Their critical attitude, he argues, 'prepared and made possible the ethical rationalism of Socrates'.

Our particular concern is to see how near these early thinkers got to the notion of treating a theory as a hypothesis in the sense that it is a provisional theory subject to confirmation or refutation and, moreover, capable of being tested for that purpose by some recognised method. It is clear that in the fifth century B.C. the natural philosophers in Greece made some progress towards this notion. For it is clear that, especially in the period from Parmenides' theory to that of the Greek atomists, there was a *progressive* attempt to solve fundamentally the same problems, the progress consisting in the continual modification of successive theories. The criteria used for testing a theory were admittedly of a negative and very general kind. They were that a theory must be free of logical inconsistencies and must not contradict the obvious fact that the observable world is a world of motion and change. But, whatever their failings as far as having a recognised experimental method is concerned, there is no doubt that by the end of the fifth century these Greek thinkers were accustomed to treating a general theory as capable of being refuted or confirmed, and, if refuted, of being replaced by a 'better' theory which avoided the refutation. And the Sophists extended this manner of treating a thesis to other fields of inquiry, as we have already seen.

We do not have evidence, however, to show that any one of the pre-Socratic thinkers was critically aware of the procedures of a method which advanced a theory as a working hypothesis and subjected it to the kind of critical testing which would explore possible contrary hypotheses and suggest progressive modifications. These thinkers treated the theories of others as capable of refutation and of radical modification. To this extent they treated theories as hypotheses. But the method of a Zeno or a Protagoras is a method of refuting or of substantiating a single given thesis. What is lacking is evidence of any one thinker's awareness of a systematic method of adopting a theory provisionally and testing it as a hypothesis in the modern sense.

It is this sort of awareness which is evidently shown by Socrates in his combination of the *elenchus* with a method of hypothesis in the arguments of Plato's early dialogues. The *elenchus* has its basis in the 'contradictory arguments' of the Sophists. But in Plato's Socrates we see it serving the constructive aim of seeking the truth by using a true conclusion not only to refute a false one but also to suggest modifications in the premises which yielded the false conclusion. And I am inclined to think, with Popper, that reflection on the critical method of hypothetical thinking implicit in the theorising of the natural philosophers played some part in shaping Socrates' hypothetical method of argument.

This does not mean that Socrates was the first to use the term 'hypothesis' in the modern sense. It is possible that he, rather than Plato, was the first. But we have no good evidence to guide us here. Xenophon, most probably relying for his terminology on Plato's dialogues, mentions 'hypothesis', as we noted, in connexion with Socrates' method, but does not use it in the modern sense. Xenophon's reference is still important. It is likely that he recognised in what Plato says about the method of hypothesis 'something familiar to him in his association with Socrates, though very likely not well understood by him'.[51] It is thus some confirmation that Socrates' use of a method of hypothesis in Plato's early dialogues is not simply a piece of Platonic sophistication.

But it can hardly be taken as confirmation that Socrates invented the term 'hypothesis' in its modern sense.

So we must leave undecided the question whether Socrates or Plato was the inventor. The more important question is whether Socrates or Plato first systematically used a method of hypothesis in the modern sense as a method of philosophical analysis. Here we are on rather firmer ground. Both in Xenophon's *Memorabilia* and Plato's early dialogues we find Socrates practising it. And he practises it here in intimate connexion with those other features of his method which the independent testimony of Aristotle ascribes to him. It is true that, as in the case of the *elenchus*, Xenophon's illustration of it is neither so extensive nor so precise as Plato's. Xenophon remains the practical moralist, essentially uninterested in questions of philosophical method. But we can see in exchanges such as those between Euthydemus and Socrates at *Mem.* IV 2 the basic pattern of the method.

The importance of the method of hypothesis in Socrates' arguments is that it enables the results of applying the *elenchus* to a particular thesis to be used progressively to further the aim of reaching a satisfactory definition. The *elenchus*, in setting a true proposition against a false one, does not remain simply a method of refutation but becomes, within the method of hypothesis, a means of suggesting modifications in the refuted thesis. The modified thesis can then itself be subjected, as a further provisional hypothesis, to examination. And as further inconsistencies are revealed, the process of refinement can be continued towards the final aim of a definition free from contradiction. Thus the method becomes a genuinely experimental method, tentative and exploratory in its approach, and ready to take into account all possible alternative solutions to the problem under discussion. We may sometimes feel dissatisfied with the criteria used by Socrates in deciding between alternatives when a contradiction has been revealed. But his method is in principle a most valuable method of analysis. And he practises it with a sincere concern for establishing the truth.

As an illustration of Socrates' use of it, let us look at the argument of Plato's *Euthyphro*. Euthyphro is attempting to define piety. His proposed definitions are 'hypotheses' (11c), subjected to Socrates' *elenchus*, and progressively refined. Here is an analysis of the argument:

5d 1–5   I   Two assumptions are made:
       (*a*) that piety is a characteristic belonging identically to *all* instances to which the term 'pious' is properly applied.
       (*b*) that possession of the characteristic of piety excludes the possession of its opposite, impiety.

5d 7–e 2   II   (*a*) Euthyphro proposes the following definition:
       'Piety is prosecuting any person guilty, as his own father is, of murder, sacrilege, or similar offences.'

5e 2–6a 5   (*b*) To support his definition, Euthyphro argues from the behaviour of gods to that of men in order to show that it is pious to prosecute one's father for murder.

6b 3–c 7   (*c*) It is established that Euthyphro believes in the old mythology, including its stories of disagreements between gods.

6d 1–e 6   (*d*) Socrates objects that Euthyphro, in giving the definition under II(*a*), has given merely an example of what is pious, without attempting a general definition, as demanded by I(*a*) (Euthyphro agrees that there are many actions properly called 'pious' other than those specified by his 'definition').

6e 10–7a 1 III   Euthyphro now proposes the following general definition:
       'Piety is what is dear to the gods; impiety is what is hated by the gods'.
       Socrates argues that:

7b 2–4   (a) Euthyphro has assumed that the gods have disagreements (II(c)).

7b 6–e 4   (b) If the gods disagree, they must disagree about what is just and good and fine (Socrates here argues from men's behaviour to gods' behaviour, eliminating as possible subjects of the gods' disagreement subjects about which men do not disagree).

7e 6–7   (c) If x is thought to be just or good or fine by a god, then x is loved by that god.

If x is thought to be unjust, bad or disgraceful by a god, then x is hated by that god.

7e 9–8a 9   (d) It follows from III(a) and (b) that the same action may be thought just by some gods, unjust by others.

(e) And it follows from III(c) and (d) that the same action may be loved by some gods, hated by others.

(f) And it follows from III(e) and Definition III that the same action may be both pious and impious.

8a 10–b 6   (g) But this is inconsistent with assumption I(b), which Euthyphro had accepted.

8b 7–9   (h) Euthyphro, in an attempt to avoid the inconsistency, suggests that all the gods would (i) agree that someone who kills a man unjustly should be punished, and hence (ii) implicitly condemn unjust killing as impious ((ii) follows from (i) in view of (c) and Definition III; see 9c 6–7).

8b 9–9c 8   (i) Socrates points out that this is a truism, which adds nothing to the argument. For it has been agreed by Euthyphro (III(c)) that 'x is thought unjust by gods' implies 'x is hated by gods', which is equivalent, by his Definition III, to 'x is impious'.

Thus: (*a*) all that Euthyphro's suggestion amounts to is that gods disapprove of impious acts; and this is already assumed in Definition III.

(*b*) the suggestion does not help to specify *what kind of things* all the gods think unjust; in fact III(*a*) and (*b*) together make this impossible.

(*c*) hence, without the possibility of such specification, one can say only that a chance agreement between all gods may occur with regard to a particular action; and disagreement will still occur with regard to other actions, and to these the objections under (*f*) and (*g*) will still apply.

9d 2–e 2 IV Socrates allows a provisional amendment to Definition III, which now becomes: Piety is what all the gods love; impiety is what all the gods hate. He now wishes to show that, assuming consistency and unanimity in the approvals and disapprovals of the gods, this approval or disapproval is not in itself sufficient to constitute an action approved or disapproved as pious or impious. The unanimity and consistency of approval and disapproval must be directed by principles and standards external to the gods themselves.

10a 1–11b 1 He uses an inductive argument to show that 'being loved by the gods' is a *consequential* characteristic, i.e. consequent on the act of loving. Hence to adopt Definition IV is to assume that pious actions have no intrinsic characteristics constituting their piety independently of the approval of the gods. But this is inconsistent with the assumption (made by Euthyphro, in agreement with Socrates, at 10d 4–7) that 'what is pious is loved by the gods because it is pious'. For this is an assumption that 'if x is pious, x is loved by the gods because it possesses certain intrinsic characteristics constituting its piety antecedently to the act of loving'. Hence Definition IV is unacceptable. It fails to specify in any way what are the characteristics in virtue of which the gods approve certain actions. The discussion therefore turns to the attempt to specify what these are.

This passage illustrates admirably the various features which we have so far argued to be characteristic of Socrates' method. The argument is given direction by Socrates' aim to reach a general definition. The principle that the definition must be a universal definition is introduced at the start. Then Socrates characteristically brings home to his interlocutor the importance of distinguishing between universal and particular, and of viewing his particular problem in relation to some general principle.[52] Characteristic too is Socrates' facility in calling up a variety of particular instances relevant to his argument, e.g. in determining the area of the god's disagreement at 7b–e, and in showing inductively at 10a–11b that 'being loved by the gods' is a consequential characteristic. And throughout the argument he shows his considerable skill in applying his *elenchus* and adding up the admissions of his interlocutor in order to convince him of inconsistency and also to suggest modifications in his thesis.

Finally, there is the important element of progression in his method. Socrates treats the successive proposals of Euthyphro as provisional hypotheses. Each hypothesis is subjected to the critical analysis of the *elenchus*. And each contradiction revealed by the *elenchus* suggests an amended hypothesis. So there is a constant process of improvement towards a satisfactory definition. Socrates draws attention to the status of Euthyphro's proposals as 'hypotheses'. When Euthyphro tries to answer the criticism of his proposed definition of piety as 'what is dear to the gods',

Socrates asks him if he is now proposing to 'amend' his earlier definition and to 'hypothesize' that piety is 'what all the gods love'. If he is, the correctness of this hypothesis must in turn be examined. The hypothesis cannot, says Socrates, simply be accepted or assumed to be true; it is essential to consider precisely what its significance is and what is implied by it in order to establish whether it is right or not (9d–e).[53] And when this hypothesis too is found to be unacceptable, Socrates comments on the difficulties of establishing the truth of Euthyphro's 'hypotheses' and of making them 'stay put' (11b–c). Constant refinement is necessary.

It is clear from this that the Socratic *elenchus* has a constructive as well as a destructive purpose, and that its constructive role comes to it from its association with a progressive method of hypothesis. It is also clear that the significance of calling Socrates' method constructive is that it is designed to establish the truth. This above all distinguishes his method from the method of the Sophists. The Sophists' art of constructing contradictory arguments and of 'making the worse cause appear the better' was a valuable stimulus to philosophical analysis. But the Sophists present contradictions and puzzles as a means of displaying their rhetorical skill. They have no concern for the possibility of resolving them in order to determine the truth. Hence they are not concerned to devise a method for doing so. It is Socrates' concern for the truth in ethics which prompts him to develop a method of both revealing inconsistencies and resolving them. This gives to his method a superiority in technique over that of the Sophists and at the same time a more serious and valuable philosophical purpose.

Moreover, the question-and-answer form of argument gains considerably in value once it is divorced from the rhetorical aims of the Sophists and related to the aims of Socrates' method. Question-and-answer eristic did, as we saw earlier, have an educational aim. In the *Euthydemus* Dionysodorus and Euthydemus claim to be teachers of a particular kind of human excellence (*aretē*). This excellence is skill in persuasive argument.

And the question-and-answer form of instruction is essentially a form of *display* of this skill in arguing persuasively and victoriously for or against *any* thesis. The primary purpose of the exercise is not to sharpen the respondent's wits in attempting to avoid contradiction. Its rules, as the *Euthydemus* shows, are so rigid as to take away from the respondent any initiative in the argument and any chance of qualifying his answers. What it does aim to do is to teach others, through the dramatic display of question-and-answer examples, the art of arguing to win in attacking or defending any thesis, whether as questioners in question-and-answer eristic or as long-speech debaters.

Socrates' educational aim is quite different from this. He is well aware of the danger that the young people he is trying to benefit will pervert the aim of his method and attempt to act as questioners themselves in a win-at-any-price game of trapping others into contradiction. In defending himself against the charge of corrupting the young he complains of young people who try to copy him and 'try their hand at examining others on their own account'.[54] Elsewhere he refers to the misguided imitation of his method by those who treat it as a game to play at the expense of others.[55]

But it was no part of Socrates' aim to teach men to practise his method on others as an eristic-type game. His aim was to stimulate them to seek out the truth for themselves. As we saw in discussing his justification of his use of the *elenchus*, he thought of this aim as a moral as well as a scientific one. He was able to do this because of his conviction that knowing what was good was a necessary and sufficient condition of being good. So he could legitimately claim for his method a moral aim in so far as its aim was to provide knowledge. But we may neglect the specifically moral aim in assessing the value of the question-and-answer form of argument in Socrates' method. It is enough to assess this in relation to the truth-establishing aim.

Let us assume, then, with Socrates, that the pursuit of truth in ethics is a valuable activity, since to have right opinions in this is preferable to having wrong ones. Let us also assume with him that there are numerous inconsistencies in men's moral views which stand in the way of their realisation of the truth, and that the particular inconsistencies differ from individual to individual. And let us assume finally with him that men are unaware of these inconsistencies.

Now the *elenchus* is designed to reveal these inconsistencies and to point the way to resolving them. It is designed, moreover, to confront the *individual* with the inconsistencies in his own views, and to stir his intellectual desire to resolve them. It is for this purpose that Socrates thought that a question-and-answer technique of examination was essential. *Elenchus* and question-and-answer and the hypothetical method were for him inseparable features of his method of education. He thought that the provocative shock to the individual provided by the *elenchus*, and the realisation of the individual's desire to resolve contradictions could be effective only through direct personal questioning. Hence, on the basis of the assumptions we noted above, he placed a high value on question-and-answer argument and claimed that as an intellectual gad-fly in persistently questioning others he was doing a valuable service to the state.[57]

These *educational* claims for the value of his question-and-answer technique are justifiable ones. They are, roughly, the claims that can be made for the value of the individual tutorial as opposed to the formal lecture. A long speech, says Socrates in Plato's *Protagoras* (329a), is like a book. It is not open to questioning and it does not ask questions.[58] His own role as an educator is to do what he thinks the long speech or the book cannot do. And he does it well. By dealing directly with the individual's own opinions and admissions, and the individual's own reasonings, he is able by question-and-answer to reveal inconsistency and to stimulate search for the truth more forcibly than by any other means. In this way a question-and-answer method gains a value in relation to Socrates' educational aims which it lacks in relation to the Sophists' aims. For the Sophists it is a dramatically appropriate form for displaying their persuasive skills. For Socrates it is the essential form of a method of analysis which aims to help others to see the truth for themselves.

Richard Robinson has argued that the *elenchus*, by addressing itself through question-and-answer always to the individual, is 'a very personal affair' and 'takes on particularity and accidentalness, which are defects'. He is thinking of Socrates' method here in contrast to 'the impersonal and universal and rational mark of a science axiomatized according to Aristotle's prescription'.[59] But it is proper to assess the defects of a method only in relation to the method's aims. The particularity and the personal application of the *elenchus*, together with its question-and-answer pattern, are essential to the method's educational aim. And it is abundantly clear that the further stages in realising this aim are designed to take the individual away from the particularity and uncritical personal nature of his views to the generality of principles which are free from contradiction and prejudice. Robinson does suggest that Plato might urge that 'the elenchus is the means by which the irrational and accidental individual is brought to the appreciation of universal science, brought out of his individual arbitrariness into the common world of reason'. [60] Socrates' practice shows that this was in fact an essential aim of his own *elenchus*.

It may seem surprising that Aristotle, while he mentions the question-and-answer form of Socrates' method, makes no mention of the *elenchus* or of the method of hypothesis in connexion with Socrates. For Aristotle's own dialectical method of inquiry, exemplified perhaps most effectively in his ethical works, owes a great deal to the Socratic method exemplified in Plato's early dialogues. Like the Socratic method it is tentative and exploratory, rejecting and refining possible hypotheses, and moving progressively to a satisfactory solution of a problem. Admittedly Aristotle's uses of the term 'hypothesis' do not include the use we have been discussing in connexion with Socrates' method. But though this might make Aristotle hesitate to describe the Socratic method from his own point of view as a method of hypothesis it obviously would not prevent him describing it at all and acknowledging its originality.

Why, then, does he not mention either the *elenchus* or the method of hypothesis? Almost certainly the explanation is the same as the explanation for his failure in the *Metaphysics* to ascribe 'dialectical power' to Socrates, and for his claim (in the *Topics* and *Sophistici Elenchi*) to complete originality in providing a theory of dialectic and formulating its rules (*Soph. El.* 164a). As we saw in the first section of this chapter Aristotle recognises between scientific method and dialectical method a distinction which he considers important and which he does not find either in Socrates and Plato. Moreover he considers the method of Socrates to be scientific in its aim, and assesses it and implicitly criticises it from the standpoint of his own conception of scientific method. And in assessing it as a method which, from his own point of view, is non-dialectical, he too readily overlooks its properly dialectical features. His failure to pick out the *elenchus* and the method of hypothesis as original features of Socrates' method is to be explained therefore on the same grounds as his charge that Socrates lacked 'dialectical power'.

So we need not infer from Aristotle's silence about them that they were neither original nor important elements in Socratic method. And we should not, of course, infer from this silence that they formed no part at all of Socrates' method. Aristotle ascribes to Socrates virtually all the points of method and doctrine which we find in the portrayal of Socrates in Xenophon's *Memorabilia* and Plato's early dialogues. He mentions the search for definitions, the inductive arguments, the question-and-answer technique, Socrates' role as questioner, the profession of ignorance, the concentration on moral problems, the moral paradoxes. The agreement between Xenophon, Plato and Aristotle is here extensive. And the two features which Aristotle does not mention – the *elenchus* and the method of hypothesis – belong so intimately and naturally, in the portraits by Xenophon and Plato, to the rest of Socrates' method and philosophical aims that it is

barely conceivable that Aristotle's silence about them is an
implicit denial that Socrates practised them.

F. WAS SOCRATES A SCEPTIC?

We have now reviewed the main features of Socrates' method.
We have also tried to distinguish his method from that of the
Sophists and to show in what respects it is superior.

There remain several important problems about the aims of
the method. We have looked at the educational aim, and we have
seen that it is linked with a scientific aim. For the educational aim
is to stimulate others to search out the truth for themselves. But
Socrates sometimes seems to be assuming for his method an aim
which is much more directly scientific. He sometimes seems to
assume that the method will enable a person who practises it
properly to discover the truth. This is to assume that it is not only
a method of educating others to discover the truth for themselves,
but also a method of discovering the truth for oneself.

This raises the first of our problems about the aims of the
method. Did Socrates really believe that his method was a method
of discovery? One possible indication that he did believe this is
his familiar 'confession of ignorance'. Aristotle mentions this
(*Soph. El.* 187b), and remarks that Socrates' art of interrogation
does not assume any knowledge of the subject under discussion.
Plato makes several references to it (*Apol.* 21b ff., *Charm.* 165b,
Symp. 216d, *Gorg.* 509a). And it is possibly implied in Hippias'
complaint to Socrates in Xenophon (*Mem.* IV iv 9) that he is
always questioning others without ever declaring his own
opinion. It allows Socrates to present himself to his interlocutors
as a person joining with them in an inquiry which seeks the truth
on a particular problem, not as a person already in possession of
this truth and concerned only to lead them to see it for themselves.

The confession of ignorance does, of course, indicate that

Socrates starts a discussion with one advantage over his interlocutors. Unlike them he is aware of his ignorance. He 'knows
that he does not know'. And he aims, through the *elenchus*, to
make others confess their ignorance and thus to prompt them to
seek out the truth. As we have seen, he considered this to be an
essential first step on the road to knowledge. At the same time
Socrates professes to be seeking out the truth for himself as well
as for his interlocutors. He claims to be following the argument
with them wherever it leads (*Rep.* 394d) in the hope of finding
the truth, and not to be acting simply as a teacher who knows the
solution in advance of the inquiry. From this point of view it
may be argued that he treats his question-and-answer method as
a method of discovery, and not only as a method of education.

Another possible argument in favour of this is that Plato
certainly treats his own art of dialectic, which proceeds by
question-and-answer and is clearly based in its other main
features on Socrates' method, as a method of discovery. Indeed,
Plato considers the question-and-answer technique to be such a
fundamental feature of his ideal method that he defines the
dialectician, the person with supreme ability to gain insight into
the truth, as the person skilled in asking questions and giving
answers (*Crat.* 390c).[61] Is it not then reasonable to argue that, in
treating the dialectical art of question and answer as a method of
discovery, Plato is simply following Socrates' lead, as he certainly
does in many other aspects of his method?

Let us look first at the question of Socrates' sincerity in confess-
ing himself ignorant. Is this confession simply an example of
Socrates' slyness or 'irony'? Some of his interlocutors seem to
have thought so; they are represented as accusing him of being
sly and playful (Plato *Symp.* 216e; *Rep.* 337a ff.; Xenophon
Mem. IV iv 9). They assumed that his readiness to refute the
opinions of others and his reluctance to offer any opinion of his
own sprang from a desire to avoid having his own positive
convictions criticised, and not from any recognition of his own
ignorance. Hence the ascription to him of slyness or 'irony'.

Yet Plato himself represents the profession of ignorance as perfectly sincere. He depicts Socrates' slyness as a characteristic ascribed to him by others because they failed to understand his genuine humility and his disinterested concern to elucidate by question and answer what was not initially clear to him.

Why, then, should we hesitate to accept that the profession of ignorance is perfectly sincere? The main reason is that it is hardly consistent with the way in which Socrates manages his arguments. Both in Xenophon and Plato the control and direction of Socrates' arguments bear all the marks of conscious manipulation towards just those positive doctrines in ethics which we find ascribed to Socrates by Aristotle. From very different starting points the arguments move with such consistency to fundamentally the same conclusions that it becomes implausible to take seriously Socrates' contention that he is impartially following the argument wherever it leads.

The same can be said about the negative and destructive manipulation of the *elenchus*. Socrates' contention that his skill in refutation is 'involuntary' (*Euthyphro* 11d), as though he did not desire and could not foresee the refutation of his respondent's hypothesis, seems implausible when set against the vigorous and systematic manner in which he carries it out. Robinson concluded that Socrates' contention is insincere. 'The arguments', he says, 'could not be so workmanlike and purposeful, the results could not be so invariably negative, by divine inspiration or by mathematical probability.'[62]

Thus Socrates' actual practice in argument, as depicted by Plato and Xenophon, suggests much more forcibly that Socrates' question-and-answer method is educational in its aim than that it is a method of discovery. Are we then to infer from this that Plato's notion of dialectic as a method of discovery is essentially his own, and not derived from Socrates? Such an inference can be supported by other considerations. Plato does not introduce this notion until his own metaphysical theory has been introduced, i.e. until the thought of the dialogues has reached a stage which, as

Aristotle's testimony makes clear, goes beyond what can be ascribed to Socrates. When Socrates is explicit about the aims of his method in Plato's early work, it is the educational aim of the method which he mentions. It is on educational grounds that he justifies his use of it and defends its value in the *Apology*.

It seems probable, then, that Socrates thought of his method of question and answer primarily as an instrument of education. If he did, we can add to the many technical virtues of his method the virtue that he restricts its aim to an educational aim. His 'art of interrogation' has obvious merits as a method of teaching others how to think precisely and consistently. It has been commended, with much justification, as 'the only method for teaching philosophy'.[63] But, considered as a method of discovery, its question-and-answer form seems to be an equally obvious defect.

To see that this is so it is necessary only to consider what justification Socrates could have given for a claim that his method was a method of discovery in ethics. To make this claim is to claim that the best way to discover the truth in ethics is to engage in question-and-answer exchanges with someone. The only plausible justification for this would be that serious philosophical discussion between two or more people on problems in ethics is always more likely to yield the truth than a method of analysis practised by a single person. A condition would be that those engaged in the discussion should be genuinely concerned to find the truth and highly and equally gifted in analysis. This sort of justification would not, perhaps, convince many people. But it is the best and the only plausible one that could be made. It is the sort of justification that Socrates would naturally have been prompted to offer if he had thought of his method of question-and-answer as a method of discovery.

But we should then expect to find some reflection of this ideal in Socrates' actual practice in discussion. And there is no such reflection. In Xenophon's and Plato's portraits the relation between Socrates and his interlocutor is essentially that of tutor and pupil. Many of his interlocutors are singularly deficient in acumen of any kind. A few, like Protagoras, are more of a match for him and are represented as such. An interlocutor of Protagoras' standing is in fact represented as pointing out flaws in Socrates' reasoning. Yet even with Protagoras Socrates' aim is obviously educational – to make Protagoras realise the inconsistencies in what he professes to believe and to suggest a means of resolving them. With less competent interlocutors the educational aim is clearer still. Socrates' conversations are not intended to be philosophical discussions between equal minds with a heuristic, rather than an educational, aim.

To recognise that Socrates' method is specially valuable as an instrument for teaching others to think for themselves does not mean, of course, that its value is *restricted* to its educational uses. It is only the question-and-answer form which is the stumbling block to thinking of the method as more than an educational method. Apart from this feature, the method is quite clearly a model for the kind of precise critical analysis which is likely to yield fruitful results in philosophical thinking. Its *elenchus*, its searching use of examples and analogies, its tentative and exploratory use of hypotheses, and its general aim to elucidate the meaning of the most central concepts within its field of study – these are features of Socrates' method which first clearly establish a method of critical analysis as the ideal method of philosophical inquiry. And these procedures do not demand an interlocutor for their exercise.

So we must not, because of the question-and-answer form which Socrates gives to his method in order to further his educational mission, think that the method is to be valued only as an educational tool. Nor must we think that Socrates valued it only as such. One thing he is doing as an educator is introducing others to a method of critical analysis which he has himself, independently of others, found to be valuable in his own thinking. He is also introducing others to some of the valuable insights which the use of the method has yielded. The question-and-answer technique of cross-examination is the form he gives to his method when he wants it to serve educational purposes.

So far we have argued that neither Socrates' confession of ignorance nor Plato's claims for his art of dialectic can be taken as indications that Socrates' method of cross-examination was considered by him to be a method of discovery. It was, for Socrates, the best method for educating others to think for themselves and to do that thinking precisely and consistently. But he did not consider it to be a method of discovering the truth for oneself.

Our argument does imply, however, that Socrates considered that he could himself establish important truths in ethics by a critical method of analysis. For we have argued (i) that a reason for treating Socrates' profession of ignorance as not perfectly sincere is that such a profession is inconsistent with his manipulation of the arguments in the direction of certain positive conclusions which he holds to be true, and (ii) that part of his educational purpose is to introduce others, through cross-examination, to some of the valuable insights which his own critical analysis has yielded for him. Thus his method of educating others, while not itself a method of discovery, assumes a prior discovery of the truth.

But there is one argument against this conclusion which deserves serious consideration. We noted in the last section that in his early dialogues Plato, unlike Xenophon, presents the *elenchus* as such a dominant feature of Socrates' arguments that it triumphs over all attempts to reach a positive conclusion. If we accept the Platonic portrait as faithful in this respect, then it becomes possible to argue that Socrates was an agnostic or sceptic. For, apart from the general point that the discussions are inconclusive, we find Socrates declaring his despair of ever reaching any definite truth. In the *Euthyphro* (11b–d) he says he would like to have the arguments 'immovably settled', but complains that all propositions seem to be shifting and transitory, so that they 'run away' from any systematic attempt to substantiate their truth. He also refers to the difficulty of finding any 'adequate criterion' which will enable disagreements in ethics to be resolved (7c–d).

This suggestion of agnosticism or scepticism prompts the further suggestion that Socrates' profession of ignorance, so far from implying that he considers his method of cross-examination to be a method of discovery, is a profession of agnosticism. For example, Vlastos, in discussing Socrates' method, speaks, not of Socrates' profession of ignorance, but only of his 'profession of agnosticism'.[64]

Vlastos thinks that Socrates' profession of ignorance 'makes good sense' only when seen as a profession of the limited aims of his method. For this method, he argues, 'neither assumes nor affords certainty about the truth or falsehood of any one proposition'. Its purpose 'is a more modest one; to increase one's insight into the logical relations between propositions and thus one's ability to estimate how the truth claims of one proposition are affected by those of others, implying it or implied by it'. Indeed we have only to look, he suggests, at some of the contexts in which Socrates' profession of ignorance is made in Plato's earlier dialogues, and we will see that his profession is at once a profession of agnosticism and a profession of the modest aims of his method.

He gives *Charmides* 165b as an instance. Here Socrates says to Critias: 'you deal with me as though I professed to know the things I am asking questions about and as though I could, if only I would, admit the truth of what you propose. But this is not the case. I inquire with you into the truth of whatever is proposed just because I do not myself have knowledge.' Vlastos argues that 'had Socrates thought of his method as aiming at a certain demonstration of particular truths, he would not have talked this way unless he was conceding that his previous practice of his method had been a failure, and this he would not have admitted for a moment'. And to support this he refers to *Gorgias* 508e–509a as a place where we find Socrates 'reiterating his profession of agnosticism at a moment when he feels it (namely his method) has been completely successful'.

This is not, of course, the only possible interpretation of Socrates' profession of ignorance in passages such as this. Socrates might be professing ignorance merely as an expedient to encourage his interlocutor to seek out the truth, to make him think that he is joining with Socrates in a voyage of discovery. This is the sort of interpretation our own argument would imply. It would allow Socrates to 'talk this way' *without* 'conceding that his previous practice of his method had been a failure'.

Moreover, it seems incongruous to use the *Gorgias* to support the view that Socrates' profession of ignorance is a profession of the limited aims of his method. The Socrates of the *Gorgias* is a Socrates different in attitude from the Socrates of the other early dialogues.[65] He is more positive and dogmatic in his views. His interests are going beyond the interests which Xenophon, Aristotle, and the other early Platonic dialogues agree in ascribing to him. They are interests linked in several respects to those of the *Meno*, which stands on the fringe of the dialogues of Plato's middle period. Moreover, his new confidence allows him to claim that his doctrine is irrefutably true (473b; cf. 486e, 487e). Subsequently he claims that his thesis has been 'secured and bound by arguments of iron and adamant' (508e–509a). These are not the claims of a person who does not think that his method can establish anything as certainly true. Socrates does, certainly, qualify his last claim by professing ignorance (509a). But this is very odd. Its oddness is commented on by Dodds.[66] 'It is as if', he says, 'Plato had belatedly remembered to make his hero speak in character'.

This explanation of the passage as an oddity seems to me to be the obviously right one. If it is right, it means that the passage implies nothing that is relevant to the interpretation of Socrates' profession of ignorance. So it cannot be taken to indicate, as Vlastos thinks it can, that Socrates is fully aware of 'the essential feature of his method' in that 'he has seen that its aim cannot be final demonstrative certainty'.

There is, then, nothing in the immediate contexts in which

Socrates professes his ignorance to imply that he is professing, as an agnostic, the limited aims of his method. Yet it remains true that, within the broader context of the general spirit and direction of the arguments of Plato's early dialogues, such an interpretation of his profession of ignorance has some plausibility. For the arguments, as we have seen, are inconclusive and dominated by the negative and destructive force of the *elenchus*. If we accept such an interpretation, then we can no longer maintain that Socrates' method of educating others, while not itself a method of discovery, assumes a prior discovery of the truth. For Socrates' agnosticism would presumably limit the aim not only of the educational, question-and-answer use of his method, but also of the non-conversational use of it as an independent method of analysis.

Yet, plausible though this interpretation may appear within the context of Plato's early dialogues, it loses its plausibility once it is considered in relation to the non-Platonic testimony on Socrates. For this non-Platonic testimony, so far from giving support to it, is quite incompatible with any sceptical interpretation of the method's aims.

Let us look first at Aristotle's testimony. As we have already seen, Aristotle presents Socrates' method as a scientific method which aims, to use Vlastos' words, at 'demonstrative certainty'. And in his assessment of the method in his *Metaphysics* Aristotle is implicitly criticising Socrates for failing to distinguish between the genuinely scientific method belonging to theoretical sciences and the dialectical method belonging to a practical science such as ethics, where no 'demonstrative certainty' is attainable. It is likely that, in assessing the method in terms of this distinction, he ascribes to Socrates a more precisely conceived scientific method in ethics than he is justified in doing. So we have to make some allowance for Aristotle's understandable tendency to assess the achievements of others in the light of his own philosophical distinctions.

To make such allowance is not, however, to concede that Aristotle's assessment in the *Metaphysics* totally misrepresents the aims of Socrates' method. It is consistent with this assessment that in his ethical works Aristotle makes it a major criticism of Socratic ethics that Socrates misconceives the nature of moral knowledge in that he thinks of it as a form of scientific knowledge when it is a quite 'different kind of cognition'.[67] Nor is there any suggestion, in anything that Aristotle says about Socrates, that there is any trace of scepticism in Socrates' thought. Aristotle assumes throughout that Socratic method was designed to yield certainty in ethics.

Moreover, Aristotle's assessment of the aims of Socrates' method is much more consistent than any 'agnostic' assessment with what are accepted to be the main tenets of Socrates' ethics. The main thesis of Socrates' ethics is that virtue is knowledge. It assumes that knowing what it is right to do is at once a necessary and a sufficient condition of doing it, and that doing what is wrong is invariably acting in ignorance of what is right. This is a discouraging sort of prescription if the method of inquiry into what is right is assumed to be incapable of yielding any certain knowledge. Aristotle always assumes that the possibility of acquiring this knowledge through definition of the virtues is fundamental to Socratic ethics. It is clear to me that he is right in assuming this.

Similarly in Xenophon there is no suggestion of an agnostic Socrates. Xenophon notes, as Aristotle does, that Socrates' method was to interrogate others without directly offering his own views (*Mem.* IV iv 9). It is possible that Socrates' 'confession of ignorance' is implied in Xenophon's remarks here. Even if it is, it does not in itself, as we have already seen, carry any implication of agnosticism. And nowhere in the *Memorabilia* is there any suggestion of a lack of confidence that the method will carry the respondent through to the truth. In practice the method is presented as successful in achieving positive conclusions, and it is associated in its practice with the confident presentation of Socrates' principal ethical doctrines.

Thus there is no support either from Xenophon or from Aristotle for the view that Socrates was a sceptic and that his

F

method had the limited aim of 'increasing one's insight into the logical relations between propositions and thus one's ability to estimate how the truth claims of one proposition are affected by those of others'. In so far as Plato's portrait of Socrates in his early dialogues supports such a view, it is in that respect quite exceptional. It is, indeed, so exceptional in this respect that it prompts doubt as to whether this aspect of his portrait can be taken as faithfully Socratic. It also prompts us to ask what special reason Plato could have had for his apparently sceptical orientation of Socrates' method.

The answer to this question lies, I think, in Plato's own attitude to Socrates' method. One of the most obvious and most striking differences between Plato's early dialogues and the dialogues of the middle period is that the tentative and inconclusive discussions of the early dialogues give way in the middle period to the confident presentation of ambitious speculative theories in metaphysics, in philosophy of mind, and in political theory. And with the advent of these theories Plato's attitude to Socrates' dialectical method changes. He now envisages for it a much wider field of application and a much more positive and ambitious purpose.

A ready explanation of this change would be that, once Plato has his own positive theories to put forward, he is no longer content to paint portraits of Socrates. This makes the change a change from Socratic thinking to Platonic thinking. There is something to be said for this explanation. In many respects its assumption that the early dialogues present Socratic thinking is supported, as we have seen, by the testimony of Xenophon and/or Aristotle. But it is too simple an explanation. It seems obviously unlikely that a lively and original mind such as Plato's would be content simply to present Socrates' thought and method without introducing at all his own refinements and evaluations. And we know, on the basis of Aristotle's testimony, that at least in his middle dialogues Plato is using Socrates as the mouthpiece for his own, rather than Socrates', views. So that when we find in the *early* dialogues something which is presented as Socratic and yet which neither Xenophon nor Aristotle confirms as Socratic, it seems reasonable to assume that it is something attributable to Plato's own thought.

This suggests an alternative explanation of Socrates' scepticism in the early dialogues. It is that this scepticism represents *Plato's* attitude to Socrates' method, his attitude being that the method cannot justifiably claim to yield certainty so long as it relies only on the criteria of logical consistency and agreement between the speakers. This continues to be his attitude until, in the *Meno*,[68] his own theory of Recollection enables him to justify on theoretical grounds the claim that the Socratic method of systematic questioning is sufficient to prompt recognition of the truth.

It is significant that the theory of Recollection appears for the first time in the dialogues as a theory to meet the explicit objection that Socrates' method is unable to solve the problems it discusses. The method continually generates perplexities, Meno complains, but offers no satisfactory criterion for resolving them (*Meno* 80d–e). What the theory of Recollection does, in answering this, is to demonstrate that in mathematics Socrates' method of cross-examination will lead a person to recognise that certain propositions are undeniably true. It then argues that what the method can do in mathematics it can do also in 'all other branches of learning' (85e).

Thus the context in which the theory of Recollection is first introduced suggests that it was formulated as an answer to problems which arose from Plato's reflection on the efficacy of Socratic method and his recognition of its apparent limitations. And this suggests that we should construe the change in the dialogues from a negative to a positive and constructive use of the method of question and answer in terms of developments in Plato's own thought. It follows that the sceptical orientation of the method in the early dialogues represents *Plato's* attitude at that time to the efficacy and scope of the method, and not necessarily Socrates'. The way in which Plato incorporates the purely critical and negative use of the method within his new theory is some confirmation that this view is correct. This use of it now becomes the first stage in the process of recollection (*Meno* 84a–c), to be succeeded by stages which result in true belief and finally knowledge (85c–d). It seems to me that we have here, in a nutshell, an expression of the nature and extent of Plato's own change in attitude at this time towards the method of Socrates.

We are able, then, to explain the apparent scepticism of the Socrates of Plato's early dialogues consistently with our acceptance of Aristotle's testimony that Socrates' method was a scientific method, designed to yield certainty in ethics. So we are now able to see that Socrates, when he aims as an educator to lead others to see the truth for themselves, is already convinced that his method of analysis is able, quite independently of its educational uses, to discover the truth. It is this conviction which gives strength to his further conviction that virtue is knowledge, the basis of his moral thought.

Before we examine this moral thought in the next chapter, there is one final point to be made about Socrates' method of analysis in ethics. Reference is often made to the 'rationalism' of Socratic ethics. This is properly interpreted in terms of two of Socrates' fundamental convictions. The first is that by a systematic method of analysis it is possible to establish true real definitions of the 'virtues' of moral behaviour. The second is that the knowledge thus gained is a necessary and sufficient condition of attaining 'virtue' and hence of doing what is good. The 'rationalism' of Socratic ethics means that Socrates held both these propositions to be true.

In any other sense it is misleading to speak of Socrates' rationalism in ethics. In particular we should beware of thinking of Socratic method as rationalist in the sense that it assumes that reason is a source of knowledge in ethics independently of experience. Socrates shows no awareness of the distinction involved here. Nor does his method rely on appeals to any faculty of moral intuition or insight. It assumes its self-sufficiency without asking theoretical questions about this or attempting to justify it.

2

The Moral Paradoxes

A. THE BACKGROUND

IN the discussion of Socratic method in the last chapter we noted Socrates' conviction (i) that moral knowledge is knowledge through definition of what goodness or virtue is and of what the particular virtues are, and (ii) that possessing moral knowledge is both a necessary and a sufficient condition of being good, and hence of doing what is good. (ii) is the thesis that virtue is knowledge. As a preliminary to the elucidation of this paradox, and of the other Socratic paradoxes, something must be said about the most common Greek moral concepts and about the background of moral thought in Socrates' time.

There are three basic moral concepts – virtue or excellence (*aretê*), good (*agathon*), and happiness (*eudaimonia*). The three are invariably associated with each other. Aristotle, when he attempts to formulate a definition of human goodness in the first book of the *Nicomachean Ethics* (I vii), assumes without question that he is thereby formulating a definition of happiness. He assumes further (1098a) that the definition must be in terms of man's peculiar excellence (*aretê*).

Aristotle's discussion also indicates clearly the association of good and excellence with function. Thus the adjective 'good' is explained in terms of function or purpose. If one thinks of a good flute-player or sculptor or artist, Aristotle says, or of anything that has a function or activity, the 'good' is considered to reside in the function. Similarly, in considering good as a term of commendation in reference to human behaviour generally, we assume that man *qua* man has a function. The problem of specifying man's goodness thus becomes the problem of specifying his proper function, or, more particularly, of specifying the excellence in the performance of his proper function which makes that performance good.

Plato offers much the same analysis in discussing the meaning of excellence in a passage in the *Republic* (352d ff.). Everything, he says, has its peculiar function – horses, pruning-knives, eyes, ears *et cetera*. Moreover, everything performs its function well by reason of its proper excellence or virtue. Applying this to human behaviour, we may say that a man 'lives well' by reason of his proper excellence or virtue.

Although 'good' is always associated in this way with function, it is important to note that it is not restricted, in its reference to human behaviour, to an instrumental sense which excludes its use as a term for a final end. It is certainly very often used in moral contexts in an instrumental sense of 'good for' a certain purpose, and in this sense it is used synonymously with words meaning 'useful' or 'beneficial' (*chrêsimon* or *ôphelimon*). Socrates himself, both in Xenophon and Plato, often uses it in that way (e.g. Xen. *Mem.* IV vi 8). Thus an action is describable as good in so far as it is conducive to a morally commendable end which the agent wishes to achieve. Or a person is describable as good in so far as he is the sort of person whose actions follow a consistent pattern of being conducive to such an end.

There is, however, a use of 'good' where it is not synonymous with useful or beneficial. As Plato points out in the *Hippias Major* (296e–297d, 303e), 'beneficial' is what is instrumental to 'good', or what causes good as its result. Beneficial and good are thus distinguishable as cause and effect. Here 'good' is used as a term for the end rather than as a term for what is conducive to the end. Socrates, Plato and Aristotle use it in this way when they describe the end of human action substantivally as 'the good' (*to agathon*).

The Greeks invariably specified the good as happiness (*eudaimonia*). *Eudaimonia* means, roughly, 'being blessed with good fortune'. It is often used synonymously with prosperity or 'faring well' (*euprâgia*). All the philosophical schools are agreed that *eudaimonia* is the end. As Aristotle says, it is a platitude to assert that *eudaimonia* is the chief good (*E.N.* 1097b). Similarly Plato, in his discussion of the meaning of excellence in the passage of the *Republic* (352d ff.) which we recently considered, makes a natural inference from the proposition that a man performs his proper function well by reason of his own excellence or virtue to the proposition that the virtuous man is happy (*eudaimôn*). The inference is a natural one because the Greek language allowed much the same sort of double usage of 'doing well' (*eu prattein*) as it did with 'good' (*agathon*). Just as to 'do good' is to do what is conducive to 'the good', so to 'do well' (= do what is good) is to do what is conducive to 'doing well' or 'faring well', and hence what is conducive to *eudaimonia*.

These features of the Greeks' moral language give to all Greek moral thought its broadly utilitarian character. An action is morally commendable in so far as it is conducive to happiness. The notion of 'duty for duty's sake', or of 'rightness' as an intrinsic characteristic of a particular action or class of actions is a notion foreign to Greek moral thought. Approval and disapproval of particular actions are determined by reference to the end which the action in fact promotes or is intended to promote.

With these features of the Greeks' moral language in mind, we may now consider the main problems in ethics which were being raised for the first time in fifth-century Greece. In and before Socrates' time, forms of excellence consistently admired in Greek literature were courage, piety, wisdom, moderation (*sôphrosunê*) and justice (*dikaiosunê*). It is these virtues which were canonised by the Greek moral philosophers, beginning with Socrates. But until the fifth century there is no systematic attempt to examine the basis of the belief in these virtues or to give them more precise significance within a positive moral theory. In the fifth century, however, we find the beginnings of a reasoned, critical approach to the problem of justifying any particular prescription, in terms of recommended virtues, for the attainment of happiness. This problem is at the same time the problem of resolving the moral conflicts which arise for the individual in society in assessing what it is right for him to do.

There is much explicit moralising, on the fringes of these problems, in the fifth-century Greek tragedians. The tragedians emphasise the various moral conflicts which may arise in the pursuit of happiness, the conflict between what the individual thinks is right and what the state thinks is right, between what the state thinks is right and what religion prescribes as right, between what the individual's present desire prompts him to do and what he knows the accepted conventions of his society prescribe as right for him to do. In presenting these conflicts the tragedians usually champion the virtues of wisdom and moderation as conditions of happiness. They also make some attempt to explain, in mainly religious terms, the principles which govern the distribution of human happiness and unhappiness. There is, finally, a tendency, prominent in some of Euripides' tragedies, to question the validity of any religious justification of principles of human morality.

The critical attitude of Euripides reflects in part the influence of the Sophists, who formulated in more precise terms the problems dramatically exploited by the tragedians. In general, their vocation prompted the Sophists to specify and to justify particular prescriptions for the attainment of happiness in terms of practical worldly success, within the conditions imposed by the conventions and institutions of the city-states in which they practised. This is true at any rate of Protagoras, perhaps the most influential of the Sophists, whose claim to be able to teach virtue was based on a severely practical conception of success in life. Plato, in the *Protagoras* (311d ff.), interprets in practical terms Protagoras' profession that he is able to teach men to be good citizens.

Although not all the Sophists made it their explicit aim to teach virtue, they did assume, armed as they were with specialist qualifications in the techniques of persuasive argument, that their teaching would equip men to achieve greater success in practical affairs of state. At the same time many of them questioned the validity of generally accepted moral and religious views. Their critical attitude is reflected in many ways. It is reflected in Protagoras' religious agnosticism (DK.80 B 4), and in his subjectivist thesis that 'man is the measure of all things' (DK.80 B 1). It is reflected in Critias' rationalistic explanation of the origin of religion. Critias argued that God was invented by some clever person as an expedient for deterring men from crime (DK.88 B 25). It is reflected too in the contrast made between nature (*physis*) and convention (*nomos*) by Antiphon (DK.87 B 44) and Hippias (in Plato, *Prot.* 337c–e). The thesis of Antiphon and Hippias is not merely that the generally accepted principles of morality are conventional man-made rules, but that very many of those principles are contrary to man's 'natural' rights.

The importance of this critical approach to morality is that it stimulated further examination of the problem of justifying the moral ideals generally accepted by the Greeks, and, more particularly, of the problem of giving more precise significance to them within a scheme of values prescribed on reasoned, philosophical grounds. It must not be thought that the approach made by the Sophists was necessarily destructive of those ideals or inconsistent with continued respect for them. Piety, perhaps, could not consistently be retained as a virtue if the new rationalism of some of the Sophists gained general acceptance. But it would be wrong to assert that the Sophists had any general aim to replace the traditional virtues by other virtues. Indeed, their profession was itself a tribute to the excellence of wisdom, and helped to give it a more definite significance in relation to moral behaviour. They were rather concerned to *reinterpret* the accepted virtues. They wanted to replace the hitherto vague and uncritical views about the ways in which the accepted virtues should be displayed with positive and precise moral theories.

The most prominent of these theories were theories of 'natural right', propounded in a form which provided a radical contrast to merely conventional morality. Antiphon, while championing the virtue of moderation, at the same time put forward a theory of natural right in terms of hedonism (DK.87 B 44). The doctrine that 'might is right', the advocacy of the right of the stronger to rule, which is attributed to Thrasymachus by Plato in the first book of the *Republic*, offered another criterion for the revaluation of the traditional virtues. It is a doctrine which explicitly appeals to the 'natural' basis of this right when it is presented by Callicles in Plato's *Gorgias*.

What is particularly significant about the form of the 'might is right' thesis in the *Gorgias* is that it shows how readily the 'natural right' theories of some of the Sophists could be used as grounds for the renunciation of at least some of the accepted virtues. It is true that Callicles' thesis can be interpreted, in certain important respects, as one which offers a revaluation or 'transvaluation' of the accepted virtues.[1] Thus Callicles asserts that a man is genuinely wise and courageous when he employs his intelligence and courage to achieve unrestricted gratification of his desires. But at the same time that he revalues the virtues of wisdom and courage Callicles is contemptuously rejecting the virtue of moderation. His hedonism, unlike Antiphon's, is coupled with an advocacy of self-indulgence. If one has the means to realise it, he argues, then self-indulgence, with an absolute freedom to do what one wishes, is to be identified with virtue and happiness (*Gorg.* 492c). Callicles was not a Sophist, but the influence of sophistic theory on his views seems clear.

It is easy to see why this critical reassessment of the traditional Greek moral values by the Sophists brought their profession into disfavour as an essentially subversive influence in the field of social and political allegiancies. On the one hand there were the 'natural right' theories, which rejected as conventional current evaluations of the virtues. On the other hand there were the claims to be able to 'teach virtue', associated especially with the imparting of rhetorical skills as a means to practical success in life. This was not, of course, in itself calculated to subvert accepted moral standards. What was calculated to do this was the sophistic tendency to shift from the advocacy of the importance of the art of rhetoric in practical politics to the advocacy as a moral end of what was considered to be the proper end of rhetorical skill, i.e. the power which comes from winning acceptance for any proposition and thus being able to mould the views and actions to any chosen pattern. The tendency is clearly seen in the arguments of Gorgias in Plato's *Gorgias*.[2] It is also implicit in Protagoras' attitude to the teaching of virtue. From his own subjectivist viewpoint, any proposition which he cares to persuade others to adopt is as true as any other proposition. He does indeed claim that his technique of persuasion, while it cannot substitute true beliefs for false, is directed to the substitution of 'better' beliefs for 'worse'.[3] But this is a clever attempt to square his professional claims as a teacher of virtue with his subjectivist views. What it amounts to is a thinly veiled assertion of the moral superiority of the skilled rhetorician as one who can successfully impose on others any view which he chooses to impose. Protagoras' specialised interest in the art of eristics, the win-at-any-price type of argument which was discussed in the last chapter, is in conformity with this attitude.

It is against this background of moral thought in the latter half of the fifth century that Socrates began to formulate his own theories. There is no doubt that in the development of his views in ethics no less than in the development of his methods of argument Socrates was influenced in no small way by the pioneer work done by the Sophists. They were the first to think systematically about problems in ethics, and their critical scepticism, as well as their provocative positive theories, provided an immediate stimulus to further examination of the problems which they raised. Socrates' reaction was a reaction of opposition. His method of inquiry in ethics was designed to be, not a win-at-any-price method, but a method of establishing what was true on grounds which could be seen impartially to be rational grounds for its acceptance. He was convinced, indeed, that it was a method which could yield what was certainly true. With this conviction he opposed the moral subjectivism of Protagoras, the scepticism of Gorgias,[4] and the whole general tendency of the Sophists to use persuasive techniques of argument without a serious and sincere regard for the truth of what they aimed to establish and to recommend. He opposed too the type of 'natural right' theory propounded by some of the Sophists. Such theories were, in Socrates' eyes, irrational in their basis, and liable for that reason to differ widely in their specifications of what was 'naturally' right. At the same time they were theories which found their specifications within what seemed to him to be the lower levels of human aspiration.[5]

There is one other important aspect of Socrates' opposition to the Sophists. As we saw in the last chapter, Socrates' method was designed to yield demonstrative certainty in its practical conclusions in ethics, but it was at the same time a valuable method of linguistic analysis. One of the things that Socrates is trying to do in presenting his moral paradoxes is to throw some light on the meaning of basic moral terms and to indicate some of the important relations which analysis can show to obtain between them. One feature of the use of these terms particularly occupies his attention. It is the differences between the application of terms such as 'good', 'excellence', and 'knowledge' to moral behaviour and their application to the practice of professional skills. In dealing with these differences his aim is to elucidate the significance of the moral application of these terms, but at the same time to correct what he considered to be a major fault in the arguments of some of the Sophists – the tendency to assimilate far too closely moral behaviour and the practice of professional skills. As teachers of 'virtue', the Sophists had placed too much trust in rhetorical skill as a basis of 'goodness', neglecting certain important features of moral behaviour which it was one of the aims of Socrates' analysis to reveal.

In considering in general terms Socrates' reaction to the teaching of the Sophists we have now noted two aims of his own moral teaching. The first is to establish certain basic moral principles as indubitably true. Socrates' view is that moral statements are objective statements, and that some of them can be known to be true. The second aim is to elucidate, by his method of cross-examination, the Greeks' moral terminology as a necessary preliminary to any attempt to formulate a positive theory in ethics. It is important to keep both these aims in mind when interpreting his moral paradoxes.

B. VIRTUE IS KNOWLEDGE

One of Socrates' fundamental doctrines is the thesis that virtue is knowledge. This is the thesis that knowing what is good is a necessary and a sufficient condition of possessing goodness and hence of doing what is good. Aristotle presents this as a fundamental Socratic thesis (*E.N.* 1144b, *E.E.* 1216b). So do Xenophon (*Mem.* III ix 5) and Plato (*Prot.* 352a ff.).

The thesis is based in certain important respects on the analogy of professional skills, though Socrates, unlike the Sophists, was careful to qualify the analogy in other, equally important respects. The relevance and plausibility of the analogy is immediately suggested by the way in which the principal Greek moral terms are used. We have already noted the utilitarianism implicit in Greek moral terminology, in particular the association of 'good' and 'excellence' with function, and the applicability of these terms to a wide range of activities, including professional skills, other than moral behaviour. The association of 'good' and 'excellence' with expert knowledge in their application to professional skills readily prompts the idea that in moral behaviour too knowledge is at least a necessary condition of successful practice.

In Plato's *Euthydemus* (279d ff.) Socrates develops this idea. He uses an argument from analogy to show that, just as knowledge is a condition of successful practice in professional skills, so it is a condition of success or 'good fortune' in the broader sphere of human behaviour. Arguing from examples of success in navigation, warfare, medicine, and music, he emphasises that in all these various activities it is knowledge which leads to success. More specifically, the expert knowledge of the carpenter or other craftsman enables him to use his materials and implements advantageously, i.e. to further the end of his craft. Similarly in moral behaviour it is knowledge which enables a person to use his resources – his material possessions, his physical capacities, his gifts of temperament – advantageously or beneficially, i.e. to promote the end of his moral behaviour, 'good fortune' or happiness (*eudaimonia*). Socrates concludes that knowledge is the one good (281e).

But the analogy needs qualification. In the first place moral knowledge is superior in value, Socrates argues, to any other kind of knowledge. In Plato's *Charmides* (173-4) and *Euthydemus* (291-2) it is argued that this superiority springs from the comprehensiveness in scope of moral knowledge. The argument is that its possible field of application includes that of all the specialised skills, and that it is at the same time so authoritative as to be able to exercise a directing influence on the activities belonging to those specialised skills. These characteristics belong to it because it is knowledge of the good, of what constitutes happiness (*eudaimonia*), the final end to which all human activities are directed. Thus, since moral knowledge alone is knowledge of what constitutes happiness, it is the only knowledge capable of directing all human activity correctly to the attainment of this universally desired end. Hence its comprehensive scope and its authority.

There is a further important respect in which moral knowledge is differentiated by Socrates from the knowledge belonging to professional skills. The special importance of this distinction is that it serves to emphasise his belief that knowledge of the good is not only a necessary but also a sufficient condition for the attainment of happiness. The argument of Plato's *Hippias Minor* is here important, and merits discussion in some detail.

In this dialogue Socrates considers the relations between ability (*dunamis*), knowledge, goodness, and desire in their application to the practice of professional skills; he then considers the question of whether there are the same relations between them in their application to moral behaviour. He first establishes that ability implies knowledge, and that in any professional skill the able man is the good man (365d–368a). Ability means ability to achieve one's aim, to succeed in what one wishes to do. Given the aim, the good man is able to achieve it. For example, the good runner is able to win the race, and hence satisfy his wish. The bad runner loses. What he achieves is bad. It does not accord with what he wishes. He loses 'against his will'. He could not have done any better however hard he had tried (373c–e).

In activities such as these, the link between ability and knowledge is obvious. One might argue that through force of circumstances the man with knowledge might be unable to achieve his purpose, and that in this case knowledge is not a sufficient condition of ability. But Plato excludes such cases as irrelevant to his conception of ability (366b–c), and, having defined the able man as the man who 'does what he wishes at the time when he wishes to do it', links ability with knowledge in a way which makes irrelevant to the assessment of a person's ability all factors which are irrelevant to the assessment of a person's knowledge in a particular craft. And since knowledge here means expert skill or competence in achieving a given aim and not knowledge of what the aim is (the poor runner knows that his aim is to win the race, but he is ranked as ignorant), it is not possible to argue that the man with knowledge (of what his aim is) may be unable to achieve his aim, and that in this case too knowledge is not a sufficient condition of ability.

If the kind of connexion between ability and knowledge which exists in professional skills existed in moral behaviour, it would follow that moral knowledge is a necessary and sufficient condition of ability to achieve one's aim. But Socrates thinks that at this point an important qualification has to be made. For in professional skills the ability to achieve what is accepted as the 'right' aim does not entail that the able man wishes or desires to achieve it. His ability is an ability to achieve either the 'right' or the 'wrong' aim. The runner who deliberately loses a race remains a good runner (373d–e). Thus ability is a necessary but not a sufficient condition of achieving the 'right' aim. It is a sufficient condition of achieving what the able man wishes. But the able man may wish to achieve the 'wrong' rather than the 'right' aim, and in satisfying his wish may deliberately do what is 'wrong'.

Here, Socrates thinks, the analogy between moral knowledge and the knowledge belonging to professional skills breaks down. If in this respect they were the same, it would be necessary to conclude that, just as in the practice of professional skills it is only the able and hence knowledgable and 'good' man who *deliberately* gives bad performances, so in moral behaviour it is only the knowledgable and 'good' man who deliberately does wrong. Thus the consequence of accepting the analogy in this respect would be that the morally good man is capable of deliberate wrongdoing, while the wrongdoing of the morally wicked man is always involuntary (375d–376b). Socrates' unwillingness to accept this consequence is made quite clear in his concluding remarks (376b–c).

In what way, then, does Socrates qualify the analogy and avoid this consequence? He has recognised that ability is a necessary but not a sufficient condition of achieving the 'right' aim. He recognises also that, if the further necessary condition is added that the agent has the *desire* to achieve the 'right' aim, then the two conditions together constitute a sufficient condition of achieving it. And he contends that the difference between moral behaviour and the practice of professional skills is that in moral behaviour the second condition is invariably satisfied, whereas in the practice of professional skills it is not. Hence in moral behaviour ability to achieve the 'right' aim is invariably conjoined with the desire to achieve it.

In the light of this qualification it is now possible to see the significance of Socrates' thesis that virtue is knowledge. It is the thesis that knowledge is at once a necessary and a sufficient condition of achieving the 'right' aim. It assumes that the two conditions we discussed above are satisfied in all cases where the agent knows what is good. For it assumes that in moral behaviour knowledge is invariably accompanied by both the ability and the desire to achieve what is good. Thus Socrates accepts up to a point the analogy between moral behaviour and the practice of professional skills. He believes that in both fields knowledge and ability go together, and that in both fields knowledge is a necessary and sufficient condition of ability or power to achieve what one wishes to achieve. Moral knowledge, he maintains in the *Protagoras*, is strong, authoritative, and commanding, the most powerful human agency (352b–d). What distinguishes the two fields of activity is that in moral behaviour what one wishes to achieve is invariably one's own good, and that this is the 'right' aim. Hence in moral behaviour the condition that the agent has the wish to achieve the 'right' aim is invariably satisfied.

Here again Socrates is appealing to the utilitarianism implicit in normal Greek moral usage. 'Good' is identifiable with happiness, and Socrates considers that it is 'natural' to want to be happy. It is 'not in human nature', he says in the *Protagoras* (358d), to want to pursue what one conceives to be bad, i.e. what appears not to be conducive to one's happiness. All men wish to be happy (*Euthyd.* 278e ff., *Men.* 78a). It is on this ground that Socrates is ready to assert that in moral behaviour knowledge is invariably accompanied not only by the ability to achieve what is good but also by the desire to achieve it.

Thus, for Socrates, knowledge is a necessary and sufficient condition of achieving the 'right' aim, where the right aim is what is 'really' good. One qualification to be made is that, conformably with the sense of 'ability' in the field of professional skills, external compulsion is assumed to be a factor irrelevant to the assessment of a person's ability to achieve his aim. The thesis that virtue is knowledge is, then, the thesis that *in all cases of voluntary action* knowledge is a necessary and sufficient condition of doing what is good.

There is one further important difference between moral behaviour and the practice of professional skills which is important for the understanding of the thesis that virtue is knowledge. It is the difference in the kind of knowledge employed. In discussing the case of the good and bad runner in the *Hippias Minor* Socrates presents knowledge of running as an expert skill or competence in achieving a given aim, and not as knowledge of what the aim is. The bad runner knows that his aim is to win the race, but he is ranked as ignorant. But in moral behaviour the fundamental knowledge, in Socrates' view, is knowledge of what the 'right' aim is, and not a skill or competence in attaining or achieving a given aim, whether right or wrong. That is why he presents the question of what the good is, or of what any particular virtue is, as prior to any other question about them. And the aim of his method, as we saw in the last chapter, is to gain knowledge of what the good is, or of what any particular virtue is, by defining them.

Thus in seeking knowledge of piety, Socrates seeks to know what 'piety itself' is, its 'essence' or 'form' through a general definition of it. When he has *this* knowledge, he will have a pattern or paradigm to use in classifying particular actions as pious or impious (*Euthyphro* 6d–e, 11a). Similarly, to know 'what virtue is' is necessarily prior to any determination of the best means of acquiring it (*Laches* 189e–190b). It is not that Socrates thinks unimportant the ability to apply definitions, as general principles, to particular situations or to deduce particular truths from them. But he considers that moral knowledge is essentially knowledge through general definition and that this knowledge is the foundation of all moral truth. All Aristotle's testimony on the Socratic thesis that the virtues are cases of knowledge presents Socrates' ideal of knowledge as 'scientific' knowledge of this kind.[6]

We have now considered the extent to which Socrates made use of the analogy between moral behaviour and the practice of professional skills in formulating his thesis that virtue is knowledge. Although he is careful to mark several differences between the one and the other, it is arguable that he is ready to accept the correctness of the analogy at one crucial point where it might perhaps be felt there is a fundamental difference. For although he distinguishes moral knowledge from the knowledge belonging to professional skills, he does not, apparently, consider that this difference affects the similarity between them in respect of the relation between knowledge and ability. As we have seen, he believes that in each case knowledge is a necessary and sufficient condition of ability or power to achieve what one wishes to achieve, and that in each case external compulsion is the only possible restriction on this ability or power.

The belief is well-founded as far as the field of professional skills is concerned. Here the kind of knowledge involved is an expert skill or competence in achieving certain aims. Moral knowledge is not, in Socrates' view, of this kind. It is an intellectual apprehension of the truth of certain general moral principles in the form of definitions. Yet Socrates assumes that, as in professional skills, this knowledge invariably carries with it the power or ability of its possessor to achieve what he wishes to achieve. In this he appears to be assuming too much. In particular, he assumes that what a person knows to be right is invariably what he wishes to do, and that, in any particular case, this wish is invariably the strongest of his desires. As we have seen, Socrates is here distinguishing moral behaviour in one respect from the practice of professional skills. He finds an anomaly in the notion of a man who knows what is right deliberately doing wrong, though he recognises there is no anomaly in the notion of a good runner deliberately losing a race when he knows that that is not the 'right' aim of his skill. At the same time he accepts that the morally bad man, like the bad runner, lacks the requisite knowledge. He also accepts that the ability which accompanies knowledge is definable as an ability to 'do what one wishes at the time when one wishes to do it' (*Hippias Minor* 366b) within the sphere of application of one's knowledge. Finally, he recognises that this is a consistent position to adopt with regard to moral behaviour if he assumes that what a person knows to be right is invariably what he wishes to do and that, in any particular case, this wish is invariably the strongest desire. The good man, the man who knows what is right, is always able to do what he knows to be right. He 'does what he wishes at the time when he wishes to do it'. He never willingly does wrong.

In holding this position, Socrates rules out the possibility of a person acting contrary to what he knows to be right. He thus appears to deny that there are cases of weakness of will. It is here that his position appears to be vulnerable. For if we accept his argument that all men 'naturally' desire to do what they conceive to be conducive to their happiness, it does not follow that knowing what is right and hence what is conducive to happiness is necessarily accompanied by a desire to do what is right which is stronger than any other desire. For 'knowing' is identified with an intellectual apprehension of the truth of general moral principles. And intellectual conviction does not necessarily determine desire in the way which Socrates appears to assume that it does. A man may still wish to do what, on intellectual grounds, he is sure is wrong. Thus it is arguable that Socrates has failed to qualify extensively enough the analogy between moral behaviour and the practice of professional skills. In professional skills the man with knowledge is the able man who 'does what he wishes when he wishes' within the sphere of operation of his skill. So in the sphere of moral behaviour, Socrates argues, the man with knowledge is the able man who 'does what he wishes when he wishes', the object of wish being always what is known to be right. Hence to know what is right is a sufficient defence against doing what is wrong (*Prot.* 352c).

Prima facie, then, the Socratic position appears to be exposed to serious attack at one important point. But before the weight of the attack is assessed further, it is important to consider another Socratic thesis which is closely linked with the thesis that virtue is knowledge. It is that no one does wrong willingly. Together with this thesis we will consider also Socrates' denial that there are cases of weakness of will.

C. NO ONE DOES WRONG WILLINGLY

We have seen that the thesis that virtue is knowledge is the thesis that in all cases of voluntary action knowledge is a necessary and sufficient condition of doing what is good. No one who knows what is right willingly does wrong. But the thesis that no one does wrong willingly is a more general thesis. It asserts that no one, whether knowing what is right or not, willingly does wrong.

Consider first the following argument in Plato's *Meno* (77c ff.). Meno has suggested that virtue is definable as a desire for what is good combined with the ability to achieve it. Socrates wishes to show that it is superfluous to include 'desire for what is good' in the definition. His reason is that this desire is universal and hence cannot serve as a distinctive mark of virtue. He argues as follows. If a person does what is in fact bad, it cannot be the case that he does this thinking that it is bad. He does it thinking that it is good. For to do what he thinks is bad would be equivalent to doing what he thinks will have harmful consequences to himself, which is equivalent to doing what he thinks will make him miserable and unhappy. But no one wishes to be unhappy. Therefore no one wishes to do what he thinks to be bad. Similarly, in the *Protagoras*, Socrates asserts that no one voluntarily pursues what is bad or what he thinks to be bad. It is 'not in human nature' to do so (358c–d).

The argument of the *Meno* is an attempt to refute the view that it is possible to desire what one either knows or believes to be bad. Implicit in the argument is the distinction which Aristotle makes in the *Nicomachean Ethics* (III 4; probably with Plato's *Gorgias* 466d–468a in mind) between wish for the good (the 'really' good) and wish for the apparent good. Socrates' view is that wish or desire is directed to either the good or the apparent good. The thesis that virtue is knowledge is the thesis that the person who has the 'really' good as the object of his desire (i.e. the person who *knows* what is good) invariably acts in accordance with this desire, and hence invariably does what is 'really' good. Once a distinction between the 'real' and the apparent good is recognised, it can be argued further that the person who has the apparent good as the object of his desire (i.e. the person who *believes* that the object of his desire is good, though it may be 'really' bad) invariably acts in accordance with this desire, and hence invariably does what he believes to be good. Hence (*a*) what a person desires is invariably what he knows or believes to be good, and (*b*) right action is definable as action taken to satisfy desire.

This view is attributed to Socrates by both Xenophon and Plato. In Xenophon (*Mem.* III ix 4; IV vi 6, 11) Socrates asserts that in moral behaviour it is *always* the case that people choose from *possible* courses of action what they conceive to be best for them, and do this. What is implied by 'possible' courses of action is that a person's ability to achieve what he conceives to be best for him is limited only by the force of external circumstances. The same point is made by Socrates in Plato (*Prot.* 358b7–c 1), where 'what is in one's power' is co-extensive with what is voluntary.

It follows from this that no one willingly does wrong, if we take this to mean, as Socrates intended it to be taken, that no one does willingly what he *either* knows *or* believes to be wrong. The thesis is not intended to deny that there are actions which are 'really' wrong and at the same time voluntary. It is intended to deny that there are voluntary actions contrary to what the agent conceives to be right.

It will be seen that the thesis assumes that belief, as well as knowledge, is always accompanied by the ability to achieve what one conceives to be best. It follows that moral behaviour, unlike the practice of professional skills, is not after all governed by the rule that knowledge is a necessary as well as a sufficient condition of ability to achieve one's aim. Aristotle emphasises, as a part of Socrates' position, the view that no one acts contrary to what has seemed to him to be the better course (*E.N.* 1145b 31-4). The difference between moral behaviour and the practice of professional skills in this respect has some importance. In professional skills the 'right' aim is a fixed and universally accepted aim. The problem of distinguishing between the real and the apparent 'right' aim does not arise. Moreover, ability to achieve the 'right' aim, assuming that there is the desire to achieve it, depends exclusively on the agent's possession of an expert technique for achieving it. In moral behaviour, however, Socrates recognises the legitimacy of speaking of the aim which appears to the individual to be right as the 'right' aim. And since he considers that a person invariably does what he believes to be right relatively to his individual conception of the 'right' aim, he consequently considers that his ability to achieve his 'right' aim is limited only by the force of external circumstances.

This point has to be kept in mind in examining Socrates' denial that there are cases of weakness of will. In his thesis that no one does wrong willingly Socrates is asserting that any wrong action is involuntary. For he considers that the only wrong actions are those done under external compulsion, since only those would fail to be in accordance with the agent's desire to do what he either knows or believes to be right. His denial that there are cases of weakness of will is thus a denial that there are actions, other than those done under external compulsion, which are contrary to what the agent *either* knows *or* believes to be right.

D. THE ACCOUNT OF THE TWO PARADOXES IN PLATO'S *Protagoras*

Socrates' argument that there are no cases of weakness of will is found in Plato's *Protagoras* (351b ff.). It is as follows.[7] Socrates is speaking to Protagoras.

351b I said: You would admit, Protagoras, that some men live well and others ill?

He assented.

And do you think that a man lives well who lives in pain and grief?

He does not.

But if he lives pleasantly to the end of his life, will he not in that case have lived well?

He will.

c Then to live pleasantly is a good, and to live unpleasantly an evil?

Yes, he said, if the pleasure be good and honourable.

And do you, Protagoras, like the rest of the world, call some pleasant things evil and some painful things good? – What I mean is, are not things good in as far as they are pleasant, if they have no consequences of another sort; and, again, is it not the same with painful things – in so far as they are painful, are they not bad?

I do not know, Socrates, he said, whether I can venture to assert in

d that unqualified manner that the pleasant is the good and the painful the evil. Having regard not only to my present answer, but also to the whole of my life, I shall be safer, if I am not mistaken, in saying that there are some pleasant things which are not good, and that there are some painful things which are not evil, and some which are, and, thirdly, some things which are neither good nor evil.

And you would call pleasant, I said, the things which participate in

e pleasure or create pleasure?

Certainly, he said.

Then my meaning is that in as far as they are pleasant they are good; and my question would imply that pleasure is a good in itself.

According to your favourite mode of speech, Socrates, 'let us reflect about this', he said; and if the reflection proves helpful, and pleasure and good are shown to be really the same, then we will agree; but if not, then we will argue.

And would you wish to begin the inquiry? I said; or shall I begin?

You ought to take the lead, he said; for you are the author of the discussion.

Then, I said, perhaps it will become clear to us from the following

352 illustration. Suppose someone who is trying to ascertain from a man's appearance the state of his health or some other character of his body: he looks at his face and hands, and then he says, Uncover your chest and back to me; I want to make a more searching examination: that is the sort of thing which I desire in this speculation. Having seen what

your opinion is about good and pleasure, I am minded to say to you:
b Uncover your mind to me, Protagoras, and reveal your opinion about knowledge, that I may know whether you agree with the rest of the world. Now the rest of the world are of opinion that knowledge is a principle not of strength, or of rule, or of command: they do not think of it in that way, but hold that a man may often have knowledge, and yet be governed not by knowledge but by something else, – by anger, or pleasure, or pain, sometimes by love, often by fear, – just as if knowledge were a slave, and might be dragged about by all the rest.
c Now is that your view? or do you think that knowledge is a noble and commanding thing, which cannot be overcome, and will not allow a man, if he only knows the difference of good and evil, to do anything which is contrary to knowledge, but that wisdom will have strength to help him?
d I agree with you, Socrates, said Protagoras; and not only so, but I, above all other men, am bound to say that wisdom and knowledge are the highest of human things.

Good, I said, and true. But are you aware that the majority of the world are of another mind? Do they not say that even when men know the things which are best and are free to do them, they often refuse, and prefer some other course of action? And when I have asked what
e can be the reason for this, I am told that they act as they do because they are overcome by pain, or pleasure, or some of those affections which I was just now mentioning.

Yes, Socrates, he replied; and that is not the only point about which mankind are in error.

Suppose, then, that you and I endeavour to instruct and inform them what is the nature of this affection which they call 'being overcome by pleasure', and which they affirm to be the reason why they
53 do not always do what is best, although they know what is the best. When we say to them: Friends, you are mistaken, and are saying what is not true, they would probably reply: Socrates and Protagoras, if this affection of the soul is not to be called 'being overcome by pleasure', pray, what is it, and by what name would you describe it?

But why, Socrates, should we trouble ourselves about the opinion of the many, who just say anything that happens to occur to them?
b I believe, I said, that they may be of use in helping us to discover how courage is related to the other parts of virtue. If you are disposed to abide by our agreement, that I should show the way in which, as I think, our recent difficulty is most likely to be cleared up, do you follow; otherwise I will dismiss the matter if you prefer.

You are quite right, he said; and I would have you proceed as you
have begun.

c   Well then, I said, let me suppose that they repeat their question,
What account do you give of that which, in our way of speaking, is
termed being overcome by pleasure? I should answer thus: Listen, and
Protagoras and I will endeavour to show you. When men are over-
powered by eating and drinking and other sensual desires which are
pleasant, and they, knowing them to be evil, nevertheless indulge in
them, would you not say that they are 'overcome by pleasure'? They
will not deny this. And suppose that you and I were to go on and ask
them again: 'In what way do you say that they are evil, – in that they
d   are pleasant and give pleasure at the moment, or because they cause
disease and poverty and other like evils in the future? Suppose they
simply give pleasure, and bring no evil consequences, would they still
be evil, merely because they give the consciousness of pleasure of whatever nature?' – Would they not answer that they are not evil on account
of the pleasure which is immediately given by them, but on account of
e   the after-consequences – diseases and the like?

I believe, said Protagoras, that the world in general would answer
as you do.

'And in causing disease do they not cause pain? and in causing poverty
do they not cause pain?' – they would agree to that also if I am not
mistaken?

Protagoras assented.

'Is it not then clear to you, my friends, that Protagoras and I are right
in saying that these pleasures are evil for no other reason, than that
they end in pain and rob us of other pleasures': there again they would
agree?

354   We both of us thought that they would.

And then we might take the question from the opposite point of
view, and say: 'Friends, when you speak of goods being painful, do you
not mean remedial goods, such as gymnastic exercises, and military
service, and the physician's use of burning, cutting, drugging, and
starving? Are these the things which are good but painful?' – they
would assent?

He agreed.

b   'And do you call them good because they occasion the greatest
immediate suffering and pain; or because, afterwards, they bring health
and improvement of the bodily condition and the salvation of states
and power over others and wealth?' – they would agree to the latter
alternative, if I am not mistaken?

He assented.

'Are these things good for any other reason except that they end in pleasure, and get rid of and avert pain? Are you looking to any other
c end but pleasure and pain when you call them good?' – they would acknowledge that they were not?

I think so, said Protagoras.

'And do you not pursue after pleasure as a good, and avoid pain as an evil?'

He assented.

'Then you think that pain is an evil and pleasure is a good: and even pleasure you deem an evil, when it robs you of greater pleasures than it gives, or causes pains greater than the pleasure. If, however, you call
d pleasure an evil in relation to some other end or standard, you will be able to show us that standard. But you have none to show.'

I do not think that they have, said Protagoras.

'And have you not a similar way of speaking about pain? You call pain a good when it takes away greater pains than those which it has, or gives pleasures greater than the pains: then if you have some standard
e other than pleasure and pain to which you refer when you call actual pain a good, you can show what that is. But you cannot.'

True, said Protagoras.

Suppose again, I said, that the world says to me: 'For what conceivable reason do you spend many words and speak in many ways on this subject?' Excuse me, friends, I should reply; but in the first place there is a difficulty in explaining the precise meaning of the expression 'overcome by pleasure'; and the whole argument turns upon this. And even
55 now, if you see any possible way in which evil can be explained as other than pain, or good as other than pleasure, you may still retract. Are you satisfied, then, at having a life of pleasure which is without pain? If you are, and if you are unable to show any good or evil which does not end in pleasure and pain, hear the consequences: If what you say is true, then the argument is absurd which affirms that a man often does evil knowingly, when he might abstain, because he is seduced and over-
b powered by pleasure; or again, when you say that a man knowingly refuses to do what is good because he is overcome at the moment by pleasure. And that this is ridiculous will be evident if only we give up the use of various names, such as pleasant and painful, and good and evil. As there are two things, let us call them by two names – first, good and evil, and then pleasant and painful. Assuming this, let us go
c on to say that a man does evil knowing that he does evil. But someone will ask, Why? Because he is overcome, is the first answer. And by

what is he overcome? the inquirer will proceed to ask. And we shall not be able to reply 'By pleasure', for the name of pleasure has been exchanged for that of good. In our answer then, we shall only say that he is overcome. 'By what?' he will reiterate. By the good, we shall have to reply; indeed we shall. Nay, but our questioner will rejoin with a

d laugh, if he be one of the swaggering sort, 'That is ridiculous, that a man should do what he knows to be evil when he ought not, because he is overcome by good. Is that, he will ask, because the good is or is not worthy to conquer the evil in you?' And in answer to that we shall clearly reply, Because it is not worthy; otherwise he who, as we say, is overcome by pleasure, would not err. 'But in what respect', he will reply, 'is the good not worth the evil, or the evil not worth the good? Is not the only answer, that they are out of proportion to one another, either as greater and smaller, or more and fewer?' This we cannot deny.

e 'And when you speak of being overcome – what do you mean', he will say, 'but that you choose the greater evil in exchange for the lesser good?' Admitted. And now substitute the names of pleasure and pain for good and evil, and say, not as before, that a man does what is evil, but that he does what is painful, knowing that it is painful, because he is

356 overcome by pleasures, clearly such as are unworthy to prevail. What measure is there of the unworthiness of pleasure in relation to pain other than excess and defect, which means that they become greater and smaller, and more and fewer, and differ in intensity? For if anyone says: 'Yes, Socrates, but immediate pleasure differs widely from future pleasure and pain' – to that I should reply: And do they differ in anything but in pleasure and pain? There can be no other measure of

b them. Nay, do you, like a skilful weigher, put into the balance the pleasures and the pains, and their nearness and distance, and weigh them, and then say which outweighs the other. If you weigh pleasures against pleasures, you must of course always take the more and greater; or if you weigh pains against pains, you take the fewer and the less; or if pleasures against pains, then if the pains are exceeded by the pleasures – whether the near by the distant, or the distant by the near – you must choose the course of action in which the pleasures are to be found; and

c you must avoid that course of action in which the pleasant is exceeded by the painful. Would you not admit, my friends, that this is true? I am confident that they cannot deny this.

He agreed with me.

Well then, I shall say, if you agree so far, be so good as to answer me a question: Do not the same magnitudes appear larger to your sight when near, and smaller when at a distance? They will acknowledge that. And the same holds of thickness and number; also sounds which are in themselves equal are greater when near, and lesser when at a distance. They will grant that also. Now suppose happiness consisted in doing or choosing the greater, and in not doing or in avoiding the less, what would have been the saving principle of human life? Would not the art of measuring have been the saving principle; or would the power of appearance? Is not the latter that deceiving force which makes us wander up and down and take the things at one time of which we repent at another, both in our actions and in our choice of things great and small? But the art of measurement would have done away with the effect of appearances, and, showing the truth, would have taught the soul at last to find rest in the truth, and would thus have saved our life. Would not mankind generally acknowledge that the art which would accomplish this result is the art of measurement, and none other?

Yes, he said, the art of measurement.

Suppose, again, the salvation of human life to depend on the choice of odd and even, and on the right preference of the greater or less as occasion arose, either taken by themselves or compared with each other, and whether near or at a distance; what would be the saving principle of our lives? Would not knowledge? – a knowledge of measurement, since it is the art concerned with excess and defect? And when it is concerned with odd and even, can it be any other art than arithmetic? The world will assent, will they not?

Protagoras himself thought that they would.

Well then, my friends, I say to them; seeing that the salvation of human life has been found to consist in the right choice of pleasures and pains, – in the choice of the more and the fewer, and the greater and the less, and the nearer and remoter, – must not this salvation consist in measurement, since it involves a consideration of excess and defect and equality in relation to each other?

This is undeniably true.

And since it involves measurement, it must undeniably also be an art and a science?

They will agree, he said.

The nature of that art and science will be a matter of future consideration; but the existence of such a science furnishes a demonstrative answer to the question which you asked of me and Protagoras. At the time when you asked the question, if you remember, both of us were agreeing that there was nothing mightier than knowledge, and that knowledge, in whatever existing, must have the advantage over pleasure and all other things; and then you said that pleasure often got the advantage even over a man who has knowledge; and we refused to allow this, and you rejoined: O Protagoras and Socrates, what is the meaning of

d being overcome by pleasure if not this? – tell us what you call such a state: if we had immediately and at the time answered 'Ignorance', you would have laughed at us. But now, in laughing at us, you will be laughing at yourselves: for you also admitted that men err in their choice of pleasures and pains – that is, in their choice of good and evil – from defect of knowledge; and not only from defect of knowledge in general, but of that particular knowledge which you have already admitted to be the science of measurement. And you are also aware

e that the erring act which is done without knowledge is done in ignorance. This, therefore, is the meaning of being overcome by pleasure; – ignorance, and that the greatest. And our friends Protagoras and Prodicus and Hippias declare that they are physicians of ignorance; but you, who are under the mistaken impression that ignorance is not the cause and that the art of which I am speaking cannot be taught, neither go yourselves nor send your children to the sophists, who are the teachers of these things – you take care of your money and give them none; and the result is, that you are the worse off both in public and in private life: Let us suppose this to be our answer to the world in

358 general: and now I should like to ask you, Hippias, and you, Prodicus, as well as Protagoras (for the argument is to be yours as well as ours), whether you think that I am speaking the truth or not?

They all thought that what I said was entirely true.

Then you agree, I said, that the pleasant is the good, and the painful evil. And here I would beg my friend Prodicus not to introduce his distinction of names; whether you use the word pleasurable, or delightful, or joyful, or any other conceivable name you like to call

b them, I will ask you, most excellent Prodicus, to answer according to my sense of the words.

Prodicus laughed and assented, as did the others.

Then, my friends, what do you say to this? Are not all actions honourable, of which the tendency is to make life painless and pleasant? The honourable work is also useful and good?

This was admitted.

Then, I said, if the pleasant is the good, nobody continues to do anything with the knowledge or belief that some other thing would be

c better and is also attainable, when he might do the better. And the inferiority of a man to himself is merely ignorance, as the superiority of a man to himself is wisdom.

They all assented.

And is not ignorance the having a false opinion and being deceived about important matters?

To this they also unanimously assented.

Then, I said, no man voluntarily pursues evil, or that which he thinks to be evil. To prefer evil to good is not in human nature; and when a man is compelled to choose one of two evils, no one will choose the greater when he may have the less.

All of us agreed to every word of this.

In this argument Socrates contrasts his own view with what he presents as the popular view. His own view, as we have seen, is that if a man knows what is good nothing will prevail on him to act contrary to 'what his knowledge bids him' to do; knowledge is a sufficient defence against wrongdoing (352c). The popular view is that there are many cases where a man (i) 'knows what is best', (ii) 'it is possible' for him to do what he knows to be best (the implication being that no external compulsion is brought on him to act otherwise),[8] and yet (iii) he acts contrary to this knowledge because he is overcome by pleasure or pain or some emotional urge such as anger or fear (352d–e). Socrates argues that, once we identify the good and the pleasant, it can be demonstrated that his own view is right and the popular view wrong.

In presenting his argument, Socrates first defends his identification of the good and the pleasant by showing that apparently contradictory instances can readily be analysed in a way which shows them to be confirmatory rather than contradictory instances. The analysis distinguishes the immediate pleasurable or painful effect of an action from the pleasures and pains which are the consequences of the action 'in the future'. By using this distinction it is shown that, although some things which are accepted to be good are at the same time painful, they are painful only in their immediate effects; the ground of their goodness is their pleasurable consequences. It is similarly shown that, although some things which are accepted to be bad are at the same time pleasurable, they are pleasurable only in their immediate effects; the ground of their badness is their painful consequences (353c–354b).

At the end of this part of his argument Socrates emphasises two points. The first is that even in these apparently contradictory instances pleasure and pain are the only criteria used in determining what is good and bad (354b–e). The second is that, in applying these criteria to determine what it is right to do in any particular circumstances, it is necessary to assess the amount of pleasure and pain consequent on each of the actions possible in the circumstances. For an action to be right, it must yield a balance of pleasure over pain. The implication is that to 'know what is best' in any particular circumstances is to know what action will yield the *greatest* balance of pleasure over pain (354c–e). But Socrates leaves for a later stage of his argument the interpretation of *knowing* what it is right to do in terms of a 'scientific' assessment of what will yield this greatest balance.

The analysis so far serves two purposes. It gives support to the view that pleasure and the good are identical. It also supplies the basis for the refutation which now follows of the view that a man can be 'overcome by pleasure' so that he acts contrary to what he knows to be right.

Here is the refutation. Socrates describes the *refutandum* as follows. It is the view that a person sometimes does what he knows to be bad because he is 'overcome by pleasure', or, alternatively, that a person sometimes 'is unwilling' to do what he knows to be good because he is overcome by the pleasures of the moment (355a–b). If it is agreed that pleasure and the good are identical, then to assert that a person sometimes does what he knows to be bad because he is overcome by pleasure is to assert that a person sometimes does what he knows will bring more pain than pleasure because he is overcome by a pleasure which is not 'worth' indulging, which does not 'deserve' (355d, 356a) to outweigh in his calculations the pains which he knows to be consequent on indulging it. Socrates does not provide a corresponding analysis for the alternative formulation of the *refutandum*. But it is clear what it would be. To assert that a person is sometimes unwilling to do what he knows to be good because he is overcome by the pleasures of the moment would be to assert that a person sometimes refrains from doing what he knows will yield the greatest balance of pleasure over pain because he is overcome by pleasures which are not 'worth' indulging, which do not 'deserve' to outweigh in his calculations the pleasures which he knows to be consequent on the action from which he refrains.

Socrates' contention is that it is 'absurd' (355a, b, d) to speak of being 'overcome' by pleasure in these cases. For he thinks it is absurd to say that sometimes a person will refrain from doing what he knows is more pleasant than anything else he can do, and do what he knows will involve pain not worth incurring, for the sake of a pleasure which is not worth indulging. Socrates' use here of the notions of 'worthy' and 'unworthy' is to be noted. It is clear that he thinks that their introduction helps to express more effectively the 'absurdity' of the popular view. By 'worthy' pleasure he means pleasure worthy by virtue of its amount to prevail on the agent to pursue it; its worthiness consists in its superiority *in amount* over the pleasure yielded by other courses of action possible in the circumstances. As for pain, Socrates assumes that it is always 'unworthy' to prevail on the agent to do that which has the pain as its consequence if the pain exceeds the pleasure consequent on the action (355a–356c). Thus a person who has correctly assessed what action will yield the greatest balance of pleasure over pain will know what pleasures and pains are worthy or unworthy to prevail. The popular view is that pleasure known to be 'unworthy' to prevail sometimes does prevail or 'overcome' the agent. Socrates finds this 'absurd'; no one, he thinks, will deliberately take a lesser and 'unworthy' pleasure in place of a greater and 'worthy' pleasure.

In emphasising here that a purely quantitative assessment of pleasures and pains is the only proper assessment of their 'worthiness' or 'unworthiness', Socrates notes especially that the immediacy, as opposed to the remoteness in consequence, of a pleasure or pain, does not in itself give the pleasure or pain any

H

greater weight in the assessment. The only relevant consideration is the *amount* of pleasure or pain, whether immediate or remote (356a). He goes on to develop the idea of a *science* of measuring pleasures and pains which would ensure 'correctness of choice' in moral action (356c–357b). The person who possesses this scientific skill is able to apply it to any particular situation and to *know* what it is right to do.

If this analysis was designed to show only that it is imprudent to indulge 'unworthy' pleasures and that the prudent man is the man who indulges only 'worthy' pleasures, then it would have obvious plausibility. It can reasonably be argued, indeed, that, granting the equation of pleasure with the good, the analysis cannot claim to have established anything more than this. The way in which Socrates uses the value words 'worthy' and 'unworthy' in application to pleasures and pains indicates as an implication of his argument that one *ought* to do what yields 'worthy' pleasures and to refrain from what yields 'unworthy' pain. But this is obviously not equivalent to the conclusion that a person who recognises in any particular situation which pleasures and pains are 'worthy' or 'unworthy' invariably acts as he ought to act. Yet this is the conclusion needed to refute the view that a person sometimes does what he knows to be bad and contrary to what he knows to be good because he is 'overcome by pleasure'. Although Socrates thinks the view reducible to absurdity in its moral psychology, his argument has not in fact succeeded in demonstrating that it is false.

What justification does Socrates give, then, for his assumption that pleasures 'worthy' to prevail and known by the agent to be 'worthy' to prevail invariably do prevail? Socrates obviously thinks that he has already done enough to refute the popular conception of weakness of will once he has given his analysis of 'worthy' and 'unworthy' pleasures and pains and has developed the idea of a science of measurement of pleasures and pains. At 357a–b he states that our 'salvation' in life has been shown to reside in a correct choice of pleasure and pain, and thus depends on an art or science of measuring relative amounts of pleasure and pain. He immediately adds (357b–c) that to have shown that what 'saves' our lives is a kind of science or knowledge is *sufficient* for the purpose of giving a proper account of what is popularly called 'being overcome by pleasure' and of refuting the popular conception of it.[9] For it follows, he argues, from his previous analysis that in cases where 'being overcome by pleasure' is the reason popularly given for doing wrong we should substitute 'ignorance' for 'being overcome by pleasure' as the reason (357d).

Here is the argument. It has been shown that those who err in their choice of pleasures and pains, i.e. of what is good and bad, err through lack of knowledge. But to act without knowledge is to act in ignorance. Therefore a person who errs, i.e. does what is wrong, does so because he is ignorant of what is right, never because he is 'overcome by pleasure' (357d–e).[10]

It is clear that this argument assumes that knowledge of what is right is a sufficient condition of doing what is right. It does not add any justification for the assumption. Given this assumption, it follows that wrong action is action in ignorance of what is right. Hence, Socrates concludes, ignorance of what is right is always a sufficient explanation for doing what is wrong. Hence what is popularly thought to be weak-willed action, being a case of wrong action, is sufficiently explained as action done in ignorance of what is right. Thus instances of what is popularly thought to be weak-willed action do not form a special class of instances of wrongdoing. They are to be explained, in precisely the same way as *any* instance of wrongdoing, as instances of action done in ignorance of what is right. There are no cases, then, of people doing wrong through weakness of will, knowing what is right.

With this argument Socrates considers that he has satisfactorily completed his refutation of the popular view. His interlocutors, asked if they are satisfied with his analysis, agree that they are and accept its conclusions (358a). But Socrates now makes some final observations about his analysis which not only make explicit certain points which had been left implicit in the analysis, but appeal to what are taken to be facts of 'human nature' as *confirmation* of the truth of what has been demonstrated by the analysis.

One implication of the analysis is that those who do what is wrong do so believing that what they do is right. As Socrates now makes explicit at 358c, the 'ignorance' (*amathia*) which belongs to all wrongdoing is not a simply negative 'unawareness' of what is right, but the positive holding of a false belief, a being mistaken or deceived 'about important matters', i.e. about what is right.[11] Thus men do only what they know or believe to be right. As Socrates says, no one acts contrary to what he either knows or believes to be right (358b–c), or, as he alternatively expresses it, no one voluntarily pursues what is wrong or what he believes to be wrong (358c).

Here, in his references to what a person voluntarily (*hekôn*) pursues, or is willing or desires (*ethelein*) to pursue, Socrates introduces for the first time in his analysis the notion of desire.[12] It is, of course, implicit throughout his analysis that a person desires to do what he conceives to be right. We noted in our initial discussion of the 'virtue is knowledge' thesis that the principle that all men wish to be 'happy' (*eudaimôn*) (and hence to do what they conceive to be conducive to their happiness) was one of the grounds on which that thesis was based. Socrates now asserts, in the *Protagoras*, that it is 'not in human nature' to want to pursue what one believes to be bad rather than good (358d).

Taken in conjunction with the identification of the good with pleasure, this statement becomes the statement that 'human nature' is such that in all their actions men are in fact motivated by the desire for pleasure. Thus Socrates would appear to be putting forward a doctrine of psychological hedonism. If we look back at the earlier analysis in the light of this final statement, we find that his conclusion at the end of his analysis of the 'absurdity' of the popular view at 355a–356c is that a person *must* do what he has calculated will yield the greatest balance of pleasure over pain. In weighing pleasures against pleasures, the greater *must* be taken, just as the lesser pain *must* be taken in weighing pains against pains (356b). In weighing pleasures against pains, a person *must* do what yields a balance of pleasure over pain and *must* avoid what yields a balance of pain over pleasure (356b–c).

The Greek verbal adjectives used here to express what *must* be chosen or done are ambiguous.[13] Since they are used in the conclusion of Socrates' argument about 'worthy' and 'unworthy' pleasures and pains, it seems more natural at that point to take them as expressing the idea of moral obligation. But Socrates' final appeal to the facts of 'human nature' suggests perhaps that he intends 'must' as a reference to what is psychologically necessary. Certainly he needs a conclusion here different from a conclusion expressing merely what one *ought* to do. For, as we have seen, he considers that with this argument, carrying with it the ideal of a science of measurement, he has done enough to refute the popular conception of 'being overcome by pleasure' (357b–c). There is thus some reasonable ground for interpreting the references at 356b–c to what a person *must* do or *must* avoid in terms of psychological necessity.[14]

It is important, however, if we ascribe to Socrates in the *Protagoras* a doctrine of psychological hedonism, to note the particular form of the doctrine which he is presenting. It is no necessary part of the doctrine of psychological hedonism that intensity of desire is always determined by the extent of the balance of pleasure over pain, as assessed by the agent for various possible alternative courses of action. Hence it is no necessary part of the doctrine that a person always does what he has calculated will yield the greatest balance of pleasure over pain. These are, however, parts of Socrates' doctrine in the *Protagoras*. It does not, of course, follow from this that he excludes the possibility of a conflict of desires or that he fails to take such conflict into account. The notion of choice is, indeed, prominent in his argument (355e–358d). A conflict of desires will arise whenever there is a conflict between judgments in any particular situation as to what action will yield the greatest balance of pleasure over pain. But, Socrates assumes, the conflict between judgments is always resolved by calculation in favour of a judgment, whether correct or incorrect, that there is one action which will yield a greater balance than any other possible in the circumstances. He assumes further (i) that to make this judgment is to believe that it is 'best' to perform this action, (ii) that it follows from the fact that one believes it is 'best' to do a thing that one's desire to do this is stronger than one's desire to do anything else, (iii) that the conflict between desires is thus resolved in favour of the strongest desire, and (iv) that what one most strongly desires to do is what one in fact does.

Thus the kind of psychological hedonism we have in the *Protagoras* is one which gives a supremely important place to a particular form of practical reasoning in the directing of moral behaviour. It is true that this practical reasoning serves as a handmaiden to the 'natural' desire to do what is pleasant. But its application determines the intensity of the desire to perform any particular action and hence determines, within the limits set by the identification of the good with pleasure, what action *is* performed. The conclusion which Socrates is able to draw from this is, as we have seen, that no one voluntarily acts contrary to what he has judged to be the best thing to do. On the same grounds, he is able to conclude also, once he has indicated the sense that moral knowledge has within his analysis, that knowing what it is best to do is a sufficient condition of doing it. He gets his distinction between knowledge and belief by assuming the possibility of a 'science' of measurement which enables a person to *know* what it is right to do by virtue of making a correct assessment of what action in any particular situation yields the greatest balance of pleasure over pain. If the assessment is incorrect, then the ensuing action is wrong, even though the agent believes it to be right; all wrongdoing, except wrong done under compulsion, is the result of incorrect assessment and thus of 'false belief'.

There is one final point to be noted before we consider some of the problems raised by the doctrine of the *Protagoras*. The Socratic thesis that virtue is knowledge is the thesis that knowing what it is right to do is a necessary as well as a sufficient condition of doing what is right. Now the argument of the *Protagoras* we have just examined is certainly contending that knowledge is a sufficient condition. Is it contending that it is also a necessary condition? Whether it is or not depends on whether or not it allows for the agent having a right belief, while yet not having knowledge, as to what action will yield the greatest balance of pleasure over pain. For if the agent has such right belief, then he will, given the assumptions of the argument, do what is right. In a later dialogue, the *Meno*, Plato explores the question of whether knowledge is only a sufficient, and not a necessary, condition of doing what is right. He suggests that if a person's belief as to what is right happens to be correct, then it is just as effective a 'guide' to right action as knowledge is (97a–c).

In the *Protagoras*, however, the argument appears to rule out the possibility of a person happening to hit on the right thing to do without having made the correct assessment that this is the action which will yield the greatest balance of pleasure over pain. We may fairly argue that such a coincidence is not in practice impossible. But Socrates does not entertain the possibility. He assumes that the strict correspondence between intensity of desire and rational assessment of consequences rules the possibility out. Thus he argues that any error in assessment springs from lack of knowledge, that this entails acting in ignorance (357d–e), and that ignorance is 'false belief' (358c). Doing what is right implies knowing what is right. Doing what is wrong implies believing falsely that what one is doing is right.

E. PROBLEMS IN THE ACCOUNT OF THE *Protagoras*

Socrates' argument in the *Protagoras*, for all its complexity, is presented clearly and incisively. It seeks to *demonstrate* that virtue is knowledge, that no one willingly does what he judges to be wrong, and that there are no cases of weakness of will. In examining it we have noted various features of it which help it to maintain its form as a deductive proof. There is its equation of the good with pleasure. This allows a 'scientific' criterion for distinguishing knowledge from belief to be built into the argument. There are the ambiguities in language, firstly the ambiguity of the 'must' at 356b–c and secondly the ambiguity of 'erring' at 357d–e (see note 10). It appears to be by reliance on these ambiguities that the argument manages to bridge the gap in its demonstration between recognising and performing what is right. Only after 358a, when Socrates already thinks that the demonstration has been satisfactorily completed and formally presents the conclusion that 'no one does wrong willingly', is there any explicit suggestion of that strict correspondence between reason and desire which is an essential basis of Socrates' main contentions.

The form of this proof raises a number of problems. It is a proof which can rightly claim to be 'Plato's fullest treatment of the Socratic Paradox within any single argument'.[15] This makes it particularly important to determine, as far as this is possible, to what extent it can also claim to represent faithfully the significance of Socrates' moral paradoxes and the grounds on which they were based.

In considering this, a question immediately prompted by the argument of the *Protagoras* is whether we are to count as genuinely Socratic doctrine the hedonism which appears to be an important ingredient in the argument. It must be noted at the outset that nowhere in the argument of the *Protagoras* do we find a distinction between psychological and ethical hedonism. Socrates talks of what a person 'must' do, and appeals to the facts of 'human nature' to support his general thesis. At the same time he talks of pleasures 'worthy' and 'unworthy' to be pursued. And in making his distinction between knowledge and belief he seems to imply that a person *ought* to try to attain knowledge since this is a necessary and sufficient condition of doing what is in fact good.

But he does not distinguish what a person *must* do as a matter of psychological necessity from what he *ought* to do as a matter of moral desirability.

Nor is such a distinction to be found anywhere else in the arguments of the Platonic Socrates or in any other ancient testimony about Socrates. Outside the *Protagoras*, however, it is clear that the doctrine which the Platonic Socrates has in mind in any discussion of hedonism is the form of ethical hedonism which identifies the good with pleasure and maintains that one ought only to pursue one's own pleasure. This is a doctrine which in Greek ethics can easily be confused with a doctrine of psychological hedonism. We have already seen that a psychological basis for Socrates' moral paradoxes is the principle that all men desire to be happy. And a combination of this natural 'eudaimonism' of the Greek moral outlook with a doctrine of ethical hedonism yields a doctrine very close to psychological hedonism. This makes it probable that the reason why the *Protagoras* gives the impression that it is operating with both these forms of hedonism and yet makes no distinction between them is that it fails to recognise any distinction and simply confuses them.

These considerations are important in approaching the question whether the apparent hedonism of the *Protagoras* is to be counted as genuinely Socratic. For I think they make it reasonable to assume that acceptable evidence that no form of ethical hedonism was part of Socrates' serious doctrine is at the same time acceptable evidence that no form of psychological hedonism was part of it. Our subsequent discussion of Socrates' views on moral responsibility will also have some relevance to the question. Aristotle points out that to adopt a doctrine of psychological hedonism is to deny that we are morally responsible for what we do (*E.N.* 1110b 8–15). If we find that there is no trace of determinism in Socrates' views, we may well consider it unlikely that Socrates is seriously propounding a doctrine of psychological hedonism in the *Protagoras*.

The main reason why many scholars have been reluctant to

ascribe a doctrine of hedonism either to Socrates or to Plato is
that it is inconsistent with what is presented outside the *Protagoras*
as the Socratic or Platonic moral ideal. They have pointed
especially to the direct rejections of ethical hedonism in the
Gorgias (495e ff.) and the *Phaedo* (68e–69c). And to resolve the
apparent inconsistency it has been argued *either* that the doctrine
of hedonism is presented in the *Protagoras* in a patently ironical
tone which implies that it is not to be taken as the genuinely
Socratic or Platonic view, *or* that it is presented only as the view of
'the many' or at least only as the view to which the uncritical
moral attitudes of 'the many' are reducible, carrying no implication that Socrates or Plato accepted that view.[16]

There is no weight in either of these arguments. Socrates is
represented as seriously affirming his hedonistic position at the
very start of the analysis, in opposition to the view of 'the rest of
the world' that some pleasant things are to be called bad and some
painful things good (351c). It is true that the analysis then proceeds
from the beliefs of 'the many' (351c, 352b,d), and that its inter-
mediate steps and its hedonistic conclusion are presented as
propositions which 'the many' would accept (353d ff.). But this
cannot, of course, in itself imply that Socrates or Plato does not
accept the conclusion. Socrates' preliminary affirmation of
hedonism seems enough to indicate, on the contrary, that one
purpose of his analysis is to show that the uncritical view of 'the
many' is wrong to dissociate pleasure from the good and pain
from the bad. A further indication that Plato represents Socrates
as accepting the hedonistic conclusion of the analysis is that, once
the analysis is completed, Socrates uses its conclusion to further
the argument against Protagoras, relying on a proof from
hedonism to show the unity of the virtues (358d ff.). 'The many'
are no longer mentioned. Nor is there anything to suggest that
the argument against Protagoras is conducted in a spirit of
mockery or irony.

If, however, those arguments have no weight which scholars
have based on the manner of presentation of the argument in the

Protagoras itself, there appears to be some weight in the argument that, outside the *Protagoras*, the testimony on Socrates, whether by Xenophon, Plato, or Aristotle, never ascribes to him a doctrine of hedonism. Appeals have sometimes been made to Xenophon's *Memorabilia* as evidence for Socrates' hedonism, especially to Socrates' discussion with Antiphon at I vi.[17] Yet Socrates is not, in this discussion, advocating hedonism. Against Antiphon's attempt to ridicule his poverty and frugality, Socrates replies that his way of life in fact yields more pleasure than the life of 'luxury and extravagance' of which Antiphon approves. But to say that his own way of life is the most pleasant is not to advocate hedonism. And his remarks that his pleasures arise from the consciousness that his pursuits are making him a 'better' man, and that happiness (*eudaimonia*) consists in the perfect goodness associated with God (I vi 9–10) imply that, although he considers his way of life more pleasant than any other, pleasure is not the criterion of its goodness.

Xenophon does not, then, support the view that Socrates was a hedonist. Nor does Aristotle. It is significant that, although he turns primarily to the *Protagoras* for his account of Socrates' moral doctrine, Aristotle never suggests that Socrates was a hedonist. As for Plato, in his early dialogues he attributes to Socrates, as Xenophon and Aristotle do, the view that the good and the particular virtues are to be identified with knowledge, and that this knowledge is knowledge through definition. And, outside the *Protagoras*, the Socratic search for definitions never leads to the acceptance of a hypothesis which defines either the good or any of the virtues in terms of pleasure. Where such a hypothesis is put forward (*Hippias Major* 298a ff., *Gorgias* 495e ff.) it is rejected.

Thus it seems impossible to reconcile the general testimony of Xenophon, Plato, and Aristotle with the view that Socrates was a hedonist. On that ground I think such a view must be rejected. A discussion in the final chapter of the book will attempt to show what Socratic conception of the nature of the good is indicated by the ancient testimony.

The alternative view is that it is Plato, and not Socrates, who interprets the paradoxes in terms of hedonism. It is a view which may or may not include the view that Plato himself held a doctrine of ethical or psychological hedonism to be true at the time that he wrote the *Protagoras*. Professor Hackforth considered that in the *Protagoras* Plato was 'making a serious attempt to understand for himself, and explain to his readers, what the Socratic equation (sc. of goodness and knowledge) really meant'. He considered further that Plato, although 'he soon advanced beyond this view', was making his own serious 'first attempt' to specify what the good was when he interpreted the Socratic paradoxes in terms of 'psychological hedonism'. An assumption of Hackforth's argument was that 'Socrates had left the meaning and implications of his equation of Goodness and Knowledge unexplained or, rather, inadequately explained'.[18]

This view has something to commend it. It is obviously implausible to assume that in his early dialogues Plato is representing the exact form of Socrates' own arguments. And since there is good ground, as we have seen, for thinking that Socrates was not himself a hedonist, it seems reasonable to infer that not only the sophistication and the elaborate deductive form of the *Protagoras'* refutation of the popular view are to be ascribed to Plato's refining hand, but also its hedonistic basis.

But does this imply that Plato is presenting the hedonism as his own serious doctrine? I do not think that it does. The objections to thinking that Plato was a hedonist, even for a limited period of his thought, are just as formidable as in the case of Socrates. It seems to me quite improbable psychologically that Plato should seriously advocate hedonism in the *Protagoras* as his own considered view and then, in the *Gorgias* and the *Phaedo*, dialogues not far removed from the *Protagoras* in date of composition, should explicitly refute and reject such a doctrine. And it would be agreed that the moral puritanism which characterises the attitude of the *Phaedo* is associated there with a tone of moral earnestness and conviction which does not belong to the presentation of the equation of pleasure and the good in the *Protagoras*. The attitude of the *Phaedo* is, moreover, generally consistent, unlike a hedonistic view, with the evidence of all other dialogues which present Plato's conception of the good life.

As confirmation that Plato did not consider the hedonistic analysis of the *Protagoras* a sufficient answer to the question of what was the good, there is in the *Protagoras* itself an important reservation about the sufficiency of the analysis in this respect. It is a reservation which, as far as I am aware, has been overlooked by those scholars who have looked in the text of the *Protagoras* for evidence that the hedonism of its argument is not the serious doctrine of Socrates or Plato. The reservation is at 357b. Socrates is asserting here that to have shown that what 'saves' our lives is a kind of science or knowledge is sufficient for the purpose of his demonstration. He adds that the question of the nature of this science or knowledge will be considered at some other time.

Now the proceding analysis seemed to have given an unequivocal interpretation of moral knowledge and an equally unequivocal specification of the end of moral action. Yet Socrates' remarks make it clear that, although he considers this analysis adequate *for the purpose of the particular demonstration in hand*, he does not consider it adequate as an account of the nature of moral knowledge. This implies that the apparently 'pure' hedonism of the analysis is not considered adequate as a specification of the good. For Socrates has already explained in some detail that he is interpreting the meaning of knowledge in terms of a scientific application of the hedonic calculus. And he continues to assume that such a 'science' is possible. Thus it does not make sense that Socrates, if he is assuming a purely hedonistic criterion for the good, should assert that the nature of moral knowledge has yet to be considered.

In what way are we to explain, then, Socrates' puzzling reservation? The probable explanation is that, in presenting the Socratic paradoxes in the *Protagoras*, Plato has failed to keep sufficiently distinct the thesis that pleasure and the good are identical and the thesis that the good life is the most pleasant life.[19] There is no doubt that Plato accepted the second of these two theses (see especially *Republic* IX, 580 ff.). Nor is there any doubt that from the *Gorgias* onwards he explicitly rejected the first thesis. But in speaking of the relation between pleasure and the good he does not always make explicit the sort of qualifications which would show that he is putting forward only the second thesis and not also the first. At *Laws* 732e ff. such qualifications are lacking. The passage recalls at many points the argument of the *Protagoras*, and its hedonistic tone is paralleled earlier at 663a–b in what looks very like a hedonistic formulation of the Socratic paradox that no one does wrong willingly.

Plato's tendency to express his views on the relation between pleasure and the good in a misleadingly hedonistic form becomes more understandable once we take into account some of the assumptions of his thesis that the good life is the most pleasant life. His fullest treatment of this thesis is at *Republic* IX 580 ff. There are two points in his treatment to be noted. The first is that Plato considers that the higher in value a pleasure is the greater in amount it is. Higher-value pleasures are more pleasant than lower-value pleasures. To establish this link between quality and quantity he uses terms such as true, pure, real, steadfast, and genuine of high-value pleasures, and their opposites for low-value pleasures. The second point is that mistakes in the evaluation of pleasures are at the same time mistakes as to the amount of pleasure yielded. A person may firmly believe that he is 'really' experiencing pleasure or pain when his pleasure and pain are not 'real' at all. Thus his beliefs as to what are 'genuine' pleasures and pains may be 'unsound', and, not knowing what real pleasure is, he will be mistaken or 'deceived' in his assessments (584e–585a).

It follows from this that assessing the *amount* of pleasure and pain involved as consequences in possible courses of action is dependent for its success on a knowledge of which pleasures and pains are 'true, pure, real, steadfast, and genuine', and which are not. This is Plato's view. It is consequently his view that to have determined what will yield the greatest balance of pleasure over pain is to have determined what it is right to do. This explains the occasionally hedonistic form in which he presents his arguments.

We are now in a position to solve the puzzle of Socrates' reservations about moral knowledge at *Protagoras* 357b. No reservation seemed necessary if the ideal of the 'scientific' application of the hedonic calculus was concerned with the assessment of amounts of pleasure and pain independently of the question of a non-quantitative evaluation of pleasures and pains. But it is now clear that, when Plato speaks of assessing amounts of pleasure and pain, he has in mind a conception of moral knowledge involving much more than ability to be correct in purely quantitative assessments of pleasure and pain. That is why he says that the question of what is the nature of knowledge of the good is a question for consideration at some other time.

This reservation implies, then, that the argument of the *Protagoras* should not be accepted as an argument for hedonism, and at the same time that Plato is not ascribing to Socrates a conception of moral knowledge which identifies it with a 'science' of assessing the purely hedonic consequences of possible courses of action. There is not, therefore, any incompatibility between the argument of the *Protagoras* and the conception of moral knowledge as knowledge through general definition which other evidence allows us to ascribe to Socrates. It might be argued that there is no such incompatibility even if we accept the argument of the *Protagoras* as an argument for hedonism. There the first part of the argument (353c–354e) can be viewed as an exercise in general definition in which Socrates successfully substantiates his equation of pleasure and the good. Knowledge of the good is then the knowledge that it is pleasure. And this knowledge is the essential basis of knowing what it is right to do in any particular situation. Looked at in this way, the argument serves as an illustration of the Socratic ideal of knowledge through definition.

Yet it is clear that Plato is not intending his argument to illustrate this. He associates knowledge exclusively with the 'scientific' calculation of amounts of pleasure and pain consequent on possible courses of action. It is because of this that his reservation about the nature of moral knowledge is so important. Just as we cannot infer from the *Protagoras* that Socrates defined the good as pleasure, so we cannot infer from it that Socrates viewed knowledge as a purely quantitative 'science' of assessing consequences.

However, for the purposes of refuting the popular view, Plato considers that he has said in the *Protagoras* all that he needs to say in this respect. For the same reason he does not think it necessary to discuss further the conditions of false belief or ignorance, and of being mistaken or deceived 'in important matters'. The obvious parallels between the use of these phrases in the *Protagoras* and the reference in the discussion of pleasures in *Republic* IX to unsound belief, ignorance, and being mistaken or deceived are an indication that *Republic* IX is resuming the discussion which the *Protagoras* had postponed.

The most plausible interpretation of the hedonistic form of the argument in the *Protagoras* would seem to be, therefore, that it is Plato who has given it this form and that he has failed to qualify the argument sufficiently to distinguish its thesis as the thesis that the good life is the most pleasant life. The reservation at 357b remains the only indication that such qualification is needed.

But if this is accepted, how far are we justified in assuming that in the *Protagoras* Plato is presenting the Socratic paradoxes in a form which preserves in essentials their original significance? We have already argued that there is good ground for thinking that Socrates was not a hedonist. Are we now to assume, having construed the apparent hedonism of the *Protagoras* as an admittedly misleading presentation of the thesis that the good life is the most pleasant life, that Socrates himself made that thesis the basis of his paradoxes? There is little doubt that Socrates himself put forward the thesis. Xenophon represents him as putting it forward explicitly on a number of occasions. Apart from its ascription to him in his conversation with Antiphon (*Mem.* VI v 8–9; 14) which we noticed earlier, it is ascribed to him in several other parts of the *Memorabilia* (I iii 15; III xii 4; IV v 9–10; viii 6).

The thesis is, indeed, a prevalent one in Greek ethics. It is the result of the utilitarian outlook which we considered at the beginning of the chapter. This makes 'happiness' (*eudaimonia*) the end of human action. But it does not entail hedonism. While an English utilitarian like John Stuart Mill readily assumes the identity in meaning of happiness and pleasure, the Greeks never assume this. Yet the natural 'eudaimonism' of their outlook makes them readily assume that the good or happy life is in fact the most pleasurable life. Socrates and Plato readily assume this. So does Aristotle (*E.E.* 1214a8, 1249a20–1; *E.N.* 1177a22–5).

It is not unlikely, therefore, that Socrates did sometimes make this assumption the basis of his form of explication of the paradoxes. The fact that Aristotle, while regarding the *Protagoras* as of primary importance in giving his account of Socratic doctrine, never makes any mention of this aspect of it should cause no surprise. We may assume from his silence that he did not consider that the *Protagoras* was ascribing to Socrates a purely hedonistic doctrine. We may assume from it further that, in so far as he recognised that the view that the good life is the most pleasant life played a part in Socrates' explication of his paradoxes, he did not consider this to be either a necessary or sufficiently distinctive feature of them to deserve mention.

What Aristotle's testimony *positively* shows is that in essentials the form in which the paradoxes are presented in the *Protagoras* is their distinctively Socratic form. This is especially important as far as the paradox that no one does wrong willingly is concerned. For the formulation given to this paradox in the *Protagoras* differs in important respects from its formulation in later dialogues of Plato. Hence the fact that Aristotle presents the formulation in the *Protagoras* as Socratic and nowhere suggests any alternative Socratic formulation is good evidence that in the *Protagoras* we have what is distinctively Socratic. There is some confirmation for this view from Xenophon. For he ascribes essentially the same

I

formulation of the paradox to Socrates as do Aristotle and the *Protagoras* (see especially *Mem.* III ix 4; IV vi 6, 11).

What is distinctive in the form of the paradox as we find it in Xenophon, Plato's *Protagoras*, and Aristotle (*E.N.* 1145b 21 ff.) is that it assumes that if a person does what is in fact wrong and is acting voluntarily, he is invariably doing what he believes to be right, and that if a person does what is right and is acting voluntarily, he is invariably doing what he knows to be right. Thus in all his voluntary moral actions he is doing what he either knows or believes to be right. If he acts contrary to what he either knows or believes to be right, then his action is involuntary. Hence, assuming that everybody desires to do what he knows or believes to be right, involuntary has the sense of 'not in accordance with the agent's desire to do what he knows or believes to be right'. In this sense, all wrongdoing is involuntary.

Beginning with the *Gorgias*, however, an alternative interpretation of the thesis appears, and remains the standard interpretation throughout the rest of the dialogues. In the *Gorgias* the paradox appears in the form 'no one does wrong wishing to do wrong' (509e), together with the stipulation that only what is 'really' good for the agent, and not what *seems* good to him, is an object of wish (466d–468e, to which 509e refers back).[20] Thus to say that no one does wrong wishing to do wrong is to say that if a person does wrong his action is contrary to what he wishes and hence contrary to what is 'really' good. Hence to do what is wrong is to do what is 'really' bad.

What distinguishes this formulation from the other is that in saying that no one does wrong willingly it restricts wrong to what is objectively wrong and does not, as the earlier formulation did, refer also to what is subjectively wrong. Its application of 'voluntary' and 'involuntary' is correspondingly restricted. The term 'voluntary' is restricted to 'really' good actions, the actions of those who know what the good is, since it is only those people who are capable of satisfying their 'wish'. 'Involuntary' is restricted to 'really' bad actions and is applicable to all such actions.

They are actions committed in ignorance of what is good by those who 'really' want to do what is good and would do so if they knew what was good. For the new-style 'no one does wrong willingly' thesis may be viewed in the hypothetical form that no one acts against what he would wish to do if he knew what was 'really' good. At *Laws* 731c the thesis is presented in a form closely approximating to this. The sense of 'involuntary' thus becomes 'not in accordance with the aim which the agent's desire would have had if he had known what was really good'.

Now it is this distinction between voluntary and involuntary which Proclus, in his commentary on the *Republic*,[21] presents as Plato's. He notes that 'what is in our power' and what is voluntary (*to hekousion*) are not, for Plato, equivalent terms. For in Plato's view, he says, the wrongdoer deliberately chooses to act as he does in ignorance of what is right. It is 'in his power' so to act. But his action is involuntary in the sense that it is 'not in accordance with what he really wishes' (*aboulêton*). Only good actions are properly to be called voluntary.

If we look back to the sense of 'involuntary' and 'voluntary' yielded by the account of the *Protagoras*, we see that here 'what is in our power' *is* co-extensive with what is voluntary. A person invariably wants to do what he knows or believes to be the best out of all actions possible (*dunata*)[22] in any particular situation, and invariably does this. Thus the view of the *Protagoras* is in these respects directly contrary to the view which Proclus ascribes to Plato. The view of the *Protagoras* is, indeed, one which Proclus is careful to dissociate from Plato's. This is added confirmation of what is already suggested by the evidence of both Xenophon and Aristotle – that the *Protagoras*' interpretation of 'no one does wrong willingly' is, in the important respects we have been considering, not the Platonic but the distinctively Socratic interpretation.

This distinction between the Socratic and Platonic interpretations is essential for a proper understanding of what is implied by the thesis about moral responsibility. In the *Protagoras* the thesis carries no suggestion that the person who does that which he believes to be right and which is 'really' wrong is not responsible for his wrongdoing. His action is explicitly described as voluntary, and an implicit corollary of the thesis seems to be that the person who acts in ignorance of what is 'really' good is responsible for his ignorance. According to the Platonic thesis, however, beginning with the *Gorgias*, his action is classified as involuntary. In many ways this seems to be an awkward application of 'involuntary'. It means, as we have seen, 'not in accordance with the agent's "real" wish', although the involuntary action is, of course, in accordance with what the agent actually desires at the time. This sense of involuntary, in view of the corollary that knowledge of what is good is a necessary and sufficient condition of achieving what one 'really' wishes, implies that the wrongdoer's ignorance is involuntary.[23] He 'really' wishes to have knowledge; if he had realised that he was ignorant, he would not have wanted to remain so.

What is awkward about this is that, in the *Gorgias* at least, Plato seems to be arguing that the wrongdoer's ignorance is at once involuntary and blameworthy. Aristotle would count this application of 'involuntary' improper. He makes the point that, ignorance of the 'right' moral principles being blameworthy (*E.N.* 1110b32-3), then to classify as involuntary action done in ignorance of those principles is contrary to the proper usage of involuntary (1110b30). I suspect that part of the explanation of Plato's first application of involuntary in this unusual way is that he was exploring the analogy between moral behaviour and the practice of professional skills. Just as the bad runner 'really' wants to win the race and loses it 'against his will', so, Plato suggests, the morally bad man 'really' wants to do what is good and does wrong 'against his will'.

Any awkwardness belonging to Plato's interpretation of the Socratic paradox disappears, however, once it is assumed that wrongdoing, and the ignorance inseparable from it, are non-blameworthy. For a natural corollary of the thesis that all wrongdoing is involuntary is that all wrongdoing is non-blameworthy. It is not surprising to find, therefore, that it is this corollary which Plato begins to make explicit in his further discussion of the paradox in later dialogues. In the *Republic* (382a–c; cf. 412e–413a, 589c) and the *Sophist* (228c–d, 230a) he continues to assume that ignorance is involuntary. At the same time he assumes that it is not blameworthy. Thus the *Sophist* assumes that it is not punishable (229a–d; cf. *Laws* 864a, 908b–909a).[24] The appropriate discipline for the correction of ignorance is education.

The implication here is that, since everyone naturally wishes to have knowledge and to overcome ignorance once he realises that he is ignorant, it must be the restricting influence of factors beyond our power to control which prevents us both from realising and from overcoming our ignorance. The most important factor, in both the *Republic* and the *Sophist*, is the lack of adequate education. Thus the ignorance is not blameworthy. That is why the *Sophist* describes it as deformity or ugliness rather than a vice. The *Timaeus* too assumes that ignorance is not blameworthy, and specifies poor education as one of the two factors which make a person bad. The other factor is bad physical constitution. It is on this basis that the *Timaeus* explains the thesis that no one is willingly bad (86d–e).

In the *Timaeus* Plato comes nearest to a doctrine of determinism in respect of human behaviour.[25] He still assumes, of course, that there are voluntary actions. Voluntary actions are good actions, done by those who know what the good is. They are voluntary in the sense that they are in accordance with what the agent 'really' wishes. But if, with Aristotle, we reject as inadequate a definition of voluntary simply as 'what is in accordance with desire' (*E.E.* 1223a21 ff.) and include in our definition of voluntary action 'what it is in the agent's power to do or not to do' (*E.E.* 1225b8–10, *E.N.* 1110a15–18), it becomes possible to argue that the *Timaeus*' explanation of the non-blameworthy nature of bad actions implies that good actions are at once not praiseworthy and not voluntary. For if the two factors which control our character and conception of the good – education and physical constitution

– are, as Aristotle would put it, things which do not depend on ourselves, then we are not responsible for what we are. And in that case, Aristotle argues, virtue is no more voluntary than vice (*E.N.* 1114a31–b16).

Plato himself would certainly have rejected such an assessment of his doctrine. But it was important to see in what way the Socratic paradox was developed by Plato to a point where it became possible to associate it with a denial of moral responsibility. For it was important to dissociate the Socratic from the Platonic interpretation in this respect, and thus avoid the sort of confusion which even in antiquity allowed the Socratic paradox to be associated with determinism. An instance of this confusion is found in the *Magna Moralia*. At 1187a5–13 the author ascribes to Socrates the view that being good or bad is not something which depends on us, giving as Socrates' ground for this view the argument that no one would wish to be unjust rather than just, or bad in any respect rather than good. The conclusion he draws from this is that no bad person would be voluntarily bad, and hence that no good person would be voluntarily good.

Both in its formulation and in the conclusion which the author thinks plausible to draw from it, this account of the paradox looks back to what we have now seen to be the Platonic rather than the Socratic interpretation. The fact that the former interpretation is here wrongly ascribed to Socrates underlines the importance of distinguishing clearly between the two and of emphasising that no suggestion of determinism belongs to the *Socratic* paradox that no one does wrong willingly.

Two final points are worth noting in concluding this discussion of what is implied about moral responsibility by the Socratic paradox. In the *Nicomachean Ethics* Aristotle suggests that a doctrine of psychological hedonism might be used as the basis for an argument that the pleasure motive necessarily determines all that we do in a compulsive way which shifts responsibility for our actions from ourselves to 'external circumstances' (1110b8–15). Aristotle firmly rejects both the doctrine of psychological hedonism and the argument for determinism based on it. Socrates would have rejected them equally firmly. He would have rejected also the argument that his paradox that no one does wrong willingly was reducible to a doctrine of what might be called, using the Greek word for good (*agathon*), psychological agathism. Aristotle notices this doctrine too as a possible basis for the compulsionist argument (*E.N.* 1110b). It is true that Socrates considered it a fact of 'human nature' that in his voluntary actions everybody invariably does what he knows or believes to be best. But his distinction between knowledge and belief, together with his assumption that moral ignorance is voluntary, indicates clearly his view of the nature and extent of our responsibility for the direction of our moral behaviour.

The second point is the question of the type of circumstances which would, in Socrates' view, make an action involuntary. We have already seen that the sense of involuntary in the Socratic thesis that all wrongdoing is involuntary is 'not in accordance with the agent's desire to do what he knows or believes to be right'. This immediately limits to very small proportions the class of involuntary actions. For what the agent so desires to do is, for all his intentional actions without exception, what he in fact does. It would appear, then, that the only kind of restraint or compulsion which would make an action involuntary would be the kind of external compulsion described by Aristotle at *E.N.* 1110a. That is compulsory, Aristotle says, of which the moving principle is external to the agent, the kind of principle in which nothing is contributed by the agent, e.g. 'if he were to be carried somewhere by a wind, or by men who had him in their power'. Socrates himself was never explicit in this way, but it is obviously implicit in his paradox that he would have agreed substantially with what Aristotle has to say about the distinction between voluntary and involuntary at *E.N.* III 1. Plato's interpretation of the paradox widens the class of involuntary actions to an extent which both Socrates and Aristotle would think improper.

We have now discussed two important questions arising from

the presentation in the *Protagoras* of the Socratic paradoxes that virtue is knowledge and that no one does wrong willingly. One was the question of whether its account amounted to a declaration that hedonism was the basis of the paradoxes. The other was the question of what was implied by the paradoxes about moral responsibility. In answering these questions we have been able to establish that the account in the *Protagoras* faithfully represents in essentials the significance of the paradoxes as propounded by Socrates. It is likely also, in view of the evidence outside the *Protagoras* about the kind of thinking which went to the formulation of the paradoxes, that Plato reproduces in essentials a typically Socratic form of argument in support of the truth of the paradoxes. The only aspect of the form of argument which occasions serious misgivings is, as we have seen, the misleading and exaggerated hedonistic basis. We suggested, particularly in view of the partial parallels in argument in admittedly non-Socratic dialogues such as *Republic* and *Laws*, that the severely hedonistic form is more likely to be a Platonic rather than a Socratic variation.

With this reservation, we may conclude that in the *Protagoras* we have 'a particularly ripe and masterly exposition of the Socratic moral theory'.[26]

F. ARISTOTLE'S CRITICISMS OF THE TWO PARADOXES

At the end of our discussion of the 'virtue is knowledge' thesis in the second section of this chapter, we noted that it was primarily in his conception of the nature of moral knowledge that Socrates' thesis appeared to be vulnerable. For 'knowing' is identified by Socrates with a severely intellectual type of apprehension of general truths in the form of definitions. At the same time Socrates assumes that this knowing determines desire in such a way that a person invariably desires to do what he knows to be right and invariably has a stronger desire to do this than any other action possible in the circumstances. An obvious objection to this appears to be that Socrates, in building into his thesis that virtue is knowledge this 'intellectualist' conception of moral knowledge, is asserting, as Vlastos has put it,[27] 'the conjunction of two logically distinct things, an intellectual state (knowing . . . something), and an emotional one (one in which there is the affective backing for doing the thing one knows . . . one ought to do).' The objector can readily counter, we feel, Socrates' appeal to 'human nature' for the truth of his thesis by asserting that it is a fact of human nature that people sometimes act contrary to what, on intellectual grounds, they are sure is right.

Aristotle recognised that the vulnerable point of the Socratic thesis was its conception of moral knowledge, and consequently made this the primary target of his criticisms. It is to the examination of these criticisms, and an assessment of their fairness, that we must now turn. We will first consider Aristotle's criticism of Socrates' denial in the *Protagoras* that there are cases of weakness of will (*akrasia*). Aristotle makes this criticism in the course of his own account of weakness of will in the *Nicomachean Ethics*. As a preliminary to the examination of this, something must be said briefly about Aristotle's conception of moral knowledge.

The term which Aristotle uses for moral knowledge, i.e. the knowledge which a person exercises when he knows what it is right to do in any particular situation, is *phronêsis*, often translated as 'practical wisdom'. For Aristotle, it is one of the two virtues or 'best dispositions' of human reason. The other is *sophia*, philosophic wisdom, which is exercised in theoretical sciences (e.g. metaphysics and mathematics) and not in determining what it is right to do in the practical sphere of human behaviour. *Phronêsis*, unlike *sophia*, is essentially a deliberative excellence, the deliberation being directed to the assessment of the best means, in any given circumstances, to the realisation of what is the agent's good (*E.N.* VI 5, 7, 8).

Aristotle emphasises, however, that in speaking of deliberative excellence he does not mean simply a disposition to be always correct in one's calculation of means to *any* moral end. The excellence is not a mere technical excellence in calculation. The person whose conception of the good is not of what is 'really' good but only of 'the apparent good' may have the disposition to be right in calculating the means to realise this apparent good. But he will not have *phronêsis*. For by deliberative excellence Aristotle means excellence in calculating the means to realising what is 'really' good (*E.N.* VI 9).

It follows that one cannot possess *phronêsis* unless one is right in one's conception of what the good is. And since it is Aristotle's view that a person's conception of what is the good is determined by his character, it follows further that it is impossible to have *phronêsis* without having excellence of character, or 'moral virtue', as well as technical excellence in calculation. As Aristotle puts it (*E.N.* 1144b30–2), 'it is not possible to be good in the strict sense without practical wisdom, nor practically wise without moral virtue'.

Thus *phronêsis* is not a merely intellectual disposition. In the sphere of the theoretical intellect, Aristotle says, the goodness or badness of any theory formulated depends on whether that theory is true or false, irrespective of the desires or emotions of the person who formulated it. But in the sphere of the practical intellect this is not the case. Here the criterion which determines whether a person has 'got it right' in choosing what to do is 'truth in agreement with right desire' (*E.N.* 1139a21–31). The disposition to 'get it right' is *phronêsis*.

This notion of 'truth in agreement with right desire' expresses Aristotle's view that it is not possible to claim to *know* that a certain course of action is right unless (i) the deliberative assessment of what it is right to do, relatively to a given end, is correct; (ii) the resultant judgment is, as we might put it, 'characteristic of' the agent and hence, because of this accord with his character, represents a genuine conviction; (iii) the agent's character is good and thus gives him a right conception of the good. It is because *phronêsis* invariably reflects in its judgments the character of the agent and hence his desires that it is what Aristotle calls 'epitactic', i.e. its judgments as to what it is right to do have an imperative force which distinguishes them from the judgments of the understanding (*synesis*). For 'the end of practical wisdom is what ought to be done or not to be done, but the understanding only judges' (*E.N.* 1143a8–10). Moreover, *phronêsis*, although in its strictly deliberative activity it is a faculty which assesses the right means to a given end, includes, as an invariable part of its activity, a 'true apprehension' of the end.[28] And just as the truth which it apprehends is a different kind of truth from the truth established in the theoretical sciences, so *phronêsis* is not scientific knowledge, but 'another kind of knowledge', as Aristotle puts it in the *Eudemian Ethics*.[29]

It is from the viewpoint of this conception of moral knowledge as *phronêsis* that practically all Aristotle's criticisms of the Socratic thesis that virtue is knowledge are conducted. With the Socratic view that knowing what it is right to do is at once a necessary and sufficient condition of doing it Aristotle is in substantial agreement. For he is committed to this view by his conception of moral knowledge. In the *Nicomachean Ethics* he rules out the possibility of the practically wise man acting contrary to what he knows to be right. He considers it absurd to assume such a possibility. *Phronêsis*, he says, echoing the language of Socrates in the *Protagoras*, is the strongest of all states (1146a5–8). Similarly, in the *Eudemian Ethics*, he agrees with Socrates that nothing is stronger than moral knowledge, *phronêsis* (1246b34). But he disagrees with Socrates about the nature of moral knowledge. He thinks that Socrates failed to appreciate the distinctive features of moral knowledge as a 'kind of knowledge' quite different from scientific knowledge, and that he consequently made the mistake of building into his thesis that virtue is knowledge a conception of moral knowledge which made the thesis false.

If we now look at Aristotle's discussion of weakness of will (*akrasia*) in Bk. VII of the *Nicomachean Ethics*, we find that he disagrees with Socrates' assertion 'that there is no such thing as incontinence', but that he makes no attempt to press what is elsewhere his major objection to Socrates' moral doctrine, i.e. the objection that Socrates misconceives the nature of moral knowledge. He begins by arguing that Socrates' denial that there are cases of weakness of will is a clear contradiction of 'the plain facts' (*E.N.* 1145b25–8). His own position is, as we have seen, that there are no cases of weak-willed action among people who know, in the full sense which belongs to *phronêsis*, what it is right to do. But he does not think that this entails that there are no cases of weakness of will. For 'the plain facts' are that there are recognised cases of people who, through weakness of will, act contrary to what they know or believe in some sense to be right. The problem of explaining these cases becomes for Aristotle the problem of determining in what sense they can be said to know or believe this at the time that they act.

The solution which he offers of this problem is not, however, one which is intended to suggest that Socrates in his thesis used 'knowledge' in too weak a sense to rule out the possibility of a person acting against what he knew to be right. This is made clear by the concluding remarks in his analysis (1147b14–17). His main criticism of Socrates is that, although he was correct in his view that no one acts contrary to what he 'really' knows to be right, he should have recognised that it still makes sense to say that a person may, through weakness of will, do what he *believes* to be wrong. This criticism involves no criticism of the Socratic thesis that virtue is knowledge. But it does constitute a criticism of the thesis that no one does wrong willingly, inasmuch as that thesis asserts that no one acts contrary to what he *believes* to be right.

What is particularly important in Aristotle's analysis is the use which he makes of the notion of conviction (*pistis*). He introduces the notion initially in discussing the relevance to the problem of weakness of will of the distinction between knowledge and belief. Socrates' contention, he points out, that no one acts against what he judges best is the contention not only that 'nothing is stronger than knowledge' but also that 'no one acts contrary to what has seemed to him the better course', i.e. that no one acts contrary to what he *either* knows *or* believes to be best (1145b26–35). This is the doctrine of the *Protagoras*. A different possible contention,[30] Aristotle suggests, is that, if we assume that a strong conviction belongs to knowledge and only a weak conviction to belief, then no one will act contrary to what he *knows* to be best but some people will act contrary to what they *believe* to be best.

But Aristotle refuses to accept the assumption on which this contention is based. There need be no difference, he says, between knowledge and belief in respect of strength of conviction. Some men 'are no less convinced of what they think than others of what they know'. Though they have only belief as to what it is right to do, they have no doubt or uncertainty about this. They 'think that they know exactly' (1146b24–30).

In discussing the assumption in this way, it is clear that Aristotle is unwittingly granting the strength of the assumption which his argument is designed to reject. For in associating with strength of conviction lack of doubt or uncertainty and a belief that one 'knows exactly' he indicates how natural it is in the case of moral knowledge to make strength of conviction the criterion for distinguishing between knowledge and belief. His reason for rejecting the assumption is that he would have been committed to some form of subjectivist moral doctrine if he had accepted strength of conviction as the basic criterion of distinction.

Aristotle does, however, accept strength of conviction as a criterion for distinguishing weak-willed actions from other moral actions. The distinction between the self-indulgent man and the incontinent man, says Aristotle, is that the former deliberately pursues his pleasures from conviction that it is good for him to do so, while the latter acts without any 'conviction that he ought' to be doing what he does. The self-indulgent man has 'conviction' because 'he is the sort of man' to do what he does. The weak-willed man, lacking any firm dispositions of character, lacks conviction of the rightness both of what he is doing and of what he has failed to do (1146a31–b2, 1151a11–26).[31]

Here is Aristotle's example of a weak-willed action. Suppose a person believes that sweet things ought not to be tasted, and believes at the same time that everything sweet is pleasant. Suppose further that he is weak-willed. If he comes across something which he judges to be sweet, his desire to taste it will give to his belief that everything sweet is pleasant an 'epitactic' or imperative force which will outweigh any such force belonging to his belief that sweet things ought not to be tasted. Thus he will subsume the minor premiss that 'this is sweet' under the 'wrong' major premiss to form his practical syllogism. He will taste the sweet thing (1147a29–b3).

It is assumed here that if the agent had had the *conviction* that sweet things ought not to be tasted he would not have tasted the sweet thing. Aristotle characterises his state of mind with regard to this major premiss as akin to that of a person reciting a scientific proof or a poem without a grasp of its significance (1147a19–21). It is precisely the state of mind which he earlier associates with lack of conviction (1142a19–20). In the situation envisaged in Aristotle's example the major premiss lacks effective moral significance for the agent because it lacks sufficient affective backing from his desire to give his belief in it conviction. It must be added that, in Aristotle's view, the agent in this case lacks the conviction also that it is right to taste this sweet thing.

What criticism of Socratic doctrine is implied by this analysis? Aristotle makes it clear immediately that the weak-willed man's state of mind with regard to the universal major premiss is such that he cannot be said to *know* it at the time of his action. Thus he cannot be said to be acting contrary to what he *knows* to be right. The only knowledge which Aristotle grants to him is the non-moral 'perceptual knowledge' that 'this is sweet'. Thus Socrates is right to deny that there are cases of people acting, through weakness of will, contrary to what they *know* to be right (1147b13–17). Aristotle readily grants this, nor is he concerned here to question the adequacy of Socrates' conception of moral knowledge.

What Aristotle does not grant is the Socratic contention that no one acts contrary to what he *believes* to be right. For he considers that, if the belief lacks conviction, it can be 'mastered'. Aristotle's position, as we have seen, is that, while conviction always belongs to moral knowledge, it does not always belong to moral belief. Conviction is not sufficient to distinguish knowledge from belief, but it is at least a necessary condition of possessing moral knowledge. Belief, however, is either strong or weak. A strong belief constitutes conviction, a weak belief implies lack of conviction.

It is difficult, of course, to give precision to this. But Aristotle's point in criticising the Socratic thesis that no one does wrong willingly is that the difference between having a 'strong' belief in a moral principle and having a 'weak' belief in it is recognisable as the difference between the continent man's and the incontinent man's attitude to it. His contention is (i) that a necessary condition of being able to stick to a moral principle in one's actions is 'really' believing in it or being *convinced* of it; (ii) that a necessary condition of being convinced of it is that one's belief in it is 'part of one's nature' or character, as Aristotle puts it at 1147a22; (iii) that, since these conditions are not always met, some people act contrary to what they believe to be right, and do so voluntarily (1152a15–16). Hence Socrates is wrong to deny that there are such people.

If we look again at Aristotle's example of weak-willed action, we see that it is a case of conflict between two 'weak' beliefs in a person of weak character. The weak-willed man has the belief 'present in him' that sweet things ought not to be tasted. He has also the belief, given some imperative force in this particular case by his present desire for what he recognises to be sweet, that sweet things are pleasant. His action is prompted by this latter belief, to the neglect of the former.

Socrates would have said that here the agent does what he believes to be right, satisfying his strongest desire at the moment. Aristotle says that the agent does what he believes to be wrong, satisfying his strongest desire at the moment. He argues that the agent does not 'really' (i.e. with conviction) believe that it is right to do what he does (1151a22–4). And although he grants that the agent does not 'really' believe at the moment of action that it is wrong to do it, he considers that the agent is doing what he believes, but is not convinced, that he ought not to do (cf. 1136b6– 9). Moreover, all weak-willed men (unlike the wicked) are 'given to repentance' (1150b29–31). Though neglecting what they ought to do at the moment of action, they soon fully realise that what they did was wrong, and are sorry for it. It is contrary to what they normally 'really' believe to be right.

On these grounds Aristotle thinks that in a case of weak-willed action the belief as to what it is right to do is properly identified with the belief which does not prevail, and not, as Socrates argued, with the belief which does. Whether we prefer Aristotle's analysis to Socrates' depends largely on whether, on introspective grounds, the one appears truer than the other as a piece of psychological analysis. Aristotle is obviously more sophisticated in his analysis than Socrates, and his use of the notion of conviction in relation to moral belief and moral character is an important contribution to the analysis of weakness of will. It seems to me that Aristotle successfully shows the over-simplification in Socrates' contention that no one acts contrary to what he believes to be right. Socrates assumed that what a person believes to be the best thing to do in any particular situation is invariably what he has a sufficiently strong desire to do. Aristotle shows, by his analysis of weak-willed action, that this is not invariably the case.

Aristotle does not, however, here criticise the Socratic view that no one acts contrary to what he *knows* to be right, which is the other half of the thesis that no one does wrong willingly.

It is to the *Eudemian Ethics* that we have to turn to see what assessment Aristotle gives of Socrates' thesis that virtue is knowledge.

In a familiar passage (1216b3 ff.) Aristotle gives the following account of Socrates' aims:

Socrates thought that the end is to know virtue, and sought to find out what justice and courage and each of the divisions of virtue are. This was a reasonable procedure, since he thought that all the virtues were instances of knowledge, so that to know justice is at the same time to be just. For to have learned geometry and house-building is at the same time to be a geometer and a house-builder. Hence he used to inquire what virtue was, but not how and from what sources it came into being. His thesis is valid in the case of the theoretical sciences, since astronomy and natural science and geometry have no other end except to gain knowledge of, and to contemplate, the nature of the things which are the subjects of the sciences. But the end of the productive sciences is something different from science and knowledge. For example, the end of the science of medicine is health, and that of political science ordered government or something of that kind. So, while it is a fine thing to gain knowledge of all that is fine, yet it is not knowledge of what it is which is the most valuable thing in the case of virtue, but ascertaining what the sources are which bring it into being. For we do not want to know what courage is but to be courageous, nor to know what justice is but to be just, in the same way as we want to be healthy rather than to get to know what health is, to be in good disposition rather than to get to know what being in good disposition is.

Here Aristotle is using his own distinction between theoretical and practical sciences as the basis of his criticism of Socrates. The distinction[32] includes a distinction between the ends of these sciences. While the theoretical sciences aim at knowledge for its own sake, the practical sciences have as their end a 'product' (*ergon*) which is apart from the knowledge itself.[33] In the case of the practical science of ethics, the 'product' which constitutes the final aim is goodness or good conduct. Of his own inquiry in the *Nicomachean Ethics* Aristotle says that 'we are inquiring not in order to know what virtue is, but in order to become good' (1103b27–8). That is why, he says later, a study of politics is a necessary complement to his inquiries in the *Ethics* (1179a35 ff.). Political science is, for Aristotle, the 'master art' (1094a26–8). For while it is important to determine what goodness is, the further aim must be to determine and to establish the conditions for realising or 'producing' human goodness in society (1179b31–1181b22).

His criticism of Socrates in the present passage of the *Eudemian Ethics* is that, in making knowledge of what the good is and not goodness itself his final aim, he is mistakenly treating ethics as if it were a theoretical science. In one respect the criticism appears to misrepresent Socrates' position. For it is not strictly true to say, as Aristotle does, that Socrates made knowledge of what the good is, *rather than* goodness itself, the end. We have already considered in detail the significance of Socrates' thesis that virtue is knowledge. It is the thesis that knowing what is good is a necessary and sufficient *condition* of being good. Both Xenophon and Plato interpret it as such. It is difficult to suppose that they are both systematically misrepresenting it. Thus in Plato's *Euthydemus* (279a ff.) knowledge (*sophia*) is the answer given to the question of 'what is sufficient for the attainment of happiness'. Similarly, in the *Meno*, it is 'under the guidance of knowledge' that moral behaviour is said to terminate in happiness (88c). In the *Protagoras* knowledge is presented as the 'salvation' of life, in the sense that it is a sufficient defence against wrongdoing and a sufficient guarantee of 'prosperity' or happiness (352c, 356d ff.). Xenophon's interpretation is essentially the same (*Mem.* III ix 4–5; cf. IV vi 6, 10–11).

Thus Socrates is in agreement with Aristotle in thinking that goodness or happiness is the end, and that knowledge is a condition of it. It is true that Socrates states his thesis in a form which might suggest that knowledge is to be identified with virtue and made definitive of it, but his explanations of the thesis make clear what is its proper significance. When Aristotle criticises Socrates in the *Nicomachean Ethics* (1144b17–30) for identifying the virtues with knowledge instead of making knowledge a necessary condition of virtue he is guilty of the same sort of misrepresentation as he is in the *Eudemian Ethics* when he criticises Socrates for making knowledge the end.

The fundamental criticism in this passage of the *Eudemian Ethics* is, however, that Socrates was wrong to make knowledge of what virtue is a sufficient as well as a necessary condition of being virtuous. For this is the criticism which Aristotle is making when he says that 'it is not knowledge of what it is which is the most valuable thing in the case of virtue but ascertaining what the sources are which bring it into being'. Aristotle is thinking here, of course, of Socrates' search for general definitions of the virtues. And he considers that the attempt to establish what a thing is by general definition is a theoretical type of study (*theôria*) which has far less importance in ethics than Socrates had attached to it.

Several passages in the *Nicomachean Ethics* make clear his attitude to what he describes as 'theorizing' in ethics. There is the passage (1103b26-9) which we recently noted, where he says that his own inquiry does not aim at any theoretical kind of knowledge (*theôria*), since its aim is not to know what virtue is, but to achieve goodness. A little later (1105b12-18) he speaks of people who 'take refuge in theory and think they are being philosophers and will become good in this way, behaving somewhat like patients who listen attentively to their doctors but do none of the things they are ordered to do'. Most instructive of all for an understanding of his present criticism of Socrates are his remarks at the end of the *Ethics*, when he is commenting on the need to complement his inquiries in ethics by a study of politics. Here (1179a35 ff.), in terms almost exactly the same as those which he uses in criticising Socrates in the passage of the *Eudemian Ethics*, he says that in practical matters the end is not to contemplate and get to know things,[34] but to *do* them.

He then goes on to explain why he thinks that merely knowing what is virtue is not sufficient for becoming good. His argument is that theoretical arguments (*logoi*) are the means whereby one acquires knowledge of what virtue is. Thus it is possible to provide someone with sound theoretical grounds for accepting as correct a certain specification of what virtue is. Yet it is an obvious fact of experience, he says, that such arguments are not sufficient to make people good. Unless one has the dispositions of character which allow one to accept such arguments, not as a merely intellectual assent but, as one might put it, as a temperamental conviction of their rightness, of what use are they? 'He who lives as passion directs will not hear argument that dissuades him, nor understand it if he does. The character must somehow be there already with a kinship to virtue, loving what is noble and hating what is base' (1179b26–31). Knowledge, then, is not a sufficient condition of virtue. One must have the right dispositions and 'make use of them' (i.e. exercise them in action).

These remarks in the *Nicomachean Ethics* are, it is clear, an implicit criticism of Socrates' thesis that virtue is knowledge, and are making fundamentally the same point made as an explicit criticism of Socrates in the *Eudemian Ethics*. There is, perhaps, undue depreciation by Aristotle of the value of knowledge in the theoretical sense he is giving to it in the passages we have considered, especially in the concluding remarks of the passage in the *Eudemian Ethics*. For in his own inquiries in ethics he obviously 'wants to know' what goodness is, what is the proper definition of it. Indeed, good examples of the theoretical type of argument which he tends to depreciate are his own arguments in the *Nicomachean Ethics* in support of his contemplative ideal of goodness, especially the arguments based on the conclusions of his work in metaphysics and psychology (VI 7; X 7–8). And Aristotle presumably thinks that a necessary condition of a person becoming 'really' good is that he should fully understand the theoretical grounds for accepting the definition of what the 'really' good is.

However, he can still legitimately make the point against Socrates that the knowledge thus yielded is not a *sufficient* condition of becoming good, and can legitimately treat the Socratic ideal of knowledge through general definition as a theoretical type of knowledge. We saw at the beginning of the first chapter that at *Metaphysics* 1078b he implicitly criticises this Socratic ideal because it assimilates ethics too closely to the demonstrative sciences. As for his point that Socrates neglected the question of 'how and from what sources virtue comes into being', he has in mind two main points which he considers to be of the first importance for any inquiry as to how we are 'to become good'. The first is the recognition that it is a disposition to behave in a certain way which is the genus of virtue and that the 'right' dispositions is acquired by habituation (*E.N.* II 1, 5–6). The other is the need for inquiry on a political scale into the conditions under which the 'right' disposition can most readily be realised, a need which he emphasises in the final chapter of the *Nicomachean Ethics* (x 9).

In criticising in this way the intellectualism of the Socratic thesis that virtue is knowledge, Aristotle attacks the thesis at what we have seen to be its most vulnerable point, i.e. its implicit assumption that an intellectual insight, through definition, into the nature of virtue invariably brings with it a conviction sufficient to determine a person's disposition to behave in a way corresponding to that insight. Theoretical knowledge of that kind, Aristotle says, is never sufficient in itself to ensure goodness of character.

Later in the *Eudemian Ethics* he again criticises Socrates' intellectualism by comparing the Socratic conception of moral knowledge with his own. The passage (1246a27 ff.) is far from clear in its argument.[35] Here is a summary of what appear to me to be its main points.

The first main point is that the virtues cannot be identified with knowledge if that knowledge is of a scientific or technical nature.[36] The argument here is straightforward. It rests on a distinction between two possible uses of a given thing: (i) using it in its proper character and for its natural purpose, and (ii) using it in its proper character but not for its natural purpose. For example, the eye, *qua* eye, is used naturally to see things (i), but, still *qua* eye, it may be used 'to see wrong', e.g. squinting so that one object appears two (ii). Scientific or technical knowledge can be used in both these ways, e.g. the grammarian can use his knowledge either to spell correctly or deliberately to spell incorrectly. The virtues, however, cannot be used in the second way. Goodness cannot be employed to do what is bad, for it is contradictory to speak of goodness being the source of deliberately bad actions. It follows that the virtues cannot be identified with knowledge of a scientific or technical nature, because of this fundamental difference between them.

If we accept the validity of this argument against the identification of virtue with scientific or technical knowledge, we may still be reluctant to accept it as a valid criticism of the Socratic thesis that virtue is knowledge. For, as we saw in our initial discussion of this Socratic thesis in section (B) of this chapter, Socrates was careful to differentiate moral knowledge from the technical knowledge belonging to professional skills, and used the results of his examination of that difference as a basis for his thesis that virtue is knowledge. Moreover, the difference which he notes is essentially the same difference which Aristotle now notes and yet uses to criticise rather than to support or to elucidate Socrates' thesis.

This makes it difficult to assume that Aristotle's implicit criticism of Socrates here is that he *confused* moral knowledge with technical or scientific knowledge. He can hardly be thought to have confused them if he distinguished them in just that respect specified in the argument against him. It might be argued, of course, that, since it is in Plato's early dialogues that we find Socrates making the distinction, we should infer from Aristotle's apparent charge of confusion that in his early dialogues Plato is ascribing to Socrates a distinction which he, and not Socrates, was the first to make. I do not think this argument can be accepted. The *Protagoras*, in arguing against the possibility of the 'misuse' of moral knowledge, clearly assumes the distinctive nature of moral knowledge in the respects noted in earlier dialogues. And just as clearly Aristotle accepts the central argument of the *Protagoras* as a substantially faithful account of Socratic doctrine.

Aristotle is not, then, accusing Socrates of simply confusing the two kinds of knowledge, in the sense of failing to make any distinction between them. I think the most probable explanation of his argument is that he is criticising Socrates, as he did in the earlier passage of the *Eudemian Ethics*, for not making the distinction between theoretical and practical knowledge which he himself makes. His argument then becomes the argument that, because moral knowledge is, for Socrates, theoretical in its content, it must have the characteristic which Aristotle allots in the present passage to any scientific or technical knowledge, i.e. that it can be 'misused'. But to see further in what respects Aristotle thought that Socrates failed to make a proper distinction between the two kinds of knowledge we must consider the second half of his argument.

Here his main point is that the correct conception of moral knowledge is one which distinguishes moral knowledge from scientific knowledge in such a way as to rule out the possibility of its 'misuse'. He contends that Socrates did not make a proper distinction between the two and held a view about the nature of moral knowledge which was incompatible with the claim that virtue is knowledge.

As we saw in our preliminary remarks on the criticisms in the *Eudemian Ethics*, Aristotle's term for moral knowledge is *phronêsis*. In the present argument he says that *phronêsis*, though it is a form of knowledge and truth (1246b5), cannot be diverted from its proper purpose. He assumes this at the outset, contending that it is impossible to use moral knowledge for an improper purpose (i.e. deliberately to act in what one knows to be an 'unwise' or 'imprudent' manner). For the possibility of its misuse depends, he argues, on the possibility of its diversion (*strophê*) by other factors in the personality, whether rational or irrational factors. He then attempts to show that there are no factors capable of doing this.

Here is his argument. He considers first the rational factors. There are no other forms of knowledge, he argues, capable of diverting moral knowledge (*phronêsis*). Moral knowledge is 'supreme'. But he says nothing further here to elucidate or justify this. An earlier passage in the *Eudemian Ethics* (1218b) and a passage at the beginning of the *Nicomachean Ethics* (1094a–b) make clear, however, what he means by the 'supremacy' of moral knowledge. What is interesting about the first of these two passages is that, in asserting the 'supremacy' of *phronêsis*, it associates it with politics. Aristotle explains at *E.N.* VI 8 in what sense *phronêsis* and political wisdom constitute 'the same disposition'. Political wisdom is *phronêsis* exercised in the wider

sphere of politics, in legislating and making political decisions.
And at *E.N.* 1094a–b Aristotle asserts the supremacy of political
wisdom over all other forms of knowledge. It 'uses' the rest of the
sciences, ordaining which of them should be studied and who
should study them, with the supreme aim of realising 'the good
for man' in the state. *In relation to this aim* the other sciences are
subordinate to it.

With the help of these other passages we are able to understand
in what sense and in what sort of implicit context Aristotle is
asserting that *phronêsis* is supreme over other forms of knowledge.
He is not trying to say that *phronêsis* is more 'valuable in itself'
than any other form of knowledge.[37] He is making essentially the
same point which Socrates makes in Plato's *Charmides* (173–4) and
Euthydemus (291–2) when he attributes the comprehensive scope
and authority of moral knowledge to the fact that it is concerned
with the final end to which all human activities are directed. He is
also, of course, implying that in the field of moral behaviour the
only knowledge which has any authority at all and is capable of
'issuing commands' as to what it is right to do is moral knowledge.
This in itself rules out the possibility of *phronêsis* being diverted
from its proper purpose in this field by other forms of knowledge.

There is nothing in this argument which can be construed as a
criticism of Socrates' thesis that virtue is knowledge. Socrates,
as we have just noted, put forward essentially the same argument
himself. What does Aristotle say, then, about the possibility of
irrational factors in the personality diverting *phronêsis*? His argument here is a curious one. He recognises that one doesn't
'misuse' moral knowledge. One fails to put it into practice, to
stand by one's convictions. He recognises also that it is the case of
the weak-willed man which alone might be appealed to as a case
of moral knowledge being diverted from its proper purpose. He
now denies that such a case of diversion of moral knowledge is
possible. He uses a *reductio ad absurdum* argument to refute the
view that the man possessing *phronêsis* can be prompted, under
the influence of 'strong passion', to act contrary to what he knows

to be right. His argument is that, if such a thing could happen, it would be a case of vice in the 'irrational element' of one's personality overcoming a form of excellence in the rational element. But it would then be odd, he says, to maintain that a good disposition or excellence in the 'irrational element' could not prevail over 'folly' in the rational and thus convert foolish judgments to wise judgments. For if a failing can prevail over an excellence, surely an excellence can prevail over a failing?

Yet this consequence, says Aristotle, is absurd. He adds that it can be seen to be absurd by looking at what happens in other fields of knowledge. The illustration which he gives is, however, very unconvincing. He says that in the case of a specialised kind of knowledge such as medical knowledge, profligacy (i.e. vice in the 'irrational element') cannot convert a person's ignorance (i.e., presumably, it cannot convert it to enable bad ends to be furthered knowledgably), even though it can pervert one's knowledge (i.e. prompt the use of one's knowledge to further bad ends). What he wants to emphasise here is, I assume, that non-rational factors or aims are never able to convert ignorance to knowledge.[38]

What is unconvincing about this illustration is that, although it illustrates the point that non-rational factors or aims cannot convert ignorance to knowledge, it is not the right type of illustration to reinforce Aristotle's argument that moral knowledge (*phronêsis*) cannot be diverted from its proper purpose. Indeed, in one important respect it tells against Aristotle's *reductio ad absurdum* argument. For it shows that in some fields of knowledge vice in the 'irrational element' can divert knowledge *without* entailing that a disposition of the 'irrational element' can convert ignorance to knowledge. So far there is nothing in Aristotle's present argument to show what are the distinctive qualities belonging to moral knowledge which exclude the possibility of it being 'diverted'.

Nor is there anything so far which appears to be a criticism of Socrates, just as no criticism could be found in the previous argument about the 'supremacy' of moral knowledge over other forms of knowledge. Socrates denied, as Aristotle does here, that moral knowledge could be 'diverted' from its proper purpose, and so denied, as Aristotle does, that there are cases of weak-willed action by those possessing moral knowledge. But there is a sting in the tail of Aristotle's argument. He concludes his argument by agreeing with Socrates' contention that nothing is stronger than moral knowledge. But he adds that Socrates was wrong to think of moral knowledge as scientific knowledge (*epistêmê*). Moral knowledge (*phronêsis*) is not scientific knowledge. It is 'another kind of cognition'.

The only reason he gives for making this distinction is that *phronêsis* is a form of excellence (*aretê*). And the only clue which he gives to the significance he is attaching to *aretê* is his assertion that men are 'practically wise (*phronimoi*) and good at the same time', an assertion which he says is justified by his preceding argument. We would prefer to say that Aristotle is now telling us that when in the preceding argument he spoke of *phronêsis* as a form of excellence he meant by this that the rational excellence belonging to the practically wise man was always combined with excellence of character, and that it was this combined excellence which was incompatible with doing wrong. That this is what Aristotle means when he characterises *phronêsis* as an excellence is confirmed by what he says at *Nicomachean Ethics* 1142b16 ff. As we noted in our preliminary survey of Aristotle's conception of moral knowledge, this passage asserts that to speak of *phronêsis* as a deliberative excellence is not to say merely that *phronêsis* is always correct in its deliberations as to what is conducive to 'what the agent sets before himself' as the good. The excellence is the morally praiseworthy excellence which reasons correctly with regard to what is 'really' good; and so to have *phronêsis* is to have the excellence of character which yields a right conception of the good. The *Magna Moralia* says the same thing. It first points out, as the *Eudemian Ethics* does, that *phronêsis* is not scientific knowledge; it is a virtue or excellence (1197a16–17). It subsequently explains what is meant by calling it a virtue or excellence. It is not an excellence simply as a disposition to be formally correct in its deliberative capacity. It is an excellence because of its invariable association with excellences of character (1198a23–32).

Thus the sting in the tail of Aristotle's present argument in the *Eudemian Ethics* turns what appeared to be an attempt to substantiate the Socratic thesis that virtue is knowledge into a criticism of it. The form of Aristotle's argument is certainly unconvincing. But its main point – that moral knowledge is a form of excellence which connotes goodness of character – is an important criticism of Socrates' thesis. In the earlier passage of the *Eudemian Ethics* Aristotle had pointed out that Socrates' theoretical conception of moral knowledge falsified his thesis. In the present passage he indicates the quite different conception of moral knowledge which is needed to make the thesis valid. His criticism undoubtedly has some force. Yet there is some exaggeration in it. It is the same exaggeration which is found in the criticism of the *Magna Moralia* (1182a15 ff.) that Socrates, in making the possession of any virtue dependent exclusively on intellectual insight, 'did away with' feeling (*pathos*) and character (*êthos*). Socrates' thesis, as we have seen, has as one of its foundations the universality of the human desire to be happy and hence to do what is believed to be conducive to happiness. It assumes further and more questionably, with its distinction between moral knowledge and belief, that knowing what it is right to do always brings with it a desire to do what is right which is sufficiently strong to exclude acting against knowledge.

Now this is not to 'do away with' feeling and character. It is Socrates' conviction that in the field of moral knowledge the dominance of the intellect is such that knowledge can effect a conversion of character. This conviction of the *moral* efficacy of the intellectual search for 'knowledge and truth' is most clearly marked in Plato's *Apology*. Here Socrates presents his method of cross-examination as a means of 'purification' which will effect a moral improvement. He describes it with a moral fervour which condemns as 'not worth living' a life which has not subjected itself to the intellectual self-searching which will ultimately yield knowledge of the good (38a). This is, substantially, his defence against those who accused him of corrupting the young. He contends that coming to know the good is at the same time a process of becoming good and that his mission of helping others to realise that knowledge is one of moral improvement. As Robinson has said,[39] this aspect of Socrates' 'paradoxical intellectualism' is one which 'hangs together with the proposition that virtue is knowledge'.

Thus it is not entirely fair to criticise Socrates, as Aristotle does in the *Eudemian Ethics*, on the ground that he made knowledge of the good and not goodness itself the end, that he failed to consider 'how and from what sources goodness comes into being', and that his conception of moral knowledge as an exclusively 'theoretical' form of apprehension entailed neglect of the problem of moral character. The reason for this sort of exaggeration in Aristotle's criticisms is that he assesses Socrates' doctrines from the viewpoint of his own distinction between theoretical and practical sciences. He thought that Socrates was wrong in claiming that certainty was possible in ethics. Certainty, he thought, was possible only in the theoretical sciences. In ethics one could establish only what was true 'for the most part', and only what was contingently true. Aristotle's reasons for thinking so are convincing enough. He can point to the variety and fluctuation of opinion about 'fine and just actions', to the impossibility of foreseeing with any certainty the practical consequences of following one set of moral principles rather than another, and hence to the impossibility of knowing with certainty that any particular prescription for happiness is practically valid (*E.N.* 1094b11–28).

For these reasons Aristotle thought that Socrates wrongly assimilated moral knowledge to the kind of knowledge possible only in the theoretical sciences. And since he thought that this kind of knowledge is such as to be pursued always for its own sake and not for any further practical ends, he tends to assume that Socrates' thesis that virtue is knowledge entails a complete disregard of the practical problem of 'how we become good'. This assumption, as we have now seen, is not entirely justified. But the exaggeration involved in it should not blind us to the fundamental criticism which Aristotle is making of the Socratic thesis. He is not simply arguing against Socrates that knowing intellectually, through definition, what is the good is not in fact a sufficient guarantee of being good and doing what is good. He is arguing that this sort of knowing is not what we mean by 'moral knowledge', which is 'a different kind' of knowledge altogether from other forms of knowledge. Moral knowledge is not something which may or may not effect a conversion of character. Part of its meaning is having a disposition to act in a certain way. The element of character and desire is thus already included in the concept of knowing. Hence its 'epitactic' force and practical efficacy.

It is clear that in making this criticism Aristotle shows a deeper insight into the nature of moral knowledge than Socrates had done. Yet he is at the same time much influenced by the intellectualism of Socrates' ethics. It is worth considering briefly what this influence is.

In many ways the most consistent development of Aristotle's views on the practical nature of moral knowledge would have been in the direction of some form of subjectivism. He recognises that each person's conception of 'the end', of what is his good, is determined by his character (*E.N.* 1113a30-4, 1114a-b), and that character is constituted by dispositions which are formed 'by habituation'; dispositions 'arise out of like activities' (*E.N.* 1103b21-2). It would have been consistent with this for Aristotle to argue, on the basis of his own principle that 'to each person the activity in accordance with his own disposition is the most desirable' (*E.N.* 1176b), that the good is what each person conceives to be the good. He would then have presented his conception of the good in terms of contemplative activity in the final book of the *Nicomachean Ethics* as his own temperamental conviction, and would have had no need to defend it on theoretical grounds. Nor would he have needed to hesitate to use the notion of conviction (*pistis*), of which he made such effective use in criticising Socrates' denial of weakness of will, as a sufficient criterion of moral knowledge. Moreover, to have argued on these lines would have constituted the most effective criticism of the intellectualism of Socratic ethics.

But Aristotle does not choose to develop his views along these lines. He shares Socrates' views that what is good is objectively good, and that it is possible to determine intellectually what the good is. He attempts to substantiate his own specification of the good as contemplative activity, on various theoretical grounds, at *E.N.* x vii–viii.[40] This theoretical type of knowledge of the good is what Socrates understands by moral knowledge when he asserts that virtue is knowledge. Aristotle, with his conception of moral knowledge as *phronêsis*, does not share this view. But since he turns his back on subjectivism, and since he considers that moral knowledge implies a correct apprehension of what is 'really' good as well as a good character, he has to provide an objective criterion, quite independent of subjective conviction, to determine what is 'really' good and what is goodness of character.

Thus we find in Aristotle a distinction between (i) the theoretical knowledge that the good is definable in such-and-such a way, and (ii) the moral knowledge that such-and-such a course of practical behaviour is best calculated to further that good. His criticism of Socrates is that he failed to make the distinction, and confused (ii) with (i). Yet Aristotle has only partially emancipated himself from the intellectualism of Socrates' doctrine. For (ii) is obviously partially dependent on (i). And although Aristotle retains the Socratic thesis that 'nothing is stronger than moral knowledge', he can retain it only by *stipulating* that 'moral knowledge' is applicable only to cases where goodness of character (as determined in relation to (i)) is combined with excellence in deliberation (as determined in relation to (ii)).

It follows that his moral psychology (as developed, for example, in the first three books of the *Nicomachean Ethics*) is not enough to show 'how and from what sources' virtue comes into being, a question which he accuses Socrates of neglecting. For Aristotle, this question becomes the question of how to realise the combination of objectively good character and of correct apprehension of the good which constitutes moral knowledge. His answer is that such realisation is possible only through rigorous state control.

This answer is substantially Plato's answer. Like Plato, Aristotle rejects the individualism of Socratic ethics. He rejects at the same time, as we have seen, Socrates' view that intellectual insight into the nature of the good is sufficient to ensure good conduct. Yet, to make his own thesis that virtue is knowledge a practical proposition and not merely a stipulation about the meaning of moral knowledge, he has to turn to schemes of state control as a means of realising the goodness of character which will reflect in its aims what has been established intellectually to be good and will put that good into practice.

Thus he confesses, at the end of the *Nicomachean Ethics*, that the force of law is necessary to bring about the habituation which will form the right dispositions and hence the right character (*êthos*) to ensure that a person does what has been established to be good. Most people, he says, obey necessity rather than argument, and punishment rather than the sense of what is noble; for emotion (*pathos*) is curbed by force rather than by persuasion (1179b–1180b). This, in the final resort, is Aristotle's almost brutal answer to the problem of 'how virtue comes into being'. It is significant that his emphasis is on the need to control character and emotion, precisely the two factors which in the *Magna Moralia* Socrates is accused of completely leaving out of account.

Plato too hoped to find in 'the force of law' a means of making the Socratic thesis practically true. Plato never abandoned the ideal formulated in the thesis. But he makes clear, especially in the *Laws*, his view that, without the political forces of 'law and order', it can never be realised. He still proclaims (*Laws* 731c) that no one, knowing what is right, would willingly do wrong. Yet he acknowledges that in practice the individual may know the right and do the wrong. This is clear from the preface to the penal code in Book IX of the *Laws* (861e–864c). Plato there distinguishes offences committed from bad motives, by those with bad character and disposition, from offences committed simply in ignorance of what is right. Only the former are classified as acts of wrongdoing and as punishable. And they include not only impulsive but deliberate acts of wrongdoing, contrary to what is known (for they are not committed in ignorance) to be right. Indeed, Plato states explicitly that in practice knowledge of what is right does not entail either the ability or the willingness to do what is right (875a–b). He made the same point earlier (689a–e), where he said that what one conceives to be good is not necessarily what one desires to do; for a person may 'hate' the good and deliberately embrace the bad.

In these passages the insight shown by Plato into the distinction between the intellectual and the emotional conditions of right action combines with a keen awareness of the weaknesses of human nature to make him doubt the practical validity of the Socratic thesis that virtue is knowledge. His remarks imply much the same sort of criticism of Socrates which Aristotle was later to make explicit. It is only a divinely gifted person, Plato says (*Laws* 875c–d), who will have the really free and genuine knowledge which has complete mastery over his actions. And for lack of such a person, it is necessary to adopt the 'second best course' of using the 'law and order' of the state to effect that harmony of intellect and character which is a condition of realising the Socratic ideal.

Thus both Plato and Aristotle reject the combination of individualism and intellectualism in the Socratic theses that no one does wrong willingly and that virtue is knowledge. Aristotle's criticisms have a special value. This lies not only in their historical value as explicit appraisals of Socratic doctrine but also in the subtle and refined moral psychology which illuminates aspects of moral experience left out of account by Socrates' intellectualism. Aristotle shows that Socrates had expected from his method of analysis more than it could possibly yield. He had expected it to yield, through its definitions, intellectual certainty in ethics and at the same time an unswerving moral conviction. It cannot, Aristotle argues, yield either. But it did yield a valuable analysis and elucidation of the Greeks' moral language. This was the foundation of all subsequent Greek speculation in ethics.

G. THE UNITY OF THE VIRTUES

One other Socratic thesis remains to be discussed. It is the thesis that 'all the virtues are one'. Aristotle does not explicitly ascribe this thesis to Socrates. But he does so implicitly when he ascribes to Socrates the view that each of the virtues is to be identified with knowledge. For this view is the basis of Socrates' view that 'all the virtues are one'. This is made clear by Plato's *Protagoras*, a dialogue which Aristotle takes as the main basis for his presentation of Socrates' moral views. The thesis is ascribed to Socrates by Xenophon (*Mem.* III ix). It is, moreover, closely associated, as we shall see, with the thesis that virtue is knowledge.

Like the thesis that no one does wrong willingly, the thesis that all the virtues are one has its foundation in the utilitarianism of the Greeks' moral language. As we have seen, the Greeks specified the end of human action as 'happiness' (*eudaimonia*). This was 'the good'. Actions were describable as good in so far as they were conducive to that end. A natural development of this in Greek moral philosophy, beginning with Socrates, is the idea that, since 'happiness' or 'the good' is a single end of human action, then any specification of it must maintain the unity of all morally good behaviour by specifying a single kind of activity or a single state of character as constituting happiness. Human action is then morally commendable only in so far as it is conducive to that one specified end.

On this basis the various particular virtues earn their status as virtues in so far as each of them, in situations appropriate to it, is

L

exercised as good behaviour conducive to a single end. Hence the particular virtues tend to be treated as means to the end rather than as constitutive elements of the end. They are therefore different in status from 'virtue as a whole' (to use Aristotle's phrase at *E.N.* 1129b).

There were good reasons for this sort of distinction. It satisfied the Greek inclination to specify happiness in terms of a single activity or state of character. For it kept out of that specification the variety and multiplicity of the recognised particular virtues. At the same time it served to determine the proper application of such recognised virtues as courage, temperance, and justice by supplying a criterion for their application in the form of a specification of the common end to which their exercise should be directed.

This sort of scheme is readily illustrated by the moral schemes of the Athenian philosophical schools, whether in terms of the intellectualist end of the Platonic and Aristotelian schools, the Epicurean end of tranquillity or 'undisturbedness', or the Stoic end of dispassionateness. We will illustrate it briefly in terms of Aristotle's scheme.

Aristotle specifies happiness or human goodness as contemplative activity or 'activity in accordance with philosophic wisdom (*sophia*)'. On this specification the truly good man is the intellectual, the man who finds his happiness in the exercise of his intellect in the theoretical sciences. Pride of place is thus given by Aristotle to *sophia*, which he takes to be the 'most perfect' of all virtues. The other particular virtues play a subordinate role as means to the end of contemplative activity. And in virtue of their relation to that end their proper application is more precisely determinable. It lies in promoting the fullest possible exercise of philosophic wisdom. Thus a man displays 'true' courage if he always exercises that quality of character so as to promote the right end. A man is 'truly' just if he determines the fairness of his dealings with his fellows by reference to the criterion supplied by that end. And a man displays 'true' moderation if he determines what is 'too much' or 'too little' in gratifying his appetites by reference again to that end.

In a scheme of this kind it is easy to see in what sense the particular virtues may be said to be unified. In the first place they have the common characteristic of having the same relation, as means, to the same single end. In the second place, knowing what is the proper exercise of the virtues – the proper time, manner, and object of their exercise in particular situations – is in each case dependent on knowing what is the final end of human action. We have already noted that Socrates assumes, as Plato and Aristotle do, that the definition of this end is a descriptive specification of what goodness is. In view of this Socratic assumption, and in view of the relation assumed between the particular virtues and a single common end, we can see that the *full* specification of a particular virtue would include a specification of the end to which the virtue is properly directed. *To this extent* the definition of a particular virtue is at the same time the definition of any particular virtue. This, at any rate, seems to have been the direction of Socrates' thought in formulating the doctrine of the unity of the virtues.

The doctrine goes further, however, than the position we have outlined so far towards making the virtues equivalent to each other. The thesis that virtue is knowledge prompts this further step. For this thesis assumes that the dominant influence of the intellect is sufficient to convert the whole character to a pattern which excludes acting against knowledge. From this point of view Socrates feels able to dismiss as unessential to the definition of such particular virtues as courage or moderation any specification of the emotional characteristics which distinguish one virtue from the other. This leads him to declare the equivalence of the virtues. For he considers that this equivalence follows from the proposition that knowing what is the end to which the virtues should be directed in their exercise is not only a necessary but a sufficient condition of acting in a truly courageous or moderate or just or pious manner in the appropriate circumstances. This is the proposition that knowledge of the good is a sufficient condition of possessing each and all of the virtues. Socrates concludes from this that knowledge of the good is sufficient as a *definition* of each and all of the virtues. Thus all the virtues are one, for they are equivalent by definition.

Socrates' most determined attempt to demonstrate the equivalence of the virtues is found in Plato's *Protagoras*. In this dialogue Protagoras and Socrates are discussing whether virtue can be taught. Protagoras contends that it *can* be taught. Secondly, he contends that the particular virtues – justice, moderation, piety, courage, and wisdom – are essentially different as forms of virtue, and that the possession of one does not involve the possession of the others; many a man, he asserts, is courageous without being just, or just without being wise (329b–330b, 349b–c). Socrates thinks that the first contention is incompatible with the second, and that the incompatibility should be resolved by giving up the second in favour of the first. But only at the end of the dialogue, where a summary is given of the aims and conclusions of his argument, does he indicate to Protagoras the nature of this incompatibility.

This summary (361a–c) brings together the following three arguments: (*a*) that virtue can be taught only if virtue is knowledge; (*b*) that virtue is knowledge (it was argued at 351b–358d, as we saw, that to know what is good is a necessary and sufficient condition of doing what is good); (*c*) that each of the particular virtues is knowledge. The incompatibility between Protagoras' two contentions is that his second contention allows a divorce between knowledge, as one of the virtues, and the other virtues. Thus Protagoras would assert that a man may be courageous and yet ignorant. It would then follow from (*a*) that courage cannot be taught. And this is incompatible with his contention that virtue *can* be taught.

The summary indicates further that Socrates treats (*c*) as equivalent to (*b*). For the attempt to prove that each of the particular virtues is knowledge is treated as equivalent to the attempt to prove that virtue as a whole is knowledge (361b).

This must not be taken to imply that each of the particular virtues is a different constituent part of virtue as a whole, and that knowledge of all the particular virtues *adds up to* a complete knowledge of virtue as a whole. For Socrates has devoted a large part of his earlier argument to a criticism of just that view. He has criticised it by attempting to show the equivalence of each of the particular virtues. Thus, in now summarising his aim as an attempt to show that each of the particular virtues is knowledge, he is indicating his view that knowledge of any one particular virtue is equivalent to knowledge of any other. And in treating the thesis that virtue is knowledge as equivalent to the thesis that each of the particular virtues is knowledge he is combining his view that to do what is good it is sufficient to know what is good with his view that to know any particular virtue it is sufficient to know what is good.

Socrates' initial attempts (330c ff. and 349d–351b) to show the equivalence of the virtues are, however, unconvincing. The logic of his arguments is dubious. Nor is there any consistent pattern in the arguments either to suggest that they are designed to substantiate a general conclusion that each of the virtues is knowledge or to point to knowledge of the good as a general unifying principle.

Here is one of his arguments. It is not untypical of the others. Socrates wishes to show that 'wisdom and moderation (*sôphrosunê*) are the same'. He first gets Protagoras to agree that wisdom and folly are opposites. He then argues that moderation and folly are opposites. The steps in his argument are: (i) acting rightly implies acting with moderation; (ii) acting wrongly implies acting foolishly; (iii) acting foolishly implies acting without moderation. He concludes that acting foolishly is the opposite of acting with moderation. Finally, appealing to the principle that everything which has an opposite has only one opposite, he asserts that this principle is incompatible with Protagoras' view that wisdom and moderation are different parts of virtue. For, if the principle is true, then wisdom and moderation, which have the same opposite, must be identical.

It is tempting to say that here Socrates is deliberately taking advantage of the ambiguity of the Greek *aphrosunê* (folly) to force the conclusion he desires. But there is really no good ground for saying this. For why should we assume that fallacies which are obvious to us must have been obvious to Socrates? It is more plausible to assume that Socrates is here indulging his undoubted fondness for exploring logical relations between propositions without taking sufficient care either about relevant distinctions in the meaning of the terms involved or about relevant facts of moral experience. It is passages like these which prompt agreement with the judgment that Socrates 'was too fascinated by the patterns into which he could organise his propositions to reflect with the needed sensitiveness and humility on matters which can only be learned from the facts themselves or from those whose vision of the facts is more subtle and penetrating than one's own'.[41]

These passages cannot, however, fairly be taken as representative of Socrates' method or of the spirit of his moral doctrine. It is true that his arguments for the equivalence of other virtues (justice and piety at 330c–332a, moderation and justice at 333b–334c, and courage and wisdom at 349d–351d) are no less dubious in their logic and no less unconvincing than the argument just described. Moreover, they still lack any general principle of unification (though they do show that Socrates treats the principle of the unity of the virtues as the principle of the identity of the virtues). But there are indications, as we shall see, that these initial arguments for the equivalence of the virtues are merely preliminary skirmishes, designed to weaken Protagoras' resistance to the idea of the equivalence of the virtues rather than to offer a positive and serious interpretation. The basis for such an interpretation is provided with the introduction (at 351b) of the thesis that knowledge of what is good is a necessary and sufficient condition of doing what is good. This general thesis is immediately applied to the analysis of courage (358d ff.). And the summary at 361a–c implies that its application to the other particular virtues enables an analysis to be given in each case in terms of knowledge of the good. It thus enables a demonstration of the equivalence of the virtues to be given which the evidence of other early dialogues indicates to be more properly representative of Socrates' views.

Before looking at the analysis of courage in the *Protagoras*, it will be useful to look at the analysis given in another early dialogue, the *Laches*. Much of the discussion in the *Laches* is devoted to an attempt to define courage. The initial attempt (192b ff.) has many points of similarity with the initial attempt made in the *Protagoras* (349d–351d) to identify courage with wisdom.[42] Laches suggests that courage is a sort of endurance. But he agrees that endurance without wisdom is not sufficient to constitute courage, since folly is incompatible with the 'nobility' of courage. In the *Protagoras* it is agreed, for just the same reason, that confidence without wisdom is not sufficient to constitute courage.

The problem raised by this sort of qualification is the problem of what kind of knowledge constitutes 'wisdom' (*phronêsis* or *sophia*). The *Laches* firmly rejects the idea that wisdom is to be understood in terms of particular professional skills or in terms of a prudential calculus of risks involved. For the effect of such 'wisdom' is to lessen the dangers of particular tasks and correspondingly to lessen the degree of courage needed to face them. A further consequence is that the highest degree of courage is demanded of those without this wisdom. And this is incompatible with the earlier agreement that lack of wisdom is incompatible with the 'nobility' of courage.

The corresponding passage in the *Protagoras* does not, however, reject the idea that wisdom is to be understood in terms of professional skills. It makes use of just this idea to support the contention that confidence without wisdom does not constitute courage. It then extends the argument, by very dubious logic, to yield the conclusion that wisdom and courage are identical (350c). Yet later, on the basis of the thesis that virtue is knowledge, it offers an analysis in terms of knowledge of the good which is an implicit rejection of the earlier identification of courage with the 'wisdom' belonging to professional skills such as diving and horse-riding. The *Laches* offers essentially the same analysis, after explicitly rejecting an association of courage with the wisdom of professional skills. This indicates clearly enough that Socrates' initial attempts in the *Protagoras* to show the equivalence of particular virtues are not intended to represent his serious doctrine. They are merely preliminary skirmishes.

Let us now look at the *Laches* again, to see what final analysis of courage it offers. If the wisdom essential to courage is not the wisdom of particular professional skills, what sort of wisdom is it (194e)? It is suggested that its sphere of application can be indicated by specifying it as a 'knowledge of what is to be feared and what is not' (195a). But what is a proper object of fear? Knowledge of this, Socrates says, does not fall within the province of professional skills. It is true that these skills provide knowledge of the particular dangers which lie within their province. But it is only judgments of value lying outside their province which can decide what is a proper object of fear and what is not. Thus the physician knows the nature of health and disease. But his medical knowledge cannot tell him whether it is health rather than disease, or life rather than death, which is 'better' or 'worse' for a patient, less or more to be feared (195b–d).

Examples of this kind enable Socrates to show that judgments as to what is a proper object of fear are judgments of value which depend for their correctness on a knowledge of what is good and bad. What is properly an object of fear, he argues, is some impending evil. It is therefore impossible, without knowledge of what is good and bad, to know what is a proper object of fear. It follows that, if we are to define courage in terms of knowledge, then courage is definable as knowledge of what is good and bad. Yet, if this is so, is it possible to distinguish courage from virtue as a whole? For to possess knowledge of the good and the bad is not compatible with lack of any virtue. Courage, it would seem, is equivalent at once to virtue as a whole and to any virtue. A man is at once courageous, temperate, pious, and just (199d–e).

We may now compare with this analysis in the *Laches* the analysis given in the *Protagoras* (358d ff.). Socrates has just shown that no one voluntarily pursues what he knows or believes to be bad. This conclusion is now applied to the analysis of courage. If we agree that fear is definable as expectation of what is bad, it follows from the previous conclusion that no one will voluntarily pursue what he fears. In what way, then, is the brave man to be distinguished from the coward? The brave man and the coward are alike in that each is ready to do what he is confident about doing. But the brave man is ready to do what the coward is not. The thesis that no one does wrong willingly prevents us, however, from saying that, while the brave man does what he knows to be good, the coward refuses to do what he knows to be good. It must be the case that the coward refuses to do what he thinks to be bad, though in fact it is good, and is ready to do what he thinks to be good, though in fact it is bad (359c–e).

Socrates now has the distinction he needs. The confidence and fear of the coward, he says, are directed to the wrong objects and are 'base' because the coward is ignorant of what is good and bad. The confidence and fear of the brave man are directed to the right objects and are 'noble' because the brave man has knowledge of what is good and bad. Thus cowardice rests on ignorance, courage on knowledge (where knowledge is knowledge of 'what is and is not fearful' and hence of what is bad and good). Hence, concludes Socrates, equating 'that on account of which people are cowards' with cowardice (360c), cowardice is ignorance and courage is knowledge.

There is much that is commendable in this analysis of courage in the *Laches* and the *Protagoras*. For it does much to refine the popular conception of courage.[43] Socrates emphasises the moral value and significance of courage. Courage, he shows, is always directed to a noble or good end, and belongs only to those who understand the moral end to which it is properly directed. These marks of courage serve to distinguish it from mere confidence, boldness, or intrepidity. Aristotle notes them in his own analysis of courage (*E.N.* 1115a ff.). His indebtedness to Socrates in this respect is clear.

Yet in other respects the intellectualism of Socrates' analysis leaves out of account what are generally recognised to be distinctive characteristics of courage. In the *Laches* the concept of 'endurance' quietly and surprisingly drops out of the proposed definition of courage, even though the criticism of the definition is concerned with the proper interpretation of 'wise', as opposed to 'foolish', endurance, and is not a criticism of the inclusion of endurance itself in the definition. Nor does the subsequent argument make any attempt to distinguish, in respect of knowledge of the good, between that which is a necessary condition of having courage and that which is sufficient to define it. The analysis of the *Protagoras* does have a distinction between (i) 'that on account of which there is cowardice', and (ii) cowardice itself. But (i), identified as ignorance, is assumed to be a sufficient as well as a necessary condition of cowardly behaviour, and is then immediately treated as equivalent to (ii) (360b6–c7). This type of reasoning is found again in the *Meno* (88a–89a). The argument here is that only under the guidance of knowledge are the various dispositions of a man's personality 'beneficial', i.e. conducive in their exercise to his happiness, and hence properly classifiable as virtues. For example, confidence without knowledge is not beneficial, and cannot be identified with the virtue of courage. But to say this is treated as equivalent to saying that courage is knowledge.

One result of Socrates' intellectualistic interpretation of courage is that, while adding a valuable refinement to the popular conception of it, it offers a definition which in effect directly contradicts that conception. The popular conception of courage is that the brave man faces what is fearful, but the coward only what is not (*Prot.* 359c). Against this Socrates argues that no one faces what he knows or believes to be fearful. Both the brave man and the coward are in this respect on precisely the same footing. Each is confident (and hence fearless) in pursuing his ends. The only difference is that the coward is mistaken in his conception of what is the right end, but the brave man is not. This is not to deny that the brave man or the coward is ever afraid. The brave man fears and avoids what he knows to be bad; the coward fears and avoids what he believes to be bad. But it is no essential part of the brave man's courage or the coward's cowardice that it is accompanied by fear or that it is displayed in the face of what is fearful.

This aspect of Socrates' analysis emphasises its lack of any temperamental distinction between courage and cowardice. There is no distinction between the brave man who masters his fears and resolutely faces any danger or difficulty in pursuing what he believes to be right, and the coward who is weak-kneed and averse to facing danger or difficulty in pursuing what he believes to be right. It would seem that the weak-kneed man, as well as the weak-willed man, is ruled out by Socrates' analysis. In this respect Aristotle (*E.N.* 1115a ff.) offers a more satisfactory analysis. It is true that in many respects Aristotle's analysis reflects that of Socrates. Thus he emphasises that courage is essentially directed to the promotion of a 'noble' end and that it demands for its proper exercise an ability to apply the 'right rule' to particular situations. It is these marks which enable Aristotle, as they enabled Socrates, to distinguish courage from mere confidence or boldness. But Aristotle goes beyond Socrates in that he distinguishes the brave man from the coward temperamentally. Moreover he rightly concludes that the brave man displays his courage in the face of what is formidable, not in the face of what is not formidable. This is the opposite of Socrates' conclusion in the *Protagoras*.

Thus it is by leaving out of account, and hence out of their definition, what are generally recognised to be distinctive characteristics of the particular virtues, that Socrates is able to demonstrate finally that 'all the virtues are one'. The virtues have different names, but the names are, in Socrates' view, names of one and the same thing (*Prot.* 329d, 349b). For the analysis of courage in terms of knowledge of the good is an analysis applicable, with the same results, to the other virtues. The *Protagoras* assumes, in its conclusion (361b), that this is so. It is only in the *Laches* and the *Protagoras* that we find detailed analysis of that kind applied to particular virtues. But in the *Charmides* (173d–174b; cf. Xenophon *Mem.* III ix 4) Socrates indicates clearly enough the possibility of analysing moderation (*sôphrosunê*) in that way. And within the argument of *Meno* 87d–89a, a typically Socratic argument, it is assumed that particular virtues such as moderation and justice can be defined, in just the same way as courage, in terms of knowledge. The result is, as the *Laches* (199d–e) expresses it in the case of courage, that what might appear to be a distinct part of virtue can be shown in each case to be equivalent at once to virtue as a whole and to any of what appear to be distinct and other virtues. A man is at once courageous, temperate, pious and just.

This doctrine of the unity of the virtues shows Socrates' intellectualism in ethics in its most extreme form. It is the culmination of his attempt to show that the intellect has supremacy over all else in determining moral behaviour. The first fruits of his ethical analysis are found in the thesis that no one does wrong willingly. This thesis is valuable principally as a contribution to the analysis of the Greeks' moral language. As such, it is not necessarily tied to the kind of intellectualism which characterises much of Socratic ethics. More particularly, it does not depend for its validity on the kind of distinction between moral knowledge and belief which Socrates chooses to make. It is by making his ideal of knowledge through definition the basis of his distinction between knowledge and belief that Socrates contrives to build into the thesis an objectivism and intellectualism which robs it of the obvious plausibility which belongs to it as a subjectivist thesis.

With this ideal of moral knowledge as an essential part of the thesis, Socrates is, of course, now presenting his further thesis that virtue is knowledge in a severely intellectual form. For the thesis that no one does wrong willingly now includes the assertion that knowing in this way what is good is a sufficient condition of being good and doing what is good. And the thesis that virtue is knowledge yields, in turn, the thesis that all the virtues are one. Socrates shows that knowledge of the good is a necessary condition of the possession of any of the particular virtues. His thesis that virtue is knowledge allows him to say further that knowledge of the good is a sufficient as well as a necessary condition of the possession of any of the particular virtues. He concludes that each virtue is definable as knowledge of the good. Hence no virtue is distinguishable from any other. All the virtues are one.

It is especially this doctrine of the unity of the virtues which gives force to the criticism that Socrates 'did away with' character and feeling. Yet it would be an exaggeration to say that in putting forward this doctrine Socrates was indifferent to the factors of moral character and feeling. There is, clearly, an air of deliberate paradox-making about the doctrine. Socrates' primary concern is to show that, for the purpose of achieving goodness or happiness, knowledge of the good is sufficient, and hence that for this purpose there is no need to assume any distinction between particular virtues or to make an understanding of distinctions between them a condition of achieving happiness. His formal conclusion is that each virtue is definable as knowledge of the good, and hence indistinguishable from so-called 'other' virtues. This is what gives the doctrine its paradoxical air. But Socrates would not maintain that 'knowledge of the good' is completely definitive of any particular virtue, any more than he would maintain that 'knowledge' is definitive of the good in his thesis that virtue is knowledge. He is maintaining that knowledge of the good is sufficient for being good, and hence for doing what is good, in all the various circumstances which call for the display of the various particular virtues.

It is worth noting, in conclusion, that Aristotle is at one with Socrates in thinking that to have moral knowledge is at the same time to have all the virtues (*E.N.* 1144b30–1145a2).[44] Aristotle's conception of moral knowledge is very different, of course, from Socrates'. Moral knowledge is, for Socrates, a necessary and sufficient condition of goodness of character. For Aristotle, goodness of character is a necessary, if not a sufficient, condition of moral knowledge. Moral knowledge belongs only to those who have the excellence of character which embraces all the 'moral virtues'. For unless a person's assent to the view that the life of contemplation is the truly good life is completely matched by a character which gives genuine conviction of the goodness of that life, then he cannot be sure that he will invariably do what is conducive to that good. In that case, Aristotle thinks, he cannot be said to have moral knowledge.

Thus Aristotle, while accepting the Socratic doctrine of the unity of the virtues and the Socratic thesis that virtue is knowledge, modifies them in accordance with his own view of moral knowledge. His main disagreement, as we have seen, is with Socrates' assumption that intellectual insight, through definition, into the good is invariably accompanied by a desire to do what is good sufficiently strong to rule out the possibility of acting against knowledge. To assume this, Aristotle thinks, is to put the cart before the horse. Yet Aristotle is still left with the problem of 'how virtue comes into being'. Socrates had relied on the force of the individual intellect to yield goodness. Aristotle, and Plato too, relied on the educational forces of the state, backed by 'the force of law'. Neither of them had Socrates' uncompromising faith in the supreme efficacy of reason in guiding moral behaviour.

3

The Good

A. INTRODUCTION

WE saw in the last chapter that part of Socrates' purpose in presenting his moral paradoxes was to elucidate the Greeks' moral language. We also saw that his further purpose was to emphasise the supreme importance of knowledge of the good, especially in respect of its supreme efficacy in ensuring right moral conduct. What we now have to consider is his conception of the good, of the *summum bonum*.

Socrates' method of analysis assumes that it is possible to determine with certainty what the good is. His moral paradoxes, with their intellectualist conception of moral knowledge, make the same assumption. But the analysis which yields the moral paradoxes does not yield a specification of the good. For the moral paradoxes themselves are in this respect non-informative. They tell us that knowledge of the good is a necessary and sufficient condition of being good and of doing what is good. They do not tell us what the good is.

There are two places in Xenophon's *Memorabilia* where Socrates talks about the *meaning* of good. In a conversation with Aristippus (III viii) he emphasises its instrumental sense of 'good for a particular purpose'. In this sense, he argues, it can be equated with 'fine' or 'beautiful' (*kalon*); 'things which men use are considered to be fine and good in relation to that for which they are serviceable'. Similarly, in a conversation with Euthydemus (IV vi 8), he defines 'good' in terms of 'beneficial' (*ōphelimon*).

The emphasis again is on the sense of 'good for a particular purpose'. What is beneficial to one person, he says, may be harmful to another. But a thing cannot be called good which is not beneficial to someone in relation to a certain purpose. So 'what is beneficial is good for him to whom it is beneficial'.

This emphasis on the instrumental sense of 'good' is in keeping with those features of the Greeks' moral language, noted at the beginning of the last chapter, which give to all Greek moral thought its broadly utilitarian character. It illustrates how readily the Greeks used 'good' synonymously with 'useful' or 'beneficial'. And, remembering that in moral behaviour doing what is 'useful' or 'beneficial' means for a Greek doing what is conducive to happiness (*eudaimonia*), we can see that what Socrates says in Xenophon about the meaning of good is a basic part of what he is saying when he asserts that no one does wrong willingly. This becomes clear when we look at Xenophon's formulation of that paradox. At *Memorabilia* (III ix 4) Socrates says that everyone chooses from possible courses of action what he considers to be 'most profitable' (*sumphorōtata*) for him, and does this. And in Plato's *Protagoras*, in presenting the same thesis (358b–d), he links together 'fine' (*kalon*), 'good' (*agathon*) and 'beneficial' (*ōphelimon*) (358b; cf. 333d), just as he does in Xenophon in commenting on the meaning of good.

Now Socrates is not propounding a moral doctrine about what the good is when he talks about the instrumental sense of good, any more than he is propounding such a doctrine when he asserts that no one does wrong willingly. For to propound such a doctrine would be to give a descriptive specification of 'the good', considered as the end of human action, and distinguishable in this substantival use from its instrumental use as 'beneficial', 'profitable', or 'useful' (Plato, *Hippias Major* 296e–297d, 303e). Socrates' remarks are about this instrumental use, and are not concerned to specify a moral ideal.

It follows that those scholars have been mistaken who have tried to construct a moral ideal out of these remarks or out of the paradox that no one does wrong willingly. For there is nothing here which implies that Socrates was a relativist or subjectivist in his moral theory, or that he equated 'the good' with the useful or the advantageous.[1] Henry Jackson argued[2] that Socrates' answer to the question 'what is the good?' was that 'it is the useful, the advantageous. Utility, the immediate utility of the individual, thus becomes the measure of conduct and the foundation of all moral rule and legal enactment. Accordingly, each precept of which Socrates delivers himself is recommended on the ground that obedience to it will promote the pleasure, the comfort, the advancement, the well-being of the individual; and Prodicus's apologue of the Choice of Heracles, with its commonplace offers of worldly reward, is accepted as an adequate statement of the motives of virtuous action.'

The reference to Prodicus's Choice of Heracles is a reference to what Socrates is represented as narrating from Prodicus, with apparent approval of its sentiments, in conversation with Aristippus in Xenophon's *Memorabilia* (II i). The piece is in fact a recommendation of a life conscientiously devoted to the attainment of what is 'fine and good', and a condemnation of a life of maximum case and pleasure. Neither here nor anywhere else in Xenophon's portrait is there evidence for thinking that Socrates was a hedonist. We examined that point in the last chapter. He does indeed assume, in several of the conversations in Xenophon, that the good life is the most pleasant life. But this, as we saw, is an assumption readily made by the Greeks in view of the natural 'eudaimonism' of their moral outlook. Both Plato and Aristotle assume it. It does not make them hedonists.

As for the other marks which Jackson ascribed to Socrates' conception of 'the good', such marks as the 'utility', the 'advancement', the 'well-being' of the individual, these are marks of the utilitarianism of the Greeks' moral language, not peculiar marks of Socrates' conception of 'the good'. The references to 'immediate' utility and 'the commonplace offers of worldly reward' are just misguided exaggerations, prompted to some extent, perhaps, by Xenophon's own severely practical outlook. So let us not look in this direction for Socrates' answer to 'what is the good?'. And let us not criticise him, as Jackson did, from this standpoint, as having 'no conception of the graver difficulties of ethical theory' or as a person to whom morality has so become 'a second nature' that 'the scrutiny of its credentials from an external standpoint has ceased to be possible'.[3]

What answer, then, did Socrates give to 'what is the good?'. The good is for him, as for any Greek, 'happiness' (*eudaimonia*). And we saw, in discussing his paradox that all the virtues are one, that a basis for this paradox is the notion that 'the good' or 'happiness' is a single unifying end of human action. It follows that any specification of it must maintain the unity of all morally good behaviour by specifying a single kind of activity or a single state of character as constituting happiness. Such a specification would be a descriptive specification of 'the good', the same in kind as, e.g., Aristotle's specification of happiness or human goodness as 'activity of the soul in accordance with philosophic wisdom (*sophia*)'. So our concern in the present chapter is to consider what particular specification of this kind was given by Socrates in answering the question 'what is the good?'.

An immediate difficulty is that in this respect Aristotle has virtually nothing to tell us. Nor is there in Plato's early dialogues, or in Xenophon's *Memorabilia*, any full and systematic discussion of the question we are considering. We do find in these sources, however, some portrayal of Socrates' views in politics, in theology, and in what it is not too pretentious to call philosophy of mind. We must see therefore whether, within these various views, it is possible to discern a consistent conception of the good.

B. POLITICAL VIEWS

Socrates was not a practising politician. But in both Xenophon and Plato he expresses political views. He makes constitutional criticisms. He states his position with regard to matters of political concern such as 'conscientious objection', and a citizen's obligation to adhere to the laws. Finally, he indicates what he considers to be the relevance and value to the well-being of the state of his own activity as an educator of his fellow-citizens. These views are some guide to his political principles. And these principles, in so far as they reflect his moral ideals, are some guide to his conception of the good.

According to Xenophon (*Mem.* I ii 9) those who accused Socrates of corrupting the young men of Athens based their charge partly on the argument that he caused those who conversed with him to despise the established laws. Socrates is said to have maintained that it was foolish to elect the magistrates of a state by beans (i.e. by ballot), since no one would be willing to employ a pilot elected in that way, or an architect or a flute-player, or a person in any other such profession, where in fact errors caused far less harm than errors in the administration of a state. There are good grounds for thinking that this is a genuinely Socratic argument. Aristotle mentions it (*Rhetoric* 1393b), as we noted in the first chapter, as an illustration of a typically Socratic argument.

The implication of the argument is, of course, that expert knowledge is a necessary qualification for the statesman. One of Socrates' favourite analogies, the analogy between moral behaviour and the practice of professional skills, is here extended to political practice. The appeal to expert knowledge is made explicit in another part of the *Memorabilia* (III ix 10-11) where Socrates, arguing again from the practice of professional skills, asserts that true kings and commanders are 'not those who hold sceptres, not those chosen by the common crowd or elected by lot, not those who rely on violence or deceit, but those who know how to rule.'

Similarly (*Mem.* IV ii 6-7), he advocates the need for expert instruction in the art of government, an art which he subsequently characterises as the greatest art, 'the kingly art' (IV ii 11). And it is natural to associate with what Socrates says here his remarks on 'the kingly art' in Plato's *Euthydemus*. He describes this art (at 291b–292e) as a master-art which uses the results of the practice of all other arts or professional skills in the state in order to promote happiness. In developing this point Plato is possibly going beyond what Socrates himself had argued. But Xenophon's remarks are some confirmation that the notion is basically Socratic. There is no explicit specification here of what 'the good' is which the expert statesman is assumed to know and to be able to realise in the state. The *Euthydemus* (292a–e) admits this. But some definite standard of values for political practice is implicit in what Socrates says. In looking at the rest of his political views we must try to discover what these values are.

At the outset we should beware of construing Socrates' political views in terms of Plato's ideals in the *Republic*. It is easy enough to look at the thought of the *Republic* as a direct and consistent development of the political ideas which we find ascribed to Socrates by Xenophon. But closer examination will show that Socrates' notions of political reform and of the relations between the state and the individual are far different from Plato's. Professor Popper has remarked that 'the Platonic "Socrates" of the *Republic* is the embodiment of an unmitigated authoritarianism'.[4] He rightly dissociates Socrates from the Platonic Socrates in this respect. Socrates' apparent advocacy of government by experts is not intended to be the advocacy of an alternative form of government to democracy. Nor is it the advocacy of 'an unmitigated authoritarianism'.

Let us look first at Socrates' notion of political reform. The striking thing here is that, critical though Socrates is of methods of electing magistrates in a democracy, he emphatically asserts his loyalty to the laws of the state. 'He obeyed the magistrates', says Xenophon (*Mem.* IV iv 1), 'in all that the laws enjoined.' Xenophon represents him further as defining justice in terms of obedience to the laws (IV iv 18). As an example of Socrates' practice in this respect he mentions his behaviour in the public assembly when he stood alone in opposing a proposal which was

contrary to recognised law. The occasion was the trial of the
generals after the battle of Arginusae in 406 B.C. The generals
were tried and sentenced to death in a body, though the recognised
law was that they should have been tried separately (I i 18; IV iv 2;
see also Plato *Apol.* 32b–c). This was under a democratic government.

Socrates' passionate respect for the law is further shown in his
opposition to the government of the Thirty Tyrants when they
tried to implicate him in their crimes. Xenophon says that 'when
the Thirty ordered him to do anything contrary to the laws, he
refused to obey them. For both when they forbade him to
converse with the young, and when they ordered him, and some
others of the citizens, to lead a certain person away to death, he
stood alone in refusing to obey them, because the order was given
contrary to the laws' (IV iv 3; Plato *Apol.* 32c–d).

In both these cases Socrates showed considerable personal
courage and a high devotion to principle. But it was in his
refusal to escape from prison when awaiting execution that he
declared most strikingly his conviction that the laws must be
obeyed.

Plato's *Crito* is devoted to explaining this refusal to escape.
Socrates there defends his loyalty to the laws of the state by
arguing that the foundation of law is an agreement or contract
between the state and the individual, and that willingness on the
part of an individual to live in a society governed by laws implies
acceptance of that contract and hence willingness to obey the
laws. To disobey the laws is to dishonour one's agreement. The
right thing to do (*to dikaion*) is to obey them.

It seems to me that the complete consistency of everything that
Xenophon and Plato tell us about Socrates' loyalty to the laws
makes it very difficult to believe that they are not giving us a true
picture. It is possible to argue that, in their desire to show that
Socrates was unjustifiably condemned by a democratic government, both Xenophon and Plato would naturally be inclined to
argue that he was always loyally obedient to the laws of the state,

whether this was strictly true or not. But to argue in this way is to misconstrue Socrates' loyalty to the laws in one important respect.

For Socrates' loyalty is a loyalty not only to the laws of a democratic state, but to those of non-democratic states as well. Socrates, unlike Plato, does not appear to have been very interested in constitutional problems. He is not concerned to champion the case for, say, monarchy as against democracy, or vice-versa. And his opposition to any illegality is equally vehement whether it is a democracy or a tyranny which acts illegally. The examples of his opposition given by Plato and Xenophon make this clear. And since they make clear at the same time that Socrates' championing of the principle of loyalty to the laws is not necessarily a championing of democracy, it is unlikely that Plato and Xenophon are falsely insisting on Socrates' loyalty to the laws because they wish to make him out to be a loyal democrat.

It would be wrong, however, to infer from all this that Socrates approved of *all* forms of government and that he was concerned only to advocate loyalty to the laws under *any* government. In Xenophon he makes quite clear his disapproval of tyranny. And it follows from his definition of tyranny (*Mem.* IV vi 12) that his principle of loyalty to the laws has no application in the case of tyranny. Xenophon there says that Socrates considered tyranny a government which ruled men against their will and which was *not controlled by law* but only by the whim of the ruler. He considered that all other forms of government – including monarchy, aristocracy, and democracy – followed the rule of law and enjoyed the consent of those living under them.

The association made here between consent and the rule of law is in conformity with Socrates' views in the *Crito* about the implicit contract between state and individual in a society governed by laws that the individual should be obedient to those laws. Socrates, it is clear, was more broadly tolerant of different forms of government than a modern liberal democrat. He saw no incompatibility between monarchy and consent, and did not concern himself with the question of whether an aristocracy could be fully representative of the will of the majority of the citizens. The main distinction which he seems to make is between government by law and consent and government without law and consent. Under the former type of government he thinks that it is right to be loyal to the laws.

Socrates' distinction corresponds fairly closely to the distinction between 'democracy' and 'tyranny' made by Popper in discussing Plato's theory of sovereignty.[5] 'Democracy' is a type of government 'of which we can get rid without bloodshed', i.e., where 'the social institutions provide means by which the rulers may be dismissed by the ruled'. 'Tyranny' is a government 'which the ruled cannot get rid of except by way of a successful revolution – that is to say, in most cases, not at all.'

Socrates was, I think rather more naïve than Popper in his attitude to tyranny. For he seems to have thought that the arbitrary rule of a tyrant is invariably suicidal. In Xenophon (*Mem.* III ix 12) he expresses the view that the tyrant always suffers for his indifference to the advice of others, and brings immediate destruction on himself if he puts to death wise counsellors whose policy differs from his own. But what Popper says about 'democracy' expresses admirably Socrates' attitude to non-tyrannical forms of government. He says that, in making possible the reform of institutions without using violence, 'democracy' thereby makes possible 'the use of reason in the designing of new institutions and the adjusting of old ones'.[6]

This is much more explicit, of course, than anything which we can ascribe to Socrates himself. But it is undoubtedly implicit in Socrates' attitude to government. And Popper is undoubtedly right in associating with Socrates the 'personalism' of what he calls 'democracy' in its attitudes to the education of its citizens and to political reform. The personalist attitude treats the question of 'the intellectual and moral standard of its citizens' as 'to a large degree a personal problem'. Moreover, it assumes that the problem of improving 'democratic' institutions 'is always a problem for *persons* rather than for institutions'.[7]

It is in Plato's *Apology* that Socrates expresses with the most passionate conviction his sense of the importance of his mission to serve the community, not by any direct participation in politics, but by a personal approach to individual citizens. It is God's bidding, he says (30-1), that he should serve the state by questioning and examining his fellow-citizens, stirring them from their apathy and intellectual self-satisfaction. In everything he says on this score he emphasises repeatedly the individual nature of his approach (30e, 31b, 36c). I turned aside, he says, from political offices, thinking that I would best benefit the state if I went around privately to each individual and did him what I consider to be the greatest of all services – trying to persuade him not to care for what he had but for the excellence of his moral and intellectual self, nor to care for what the state had, but for 'the state itself' (36b–c).[8] There are similar sentiments in Xenophon, and a similar emphasis on the value to the state of educating the individual in 'knowing himself' through self-criticism.[9]

We see from this the kind of political significance which Socrates ascribes to his educational activities. One reason he gives for preferring to serve the state in this way rather than through public participation in politics is the severely prudential reason that it is personally safer. 'You may be sure', he says at his trial, 'that if I had attempted to enter public life, I would have perished long ago, without any good to you or to myself. No man will ever be safe who genuinely stands up against you or against any other democracy, and tries to prevent a host of injustices and illegalities being committed in the state. The man who is to fight for justice must work in private rather than in public, if he is to keep his life even for a short time' (Plato *Apol.* 31e–32a).

This is not, of course, a mere concern for his own skin. It is a concern for the well-being of the state. Indeed, Socrates' deep conviction of the importance for this purpose of his educational mission makes him ready to lose his life rather than give up his activity. Nor should we try to interpret his loyalty to the laws as an expedient for his own safety. This loyalty again belongs to his conviction that it is not by flouting the laws of the state and not by any resort to revolution that the good of the state is advanced. His respect for government by law and consent is a genuine respect. *Within* such a government, improvement must come through personal education of the citizens.

As a political programme this Socratic ideal no doubt appears unduly sanguine, as well as unduly acquiescent in its attitude of loyalty to the laws. Its expectations are, however, more readily understandable when placed within the context of the small, close-knit community of a city-state. And Socrates is confident that there will be many more besides himself ready and able to further his ideal.[10] Moreover, his loyalty to the laws does not assume that the laws are necessarily the best laws for ensuring the happiness of the citizens. In defending his loyalty to the laws in the *Crito* he makes clear that the laws are open to 'persuasion' as to what is right and just (51b–e).

Besides claiming the right to 'persuade' the laws Socrates also claims the right of 'conscientious objection' to what the laws prescribe. He states at his trial that, if he were to be acquitted on condition that he put a stop to his philosophical activities, then he would refuse to give such an assurance. As long as life leaves him the ability to do so, he says, he will never give up his philosophical activities. He will continue to try to persuade each of the citizens to care for the excellence of his moral and intellectual self (Plato, *Apol.* 29c–e). He is ready, however, to accept whatever legal penalty is imposed as a punishment for his activities. His claim for the right of defiance is not also a claim for the right to escape the punishment of the law.

This is yet a further indication of Socrates' deep personal conviction of the rightness and the political value of his mission in life as an educator. And it helps us to appreciate more clearly his ideal that the wisest should rule. He does not think this ideal incompatible in any way with his ideal of government by law and consent, or with his claims for the rights of the individual's conscience and for the individual's right to happiness. He obviously thinks of the rule of the wisest as a type of government which ensures perfect harmony between the citizen's respect for the laws and his individual right to perfect his own good. There is, however, little of the political *theorist* about Socrates. As Popper has said, 'with his emphasis upon the human side of the political problem, he could not take much interest in institutional reform'. It was 'the immediate, the personal aspect' in which he was interested.[11] The ideal that the wisest should rule is, for Socrates, not so much one particular institutional form of government. Rather, it is the end result of an educational mission which aims to bring wisdom not only to those who will rule but to those also who will elect the rulers and themselves be ruled.

From what we have now seen of Socrates' political views it is clear how radically Socrates differs from Plato in his approach to politics. Plato, as we saw in the last chapter, rejects the individualism of Socrates' ethics. He rejects, in the end, Socrates' belief in the supreme efficacy of individual reason in ensuring rightness of moral behaviour. And he rejects Socrates' belief that education is a personal affair, of individual by individual, and that education of this kind is the only proper education to promote the well-being of society. He turns instead to schemes of state control of education. And coupling with his view that only the wise should rule the view that only the few are wise, he gives to the wise supreme authority to determine the rights of the rest. In this respect the charge that Plato 'betrayed' Socrates is entirely justified.[12]

This contrast between Socrates and Plato in their political attitudes serves to emphasise what is distinctive in Socrates' attitude. What is distinctive about it is, in the first place, its individualism. This is in keeping with the spirit of Socrates' method and of his ethics. Socrates assumes the self-sufficiency of his method as a means of attaining moral knowledge. He further assumes the sufficiency of that knowledge for attaining virtue. And, finally, he assumes 'the moral self-sufficiency of the virtuous man'.[13] No evil, he says, can come to a good man, whether in life or death (Plato *Apol.* 41d).[14]

These are all marks of the individualism of Socratic ethics. It is this individualism which leads him to oppose[15] the traditional political virtue of doing good to friends and harm to enemies. For it follows from the good man's moral self-sufficiency that the only harm that can come to him is of his own making, i.e. by committing wrong himself. And if to do harm to others is to do wrong, then to do harm to those who have done wrong to oneself is to do wrong. Hence it is to impair one's own moral good. Moreover, one's moral self-sufficiency is proof against wrong done to one by others. So that it is 'better' to be wronged by others than to do wrong to others.

A corollary of this individualism is the liberalism of Socrates' attitude to politics. He considers the moral worth of the individual to be of paramount value. Hence he considers that the individual must be free to realise his own good. That is why he insists at his trial on the right of the individual to defy the state if it prescribes what he considers to be incompatible with realising that good. For it is clear from the assumptions of his own educational mission that the right he claims for himself is a right which he claims for *any* individual. Perhaps in some respects Socrates' attitude of acquiescence towards the laws of the state may appear to be unduly tolerant. Certainly his conviction of the individual's moral self-sufficiency predisposes him to think that the individual is able to realise his moral ends under most forms and conditions of government. But he always insists on the individual's right to be free to realise his own good. And he is confident that the vigorous exercise of this right will help to create the best political conditions for realising that good.

These political views of Socrates are clearly relevant to our inquiry into Socrates' conception of the good life. For they are a reflection of what Socrates holds to be valuable in human life. In the first place Socrates values the individual as an end in himself, and hence claims the right of the individual to pursue his own good. Hence he claims further for the individual the political freedom to do this. In the second place, he believes in the efficacy of reason as a means available to the individual of determining his good; he believes, moreover, in the possibility of persuading all citizens of any particular state to realise the value of applying their reason systematically, through self-criticism, to the realisation of that end.

This yields a conception of the good life as a life of free and independent criticism and inquiry, considered as the 'best' activity for the individual's self-development. Its general tendency is, of course, to emphasise the intrinsic value of the activity of impartially searching for the truth rather than its means-to-an-end value in establishing what the good is as an ultimate value. In this respect it might seem that there is some incompatibility between, on the one hand, the liberalism and individualism of Socrates' view that each person should be free to determine and to follow his own good, and, on the other hand, his conviction that there is only one proper method to determine what the good is, and that this method will yield certainty as to what it is.

The former view, emphasising the value of free and independent criticism and inquiry, seems more in keeping with the liberal ideal of morality as an individual and, indeed, private sphere of behaviour, immune from the interference of law and state; the concern here is not to evaluate the particular moral principles which the individual has determined to be the right ones for him; it is to champion the value of the individual's right to be free and independent in determining them. The latter view, in so far as it assumes that reason can establish certain principles of moral behaviour as indubitably true, seems to be more in keeping with the view that there is a rationally sanctioned code of morality which should be accepted by everybody and which law and state should uphold.[16] This is the view systematically developed by Plato. It excludes 'private morality'.

It is very unlikely that Socrates was aware of this apparent incompatibility between his individualistic views and the authoritarianism implicit in his conviction that certainty was possible in ethics and that those who had attained it should be rulers. Certainly there is much of the philosophical liberal about Socrates. This is reflected in almost all of his political views. And it is reflected also in his conception of the good in so far as this puts a high value on the activity of free and independent criticism and inquiry. But does he consider it a sufficient specification of the good to define it in terms of this activity? Or does he rather value this activity as a means to the end of establishing what the good is? Let us now look at his views in fields outside politics, to see what indications are given there about his conception of the good which might help to resolve this problem.

C. RELIGIOUS VIEWS

In a familiar passage in Plato's *Phaedo* Socrates tells how dissatisfied he was as a young man with the theories of the natural scientists of his time. They were wrong, he thought, in explaining everything in terms of mechanical causation; they should have adopted a teleological kind of explanation.

Here is his account of his reaction to the theory of Anaxagoras (*Phaedo* 97b ff.):[17]

One day I heard someone reading an extract from what he said was a book by Anaxagoras, to the effect that it is Mind that arranges all things in order and causes all things; now there was a cause that delighted me, for I felt that in a way it was good that Mind should be the cause of everything; and I decided that if this were true Mind must do all its ordering and arranging in the fashion that is best for each individual thing. Hence if one wanted to discover the cause for anything coming into being or perishing or existing, the question to ask was how it was best for that thing to exist or to act or be acted upon. On this principle then the only thing that a man had to think about, whether in regard to himself or anything else, was what is best, what is the highest good; though of course he would also have to know what is bad, since knowledge of good involves knowledge of bad.

With these reflexions I was delighted to think I had found in Anaxagoras an instructor about the cause of things after my own heart.... I imagined that in assigning the cause of particular things and of things in general he would proceed to explain what was the individual best and the general good; and I wouldn't have sold my hopes for a fortune.

And then . . . I found the man making no use of Mind, not crediting it with any causality for setting things in order, but finding causes in things like air and aether and water and a host of other absurdities. It seemed to me that his position was like that of a man who said that all the actions of Socrates are due to his mind, and then attempted to give the cause of my several actions by saying that the reason why I am sitting here is that my body is composed of bones and sinews . . . so that when the bones move about in their sockets, the sinews, by lessening or increasing the tension, make it possible for me at this moment to bend my limbs, and that is the cause of my sitting here in this bent position.

No: to call things like that causes is quite absurd; it would be true to say that if I did not possess things like that – bones and sinews and so on – I shouldn't be able to do what I had resolved upon; but to say that I do what I do because of them – and that too when I am acting with my mind – and not because of my choice of what is best, would be to use extremely careless language. Fancy not being able to distinguish between the cause of a thing and that without which the cause would not be a cause!

This is a clear and straightforward advocacy of the superiority of teleological explanations to mechanical ones. It emphasises the need to take account of the end or purpose to be realised in all natural processes, and characterises this end as 'the highest good'. It also emphasises the directive force of Mind (*nous*) in ordering these processes and realising 'the highest good'. Thus the principle that man has a realisable good is seen as part of the comprehensive principle that everything in the world is directed in its activity to the realising of a final good end.

The first thing to consider about this account in the *Phaedo* is, of course, whether it is truly Socratic. One ground for suspicion that it is not is that, after its rejection of the notion of mechanical causation, it goes on to explain its new conception of causation in terms of the metaphysical theory of Forms (100a ff.), a theory which we have Aristotle's authority for attributing to Plato, and not to Socrates. On the other hand, it is fairly certain that Socrates was acquainted with the theories of Anaxagoras. For there is a well attested tradition that Archelaus, a pupil of Anaxagoras, was the teacher of Socrates.[18] So we may reasonably ask whether it is likely that Socrates' reaction to the theories of Anaxagoras was such as the *Phaedo* describes. The fact that the later part of the *Phaedo's* discussion of causation is non-Socratic does not make it unreasonable to ask this. For that fact does not entail that the earlier part is non-Socratic.

Aristotle does not help us here. He says (*Met.* 987b1-6) that, at the time when Socrates influenced Plato, Socrates' interests were exclusively ethical and not directed at all to the world of nature as a whole. This is quite compatible, of course, with what Aristophanes' *Clouds*, Xenophon's *Memorabilia* (IV vii 4-7) and Plato's *Phaedo* all suggest – that Socrates was well acquainted with the theories of the fifth-century physical scientists and had reflected on the value of such studies. But Aristotle does not, unfortunately, make any comment about Socrates' later lack of interest in this field.

Xenophon, however, has a good deal to say. According to Xenophon, Socrates criticised the scientists on several counts – for the futility of their assumption that it was possible to achieve definite knowledge, for the lack of practical value in their studies, and for their presumption, amounting virtually to impiety, in seeking to explain the order of the universe (*Mem.* I i 11-15; IV vii 4-6). Admittedly, Xenophon has an axe to grind. He wishes to dissociate Socrates from any interests smacking of impiety, and hence from Aristophanes' caricature of him in the *Clouds* as an impious speculator in physical science. He also wishes to emphasise the practical benefits of Socrates' teaching. However, what he attributes to Socrates here is quite in keeping with what Plato's *Apology* represents him as arguing at his trial – that Aristophanes' portrayal of him is false and that it is wrong to associate him with the kind of theory he is there associated with (*Apol.* 18b–19d; 23d–e). Taken together, these passages from Xenophon and Plato give a consistent picture of Socrates' attitude to the theories of the fifth-century scientists.

Moreover, there are passages in Xenophon in which Socrates criticises these theories, just as he criticises them in Plato's *Phaedo*, on the ground of their materialism and their mechanistic explanations. These passages also attribute to Socrates a positive preference for teleological explanations of all the phenomena hitherto explained in terms of mechanical causation. Now it is easy enough to say that all that Xenophon is doing here is borrowing from the *Phaedo*. But the fact is that Xenophon goes well beyond the *Phaedo* in describing Socrates' teleological views. Some of these views have no parallel at all in the *Phaedo*. They are interesting and important.

In the first place, Xenophon (*Mem.* I iv 4 ff.) attributes to Socrates a teleological proof of the existence of a divine architect (*dēmiourgos*) of the order of the world. Socrates' argument from design appeals especially to the intricate and consistent adaptation of means to ends in the human body and personality. The major premiss of his argument here is that whatever is adapted to serve a useful purpose is the product of intelligence, not of chance (4). If then, he argues, we look at the human body, we see that the delicate structure of the different senses is adapted to man's needs and well-being. Similarly man's upright posture, his ability to speak, his intelligence are all adapted to benefit him, since they enable him to maintain himself in all sorts of conditions and to increase his happiness (5–17). Thus man is a most striking example of intelligent design. But he is only one example. Throughout the natural world an order is maintained which is evidence of a directing intelligence (8).

Thus the structure of the whole world is the product of

intelligence and not of chance. A directing intelligence (*nous*, *phronēsis*) is manifested everywhere (17). And all this points to the existence of a divine architect (*dēmiourgos*, 7), one who orders and holds together the whole cosmos (IV iii 13), exercising in the world a form of intelligent control which is conceived as analogous to the control of the human mind over the body (I iv 17).

Within this general teleological argument for the existence of a divine architect, Socrates introduces further the thesis that the pattern of adaptation of means to ends throughout the world is of a kind which shows that it is for the sake of man that the world is designed as it is. He develops this thesis at *Mem.* IV iii 3 ff. As evidence of man's privileged position in the order of the world he mentions his enjoyment of the 'gifts' of air, food, fire, of beneficial regulation of the seasons, of the use of other animals, of finely adjusted senses and intelligence, of speech, and of foreknowledge through divination of what is to his advantage. And on the basis of this evidence for man's privileged position within the cosmic pattern of means and ends, it is argued that God has a providential care for mankind and has designed the world to serve man's well-being.

If we compare the passage quoted from the *Phaedo* with these two chapters from the *Memorabilia*, we see that the arguments of the *Memorabilia* go beyond the arguments in the *Phaedo* in two main respects. The *Phaedo* argues that the order of the physical world as a whole and the purposive behaviour of human beings in particular are more plausibly explained in terms, not of a mechanical theory of causation, but of a teleological theory which recognises the directive force of mind (*nous*) in realising a good end. From this teleological viewpoint Socrates in the *Memorabilia* develops, first, a detailed argument for theism (the now familiar argument from design), and, second, a detailed argument to show that God in his providential care for man, has designed the world to serve man's well-being.

These arguments in the *Memorabilia* have a form which is closely parallel to the form of Stoic arguments to support the notion of divine providence. Indeed, in form and detail they immediately recall the arguments used by Balbus in his exposition of Stoic theology in the second book of Cicero's *De Natura Deorum*, especially those in the latter half of the book (133 ff.). The same examples are used in each case, the same conclusions are drawn. The parallel is close enough to make it likely that the Stoics made use of the arguments of the *Memorabilia* when formulating their own theological arguments. Sextus Empiricus, in his discussion of Stoic theology (*Adv. Math.* IX 92 ff.), certainly assumes this (see especially IX 101). And he gives a good deal of attention to the question of the proper interpretation of one highly important part of the argument in the *Memorabilia* (I iv 8).

In view of this, and in view also of the absence in earlier extant literature of any clear and explicit formulation of the *Memorabilia's* theistic arguments, the further likelihood is suggested that Socrates' arguments in Xenophon are in the main original arguments, and that Socrates is therefore a thinker of some importance in the development of a philosophy of theism. For there is no doubt that the two chapters of the *Memorabilia* we are considering present a theory which appears in many ways to be an 'advanced' theory for its time. The vocabulary of its account is not the least of the marks of its advanced nature. In this respect too the affinities are with later Stoic thought rather than with earlier or contemporary thought.[19] Nor, for most of the arguments of the *Memorabilia*, is it possible to find in the pre-Stoic period, whether in the Platonic theology of the *Timaeus* and the *Laws*, or in Aristotle, arguments for theism which are at all closely parallel in general form and in detail to those of the *Memorabilia*.

It has been argued, indeed, that these arguments are so advanced for their time that their place in the *Memorabilia* can plausibly be explained only by the assumption that they are late interpolations. For example, Lincke argued that the Stoic Zeno put them where they are.[20] But as alternatives to this speculative hypothesis, let us consider the probabilities of the views *either* that the arguments can be traced, in their essentials at least, to pre-Socratic thought *or* that they can be attributed, whether wholly or in part, to Socrates.

As we have already seen, it is acknowledged in Plato's *Phaedo* that Anaxagoras' introduction into his cosmogony of the element of Mind (*nous*) as that which 'arranges all things in order and causes all things'[21] suggests at once a teleological mode of explanation. But in both Plato and Aristotle the criticism is made that Anaxagoras, after introducing Mind to start the cosmic revolution, falls back on mechanical explanations in the rest of his cosmogony and makes no further use of Mind as that which 'arranges all things in order'.[22] Clearly the criticism was prompted by the lack of any use of the notion of end (*telos*) or purpose in Anaxagoras' detailed explanations.

But in the work of Diogenes of Apollonia a genuinely teleological outlook appears for the first time. Diogenes, described by Theophrastus as 'almost the youngest' of the cosmologists of the fifth century B.C., was no doubt influenced in his views by Anaxagoras' notion of Mind. Unlike Anaxagoras, however, Diogenes emphasises the conscious purpose and design to be found in nature. He assumes that this purpose is directed to the realisation of what is 'best'; this is the kind of end which Socrates, in the *Phaedo*, says that he looked for in vain in Anaxagoras' theory of causation. Finally, Diogenes thinks that the whole material world, in as much as it is infused by such purposive intelligence, is to be considered divine.

Let us see how he expresses all this. Without intelligence, he says, it would not be possible for the basic substance of the world to be distributed in such a way that it has a measure of everything – of winter and summer and night and day and rains and winds and periods of fine weather; other things too, if one cares to study them, will be found to be disposed in the best possible way.[23] Hence he describes the basic substance of the world as 'that which has intelligence'. He identifies it with air. All men, he says, are steered by this, and it has power over everything; for this itself seems to me to be God and to reach everywhere and to dispose all things and to be in everything.[24]

We can see more clearly what Diogenes means when he says that 'all men are steered by this' if we look at his account of human sensation and thought. He explains sensation in terms of interaction between external and 'internal' air. And what is especially interesting in his account is his statement that in perception it is 'the air within' which perceives, 'being a small portion of the God'; that this is so is indicated, he argues, 'by the fact that often, when we have our mind (*nous*) on other things we neither see nor hear'.[25]

What he means by this is that the divine *nous* which is operative in the whole cosmos is operative also in the act of human perception. For this act is not explicable simply in terms of interaction between external stimuli and sense-organs; for when the *nous* is directed elsewhere perception does not occur, even though physical interaction between external stimuli and sense-organs occurs. Hence 'the small portion of the God' which perceives is intelligence (*nous*). Cicero drew this conclusion from the passage when he said that it could readily be understood from it that it is the mind (*animus*) which sees and hears, not those parts which are as it were windows of the mind.[26] It affords one example of the ways in which man is 'steered' by 'that which has intelligence'.

There are obvious affinities between Diogenes' arguments and Socrates' arguments in the *Memorabilia*. In both cases there is agreement that all things are disposed 'for the best' (*kallista*: Diogenes in DK.64 B 3, Socrates in *Mem.* I iv 13), that this is a divine disposition, and that it is exemplified in the regulation of the seasons, of night and day, and of the weather, and in the human senses and intellect (Diogenes in DK.64 A 19, B 3–5, Socrates in *Mem.* I iv 8, 13, 17; IV iii 4–9, 11).

There is some agreement also in the use of the analogy between the intelligent behaviour of the human person and the orderly processes of the cosmos. Diogenes thinks of human intelligence (*nous*) as 'a small portion of the God'. And in identifying 'that which has intelligence' with air as a cosmic principle, he was certainly influenced by the connexion between air and breathing in men and animals, the further connexion between breathing and life, and, finally, the connexion between life, sensation and thought (DK.64 B 4, B 5). This kind of connexion between air and intelligence in the human personality no doubt played its part in prompting him to adopt the theory that air, possessing 'intelligence' to order all things 'for the best', is the basic substance of the cosmos.

The analogy between human and cosmic intelligence is much more explicit in Socrates' arguments. He says (*Mem.* 1 iv 17) that, just as the human mind (*nous*) directs the body, so the intelligence that pervades everything directs all things. He argues also that the physical constituents of a man are the same, though infinitely smaller in amount, as those of the cosmos, and that it is therefore arrogant to assume that, while intelligence exists in man, the order of the world is maintained without it (1 iv 8). The argument is found also in a late dialogue of Plato, the *Philebus* (28c–30b).[27]

It is highly probable that Socrates was familiar with Diogenes' work. And in view of the affinities between Diogenes' arguments and Socrates' it is reasonable to assume that *in these respects* Diogenes' arguments had some influence on Socrates. Yet there is a good deal more in Socrates' teleological thesis than in Diogenes'. It is possible to argue, of course, that if we had all Diogenes' work, we would find a fuller and more detailed exposition of his teleological views and in all probability find there an anticipation of all Socrates' arguments. For example, it might be argued that Diogenes' serious interests in physiology[28] are likely to have led him to view the structure of the human body from the standpoint of a teleological thesis about the structure of the cosmos as a whole. And it might be argued from this that Socrates' detailed arguments (*Mem.* 1 iv 5–12) – to show that there is evidence of intelligent design in the purposive adaptation of means to ends in the structure of the human body – are in all probability taken from Diogenes.

But these speculative arguments carry little conviction. If Diogenes had indeed anticipated Socrates in the full range and direction of his teleological arguments, then it becomes quite incomprehensible that Diogenes should not be mentioned along with Anaxagoras in the account of the *Phaedo* as a teleological type of thinker. For what is said in the *Phaedo* about Anaxagoras as a possible pioneer in teleological thinking seems eminently fair in its assessment and criticisms; Aristotle has much the same criticism to make, and the extant fragments generally confirm the rightness of that criticism. So is it at all likely that Plato would at the same time be so singularly unfair as to suppress all reference to Diogenes' teleological views if Diogenes had in fact been the sort of teleologist that Socrates is in the *Memorabilia*?

It seems clear, then, from Plato's lack of reference to Diogenes[29] in the account of the *Phaedo*, that Plato cannot have thought of Diogenes as at all important as a teleological thinker. The probability is that he ranked Diogenes with Anaxagoras as a natural scientist who did recognise the mark of intelligent design in the structure of the world but who was content to rely in his detailed explanations on a mechanical notion of causation. The reason for selecting Anaxagoras rather than Diogenes for special mention as a possible pioneer in teleological thinking is presumably that Anaxagoras, unlike Diogenes, introduced into his system a dualism of mind and matter[30] which seemed to be a much more promising basis for a teleological theory than Diogenes' monism.

And if Plato was so unimpressed by Diogenes as a teleological thinker, it is likely that Socrates was similarly unimpressed and that he relied much less on Diogenes for his own teleological views than some scholars would maintain. For what is really distinctive about Socrates' arguments in the *Memorabilia* is the humanistic and moral orientation belonging to them. There is nothing of this either in Anaxagoras or in Diogenes. Diogenes does indeed speak of the direction of all things 'in the best possible way'. But there is no kind of moral connotation in this. It simply means a disposition in the most orderly or regular way, with the implication that this is in itself more admirable than a state of chaos. And there is nothing in the detail of Diogenes' cosmology or his physiological theory to suggest any sort of moral interest, or indeed to suggest anything beyond the interests of a natural scientist concerned with the mechanical explanation of natural processes.

Thus, if we look for anticipations of Socrates' arguments in the work of the fifth-century natural philosophers, we find some very general anticipation of a teleological approach, but comparatively little anticipation of either the range or the direction of Socrates' arguments. Is there anything, then, in the non-philosophical literature of the fifth century that provides any sort of parallel to Socrates' arguments?

It is clear from the tragedians that there was general recognition of a range of distinctively human abilities, skills, and advantages, which allowed man to lead a civilised life superior to that of all other animals. Sometimes these were looked on as gifts from the gods, sometimes as the results of man's own persistent endeavours in adapting himself to his environment. But there is a wide measure of agreement as to the specification of them. They are, with very little variation, the 'gifts' which Socrates appeals to (*Mem.* IV iii) in arguing for God's providential care of mankind. In Aeschylus, Sophocles, and Euripides we are given much the same list – fire, water, food and shelter, the beneficial regularity of the seasons, the use of other animals, sailing in ships, speech, thought and the power of divination (Aeschylus *P.V.* 442–506; Sophocles *Antigone* 332–75; Euripides *Supplices* 201–15). The closest parallel to Socrates' argument (*Mem.* IV iii) is the argument of Theseus in the *Supplices* passage. In arguing for the view that there is a preponderance of good over evil in the world Theseus mentions as examples of the way in which God 'orders' man's life his bestowal of just those 'gifts' which Socrates mentions (IV iii 5–6, 8, 11–12).[31]

There can be little doubt that it is on these popular examples of man's distinctive advantages that Socrates draws when he formulates his argument for God's providential care of mankind. There is, moreover, an obviously moral significance in the use made of these examples by the tragedians. Man's enjoyment of these advantages makes his life 'better' than that of other animals. And the higher the development of his advantages, the happier he is. No doubt this moral significance recommended the examples to Socrates as the basis of one of his main teleological arguments.

Having now reviewed the possible sources in fifth-century philosophical and non-philosophical literature of Socrates' teleological views, what remains in those views which is distinctively original? In the first place he puts forward, *as a theological argument*, the teleological argument from design for the existence of God as an architect (*dēmiourgos*) of the order of the world. This God is both omniscient and omnibenevolent (*Mem.* i iv 18). In the second place he puts forward, *as a moral argument*, the argument for God's providential care of mankind. For he considers that this divine providence entails an obligation (iv iii 14, 17) on the part of man to 'respect what is divine' in the order of the world and to refrain from what is impious, unjust, or disgraceful (i iv 19; iv iii 14).

In this way he dissociates from the context of theories in natural science any pointers to a teleological mode of interpretation that he finds in such theories. The dualism of mind and matter which he finds in the essentially mechanical theory of Anaxagoras is given a moral and theological interpretation. And the teleological arguments within Diogenes' monistic system become part of a theology which views the order of the world in terms of a dualism. The importance of this for Socrates is that, with his exclusively moral interests, he is able to make his teleological arguments for the existence of God a basis for justifying a moral ideal. So that his originality lies essentially in the formulation of a theology which not only introduces novel arguments for the existence of God but gives a new moral significance to such arguments of a teleological kind as he takes from others.

It seems to me plausible to claim this degree of originality for Socrates. From what we know of Xenophon it is hardly conceivable that Xenophon invented any of the arguments himself. And though the terminology of the arguments still strikes me as being in some respects rather sophisticated for the time when Xenophon was writing and rather reminiscent of Stoic terminology, I am inclined to think that this is not fatal to the acceptance of the view that Xenophon, in these parts of the *Memorabilia*, is presenting genuinely Socratic views.[32] Moreover, these views are in keeping with the convictions which are the basis of Socrates' defence of his ideals at his trial. They are in keeping with his conviction that his educational mission is a divinely appointed mission, with his conviction that man's moral aim should be to care for his soul rather than his body, and, finally, with his conviction that the good man's interests are not neglected by the gods (Plato, *Apology* 28d–31c, 41d). And if we add to Socrates' religious temperament his fondness for analogical arguments, we can see how readily inclined he would be to make use of the kind of analogy he finds between the practice of professional skills and moral behaviour, and to make it the basis of his argument for the existence of a divine architect of the order of the world.

So far we have tried to establish that in his teleological arguments for the existence of God the end or purpose which Socrates constantly has in view is the end of man's behaviour as a moral being, i.e. his goodness. But what sort of moral ideal is implied by Socrates' theology? It tells us that God 'knows best what things are good' (*Mem.* I iii 2) and that in his wisdom and benevolence he has given man the abilities and advantages which will enable him to achieve happiness. But in specifying these abilities and advantages Socrates is specifying in the main what he considers to be the principal conditions for the attainment of happiness. He is not specifying the *summum bonum* itself. His theology does, however, give some positive indications of what he considers to be the peculiar excellence of man.

We have seen that Socrates' view is that the providence of God entails an obligation on the part of man to 'respect what is divine' in the order of the world. The chief defining characteristic of God is reason or intelligence (*nous, phronēsis*). And the dualism of

the ordering intelligence of God and the material world he orders
is conceived by Socrates on the analogy of the dualism of the
human mind and body. The moral significance of this for Socrates
is that man's general obligation to 'respect what is divine' entails
that he should place a far greater value on the activities of mind
than on those of body within the dualism of his own personality.
For the relation between human and divine intelligence is such
that it entails that the human mind or *psychē* (soul) is the greatest,
the most excellent element in the human personality (*Mem.*
I iv 13). For man's *psyche* is that in him which 'partakes of the
divine' (*Mem.* IV iii 14). In his *Philebus* Plato was later to argue, on
basically the same grounds, that *nous* and *phronēsis* must be
reckoned essential ingredients of the good life (28c–30b, 64b–66b).

All this clearly adds a new dimension to our inquiry into
Socrates' conception of the good. We see that Socrates views the
question of moral goodness within the context of a dualism of soul
and body, and justifies on theological grounds his view (i) that
goodness belongs to soul rather than to body, and (ii) that it is
in virtue of the *nous* or *phronēsis* belonging to the human soul that
the highest value can be placed on its activities. In order to give
more precise definition to this moral ideal we must examine in
more detail Socrates' notion of *psychē*.

D. THE SOUL

Much has been written about the development which took place
in the Greek concept of soul in the two centuries before Socrates,[33]
and the story of these developments is, in its broad outlines, a now
familiar one. But something must be said briefly about it if we are
to appreciate Socrates' distinctive contributions to the meaning
of the concept.

Furley has remarked that 'it is typical of the development of
psychē that it comes to replace other words in more and more

contexts'.[34] In Homer it is a simple notion. It is the life which distinguishes the living person from the dead person. But in post-Homeric literature it is not long before the notion of soul is associated with various experiences and activities naturally associated with the living person.

In non-philosophical literature it is associated, from the early lyric poets onwards, with certain feelings and emotions – courage, grief, love, anger, etc.[35] In philosophical literature there are several ways in which its use is extended. Within the materialistic theories of the natural scientists its primary sense of life is retained in most cases without attempts to extend its meaning. There are, however, a few exceptional cases in which soul is associated with intellectual activities. Heraclitus is one such case.[36] But the most interesting and most explicit case is the Sophist Gorgias, in a work which is essentially a rhetorical exercise but which has some philosophical interest. The *Encomium on Helen* refers to both the emotional and the intellectual effect of persuasive argument on the soul. It says that wisdom (*sophia*) is the glory of the soul. Thus it assumes that the soul is the seat of intellectual activity as well as emotion.

Assuming that the *Encomium* is a genuine work of Gorgias, there still remains the difficulty of dating it. It probably belongs to the last quarter of the fifth century B.C., and thus suggests that the notion of associating the soul with intellectual activity was by then at least sufficiently acceptable in use to allow it to figure prominently in a rhetorical exercise.[37]

Diogenes of Apollonia appears to reflect in his work this new tendency to associate soul with intellect. We noted earlier his association of air with intelligence. And though he refers to soul (*psychē*) and intelligence (*noēsis*) separately, and is clearly not *identifying* soul with mind, yet the link he makes between air and intelligence is the more easily forged because he finds it possible to use *psychē* as his middle term. Moreover, it is clear that in his view the material substance of *psychē* is air, which is 'that which has intelligence' (DK.64 B 5). So the activity of *noēsis* can be included within the activities of soul.

Diogenes' work illustrates one further extension of the application of *psychē* in pre-Socratic thought. It is the connecting of the notion of *psychē* as life and breath in the human being with the life and motion belonging to all the processes of the physical world. This cosmic significance attached to soul is already apparent in Anaximenes.[38] When it appears later in Diogenes there is added to its cosmic significance as a principle of life and motion the notion of intelligence. This marks the culmination of developments in the notion of soul within the materialistic tradition of pre-Socratic thinking.[39]

Outside this tradition there is one important development to be noted. It concerns the nature of the *psychē* which survives the death of a man. In Homer the soul survives merely as a ghost-like shade. Any thought of survival after death was naturally associated with soul, since it was the soul, as the breath of life, which deserted the body at death. But a deeper significance was given to the notion of the soul's survival by the Orphics and Pythagoreans.

This new significance is already apparent in Pythagoras' doctrine of the transmigration of souls. In a well known fragment preserved by Diogenes Laertius (VIII 36), Xenophanes tells how Pythagoras, passing by when a puppy was being beaten, took pity on it and ordered the beating to be stopped, since 'this is really the soul of a man who was my friend; I recognised it as I heard it cry out'. What is implied by this is the survival of the *personal* soul. And this idea of the retention of personality from one life to another is associated with the idea of 'punishment in the body' and with the further idea of 'purifying' the soul in the hope of escaping further incarnation. The Orphics spoke of the body as the prison or as the tomb of the soul. Plato refers to their belief that the incarnate soul is suffering the punishment of sin, and that the body is a prison in which the soul is incarcerated (*Crat.* 400c; cf. *Men.* 81a–e, *Rep.* 364e–365a).

In this way a moral significance is attached to the behaviour of the soul. But there is little reliable evidence to show that the idea of 'purifying' one's soul was associated with anything other than ritualistic procedures. It seems fairly clear that the Pythagoreans associated purification with music and poetry.[40] But whether they associated it further with scientific or philosophic studies it is impossible to say. We do know that they broadened the basis of mathematics to give it the form of a 'liberal education'.[41] But this in itself does not imply any link between mathematical studies and purification.

What is remarkable about these religious ideas of the soul and its immortality is that they stand right outside the naturalistic theories which represent the main tradition of pre-Socratic thought. When the Pythagoreans speculated about the nature of the soul within the context of their scientific and cosmological theory they advanced theories about it quite incompatible with their religious views of its nature.[42] Empedocles, who was much influenced by these religious ideas, seems to have held some naturalistic view of the nature of soul within his general physical theory.[43] But when he expresses his religious views in the *Purifications* he speaks of that which survives bodily death as the *daimōn*.[44]

Thus the position in the latter half of the fifth century B.C. was that the concept of *psychē*, while it had been examined and developed within the materialistic cosmologies of the pre-Socratics, had attracted no serious philosophical attention as a non-naturalistic concept. As such it remained a rather vague notion within a body of religious ideas which linked it with the notions of personal survival and of purification but which did not attempt any kind of theoretical justification for any of its views.

Socrates was no doubt familiar with these developments. His religious views suggest that he was familiar with the work of Diogenes, and hence that he was familiar with the notions of giving to soul a cosmic significance and of associating it with intelligence and reason. And the dualism in his religious views also makes it highly probable that he was not only familiar with, but attracted by Orphic and Pythagorean notions of the soul. It is interesting to note in this connexion that, in his caricature of Socrates' activities in the *Clouds*, Aristophanes describes Socrates' school as a 'reflectory (*phrontisterion*) of wise souls' (94). The unusual use here of 'soul' for 'person' is a possible reflection of Pythagorean ideas about the *personal* survival of the soul.

It would be wrong, however, to look for any extensive influence of Pythagorean religious views on the thought of Socrates. There is nothing at all in the ancient tradition about Socrates which links him with the Pythagoreans, though much is said about the link between Plato and the Pythagoreans. And I agree with Ross that 'this must in all probability come in the long run from a tradition in the early Academy that it was not Socrates that formed the link between Plato and the Pythagoreans; and I see no reason to doubt that Plato's interest in these doctrines was largely due to his association with the Pythagoreans of Magna Graecia several years after Socrates' death.'[45]

All that we can plausibly grant, then, in respect of Pythagorean influence on Socrates, is influence of a very general kind in turning Socrates' thought to the idea of associating moral behaviour with the soul and also of associating the personality of a man with his soul. And in view of the intellectualism of his ethics Socrates would naturally be inclined further to associate intellectual activities with the soul and would therefore be attracted by the new tendency to extend the range of meaning of soul in that direction.

We must now consider, in relation to these influences, how much originality there is in the Socratic concept of soul. We must look in particular for any developments in the analysis of it as a non-naturalistic entity, for hitherto, as we have noted, very little attention had been given to such analysis.

We have already seen that in Xenophon's *Memorabilia* Socrates says that the soul is the most excellent part of a man, and that it is that in him which 'partakes of the divine'. Elsewhere in the *Memorabilia* he emphasises the dualism of soul and body in a way which implies that for him the soul is incorporeal. Unlike the body, the soul is invisible (I iv 9; IV iii 14). It directs the body (I iv 9, 13–14). And it is because it is the seat of reason and intelligence (*nous, phronēsis*) that it is able to do this; for it is in the soul alone that intelligence resides (I ii 53; I iv 17). Moreover, a person's *moral* behaviour is the behaviour of his soul, not of his body. The 'performances that belong properly to the soul' are 'doing that which we ought to do' and 'refraining from that from which we ought to refrain' (I iv 19). In Plato's *Crito* (47e–48a) it is to the soul that Socrates implicitly refers when he distinguishes from the body 'that thing in us, whatever it is, which has to do with right or wrong'.

This dualism of soul and body is specially associated by Socrates in the *Memorabilia* with the notion of self-control or self-discipline (*sōphrosunē, enkrateia*). Self-control is, indeed, the key moral concept for Socrates in the *Memorabilia*. And he thinks of it essentially as a control of the soul over the body, just as he thinks of the lack of it as the result of a successful assault on the soul by the persuasive influences of *bodily* pleasures. Thus he says that 'pleasures that have been generated in the same body with the soul persuade the soul to abandon self-control and to gratify the pleasures and the body as soon as possible' (I ii 23). He speaks also of 'being a slave' to pleasures (I v 5), and says that every man ought to consider self-control to be the foundation of all virtue, and to establish it in his soul above all else (I v 4; cf. II i 20). It is in these terms that Xenophon claims that Socrates was superior to 'the pleasures of the body' (I v 6).

It is clear that this *moral* interpretation of the dualism of soul and body is for Socrates an additional ground for thinking that the soul, already characterised as invisible and divine, is a distinct part of a man, an entity different in kind from the body. What he says about self-control in terms of relations between body and soul constitutes in fact a new psychological argument in support of his dualistic views. And he bases on it a moral ideal, which prescribes 'care of the soul' (I ii 4) rather than of the body as the aim of the good man.

In Plato's *Apology* the ideal of 'care of the soul' mentioned by Xenophon is given an important place by Socrates in the defence of his activities at his trial. A measure of the importance which he gives to it is already indicated in Xenophon. For there it becomes apparent that Socrates uses the phrase 'the care of the soul' as equivalent both to 'the care of goodness' and to 'the care of oneself' (I ii 2 with I ii 4 and I ii 8). The same is true of what he says in Plato's *Apology* (29d–30b with 31b, 36c and 41e). He is saying that in caring for the good of one's soul one is caring for one's true self.

This identification of soul with self is the conclusion of an argument in *Alcibiades* I, a dialogue which cannot with any confidence be attributed to Plato but which presents a Socrates whose views can be matched in virtually all respects with the views of the Socrates of Xenophon and of Plato's early dialogues. One cannot confidently claim that the formal shape of its argument for the identification of soul with self is genuinely Socratic. But I think it fairly represents the sort of considerations which are at the back of what is a genuinely Socratic conclusion.

Here is the argument. If we ask what 'caring for one's self' means (127e), we must first ask what the self is (128e). It is clear that the user of anything is in all cases different from the thing used. The person who uses his hands, eyes, and so on is therefore different from the hands and eyes he uses. More generally, a man is different from the body as a whole which he *uses*. It is his soul which uses his body. And since man must be soul or body or both together, and since, as *user* of his body, he cannot be body or body and soul together, it follows that 'either man is nothing at all, or, if he is something, he turns out to be nothing else than soul'. The soul, then, is man (129b–130c).

This is just the view that Plato represents Socrates as taking at the end of the *Phaedo* (115c–d). Crito asks Socrates in what way he and his friends should bury him. 'In whatever way you like', says Socrates, 'if you can catch me'. The real Socrates, he points out, is the one at present taking part in discussion with them and marshalling the various arguments, not the one soon to be seen as a corpse. And he associates this view with the confident hope that this self will survive the death of the body.

Are we able to accept as Socratic this belief in personal immortality attributed to him by Plato in the *Phaedo*? It is certainly
a belief in keeping with the conception of soul as a divine, invisible, and non-bodily entity which constitutes the true self.
For to think of the soul in that way is to think of it as something
which is not subject to the physical laws which govern the 'coming
to be' and 'passing away' of the material body; at the same time
the 'true self' is dissociated from what is subject to those laws.
Hence it is possible to think of one's self as not subject to death in
the sense in which the body is subject to death.

Socrates seems to have been content to hope, on the basis of
these convictions, that his soul would in fact survive the death of
his body, without pretending to have any certainty that this would
be the case. This is the impression given by Plato's account in the
Apology of his concluding remarks at his trial. 'Death', says
Socrates, 'must be one of two things – either to have no consciousness at all of anything whatever, or else, as some say, to be a kind
of change and migration of the soul from this world to another'
(40c). And he adds that he would be ready 'to die many deaths'
if the latter alternative was true (41a).

It is essentially the Socratic concept of soul which Plato attempts
to justify in the *Phaedo*, on much more elaborate theoretical
grounds than Socrates appears to have done. Plato himself soon
abandoned the *Phaedo's* severely intellectual conception of the soul.
For, once he had committed himself to the identification of the
self with the substantial soul, Plato increasingly felt it necessary
to widen his conception of soul beyond its intellectual activities.
For there were non-intellectual activities which he found it
impossible to dissociate from his notion of a person. Yet the
Phaedo, while it allows us to see the difficulty of giving a satisfactory
theoretical justification of Socrates' concept of soul, is at the same
time the finest of tributes to its philosophical influence and
importance.[46]

One thing which the *Phaedo* emphasises, and which Socrates
himself emphasises, is the practical *moral* importance of under-

o

standing the nature of the soul and its relation to the body. His
ideal of 'caring for the soul' is a moral ideal. It is essentially the
same ideal which we found to be implied by his religious views.
But what Socrates says in moral contexts about the distinction between soul and body gives to this ideal a little further
specification.

For one thing, it gives practical significance to Socrates' view
of the self-sufficiency of the morally good man who 'cares for his
soul'. Like Socrates himself, such a man will be content with
small material means and will have iron self-control in respect
of all bodily pleasures (Xen. *Mem.* I ii 4–5, 14, 19–23). For to
become a slave to bodily pleasures is to 'corrupt' the soul (*Mem.*
I v 3–5). With regard to food, drink, dress, or sexual pleasures,
Socrates' view is that these are things of the body and that only a
very small regard for them is compatible with the moral self-
sufficiency which belongs to the soul (*Mem.* II i).

This is, of course, the attitude of the *Phaedo*. It is also the attitude
of the Socrates of Plato's *Apology*. Do not care, he says there, for
one's body or for money and fame and reputation, but for truth
and wisdom and making one's soul as good as it can be (29d–30b).
And Socrates himself practised what he preached. He took no
money for his instruction, and lived in poverty (19d–e, 23b–c,
31b–c).

This dualism of soul and body in Socrates' thought provides,
then, a further context within which to appreciate his conception
of the good life. It is from this viewpoint that many of the personal
habits of Socrates caricatured by Aristophanes in the *Clouds* can
best be appreciated. Negatively, the good life is a life of frugality
and abstinence as far as material possessions and the indulgence of
desires classed as bodily are concerned. Positively, it is a life
devoted to making oneself 'as wise as possible'. For to 'care for
one's soul' is to care for making oneself 'as wise as possible' (Xen.
Mem. I ii 55). And self-control, the key moral notion of the
Memorabilia, is equated by Socrates, in conformity with his thesis
that virtue is knowledge, with 'wisdom' (*sophia*) (*Mem.* III ix 4).

E. CONCLUSION

Although we are now able to form a fairly definite picture of the Socratic good, a major problem still remains. Reason and intelligence (*nous, phronēsis*), says Socrates, belong essentially and exclusively to the soul. So to 'care for one's soul' is to care above all else for the full exercise and development of one's reason and intelligence. And his own example of a life devoted to free and independent criticism and inquiry in ethics seems to be intended by Socrates to be an example of what he means by exercising one's reason and intelligence to the full. But is it a sufficient definition of the good, in Socrates' view? For it still seems legitimate to ask what we asked at the end of our examination of his political views, i.e. whether the life of unremitting and unfettered criticism and analysis, as practised by Socrates, sufficiently specifies the good life, or whether Socrates values such activity as a means of establishing what is the good.

In favour of the latter alternative it can be argued that Socrates' search for general definitions in ethics is presented by Xenophon, Plato and Aristotle as at once an example of independent criticism and analysis and a method of discovering what is the good. In favour of the former alternative much more can, I think, be said. When we looked at Socrates' political views as a guide to his moral ideals we saw that those views placed a special value on the life of free and independent criticism and inquiry. This moral estimate is entirely consistent with Socrates' speculative views in theology and psychology. For both his theology and his psychology are designed to justify the claim that supreme moral value belongs to the intellectual activities of the human soul.

Moreover, if we accept the account in Plato's *Apology* as the clearest and most direct statement of Socrates' moral convictions, we find him saying there that the post which God has assigned to him is that of 'living a life of philosophy, examining himself and others' (28e). 'The greatest of all human goods', he says later, 'is to discuss virtue and the other things you hear me arguing about in my examination of myself and others. An unexamined life is not worth living' (38a). And in his concluding remarks he expresses the hope, not only that his soul will survive the death of his body, but also that in the after-life his soul will continue its activity of critical examination. For he is convinced that even then the 'greatest thing of all' for the soul will be 'to go on examining and questioning the men of that world in the same way as the men of this, to see who is wise among them, and who thinks he is, but is not. To converse with men there and associate with them and examine them would be happiness unspeakable' (41b–c).

Thus the life dedicated to philosophy is, for Socrates, the good life. And by this he means a life dedicated to the critical analysis which he himself has practised for the best part of his life. Clearly, in the *Apology*, he thinks of this activity as constituting in itself the good, and not as a means to attaining goodness by establishing what the good is.

In the light of this, Socrates' thesis that virtue is knowledge gains an additional significance. In this thesis knowledge means knowledge of what is the good. And the thesis means, as we have seen, that this knowledge is both a necessary and a sufficient condition of being good and thus of doing what is good. We have now examined Socrates' own conception of what is the good, and we have concluded that it was Socrates' conviction that the good is sufficiently defined in terms of the philosophical activity of 'examining oneself and others' by the method of critical analysis which he himself practised. Moreover, his educational mission assumes that this specification of the good is one which is possible for others to realise for themselves to be true. Thus it is, for Socrates, an objective specification which is valid as a standard of goodness for all men.

The thesis that virtue is knowledge becomes, therefore, the thesis that knowing that the good is specifiable in the above terms is a necessary and sufficient condition of practising what is thus specified as good. For I can see no good reason for not assuming that Socrates' convictions as regards the specification of the good were considered by him to amount to knowledge of the good, and, further, that he saw his educational mission as one which aimed to realise this knowledge in others.

The thesis that all the virtues are one also takes on a new descriptive significance when it is considered in the light of Socrates' specification of the good. This specification expresses the deep moral convictions which are reflected, as we saw, in Socrates' views about the soul and in his political and religious views. Against the background of these views it is easy to appreciate that the Socratic moral ideal of wholehearted dedication to the life of philosophy embraces and unifies all the accepted Greek virtues. It is a pious life, for to practise philosophy is to care for that element in man which 'partakes of the divine'. It is a courageous life, for it is a life which in all circumstances confidently and unswervingly follows the path of goodness, even at the risk of death. It is a life of self-control, for the conviction of its goodness is always strong enough to ensure that the care of the soul takes precedence over the care of the body. And it is a just life. For it is a life which respects the right of the individual to pursue his good and shrinks from doing any wrong to others, even if others have done wrong to oneself.

It remains true, of course, that Socrates' definition of what is the good is not a formal conclusion reached by his method of analysis. It is the expression of a moral conviction which the practice of his method of analysis itself helped to create. Socrates himself did not, it is clear, analyse as fully as he might have done the grounds of his conviction that his definition of the good was certainly true. Since all his speculative thinking in ethics led him to what seemed a certain conclusion about the good, he was perhaps able to persuade himself not only that the life of philosophy was the good life but also that the practise of it served to substantiate the truth of that view.

Aristotle saw clearly enough the limitations of Socrates'

analysis. He is ready to accept Socrates' moral paradoxes except for their complete denial that there are cases of weakness of will. But he realises the need to analyse more fully the notion of moral knowledge, and is severely critical of Socrates' intellectualism in so far as it seemed to him to assume that the use of the intellect was sufficient to establish what is the good and thereby to ensure that the good is done. His criticism is valuable for the proper understanding of Socratic ethics. For quite apart from its contribution to the problem of weakness of will, its analysis of the nature of moral knowledge reveals just those features of moral knowledge which belong to Socrates' own convictions as to what the good is but which Socrates himself seems not to have recognised.

In this chapter we have examined Socrates' conception of the good, and we have argued that Socrates' moral paradoxes gain a new significance from their association with his conception of what is the good. Socrates does not think of them merely as the results of an analysis of the Greeks' moral language, nor does he consider them to be true only in an analytic sense. He considers them to be true also as practical principles of moral behaviour. For he considers that any person who is brought to share his own conviction as to what is the good will invariably practise that good. That he is able to think of his moral paradoxes as practical truths in this way is a measure of the intensity of his conviction that the good life is the life of philosophy.

This Socratic moral ideal had a considerable influence on all subsequent Greek ethics, the more so because of Socrates' remarkable personal example in remaining faithful to it in practice, even though he had to die for it. Both Plato and Aristotle were inspired by Socrates to find in the life of philosophy their ideal of human goodness. Yet his influence on their thought was much more than an influence in shaping their particular moral ideals. He determined in large part the direction of their philosophical inquiries. And in his method they found a pattern for fruitful philosophical analysis.

Notes

NOTES TO CHAPTER 1

1. For a valuable collection and review of all Aristotle's testimony on Socrates see Th. Deman, *Le témoignage d'Aristote sur Socrate* (Paris, 1942).

2. In the *Phaedo* (96a ff.) Plato ascribes to the youth of Socrates an enthusiasm for natural science; and the caricature of Socrates' activities in Aristophanes' *Clouds* (423 B.C.) appears to be some confirmation that Socrates did at one time devote some attention to scientific studies (but see Plato's *Apology* 18b–19d, 23d–24a). Aristotle, Plato and Xenophon are, however, in agreement that it was in his inquiries in ethics that Socrates showed his originality as a philosopher.

3. See also *De Part. An.* 642a24–31.

4. See especially *An. Post.* 90b23, *De An.* 402b25, *Met.* 1034a31.

5. *Soph. El.* 183b6–8. Cf. *Rhet.* 1419a8–12.

6. In *Arist. Met.* p. 741, 7–20 (Hayduck).

7. For dialectic see especially *Top.* 100a27 ff.; *Soph. El.* 165b.

8. *An. Post.* 100b3; *E.N.* 1098b3, 1139b29.

9. *E.N.* 1094b12–1095b8, 1098a21–1098b8, 1104a1–11, 1145b2–7, 1179a16–22.

10. See Ernst Kapp, *Greek Foundations of Traditional Logic* (New York, 1942), ch. i.

11. Sir W. D. Ross (*Aristotle's Metaphysics* (1924), vol. i, p. 173) suggests that Aristotle is here 'speaking with some irony' and using 'dialectic' 'in its less favourable sense'. I find this suggestion very implausible.

12. For an excellent discussion of Socratic definition in Plato's early dialogues see Richard Robinson, *Plato's Earlier Dialectic* (2nd ed., Oxford, 1953), ch. v.

13. It is possible that Plato is here adding extra refinement to Socrates' method by putting into formal dress what he recognised to be an important feature of it. Xenophon refers in a less formal way to this feature of it in one of his rare general remarks about Socrates' method (*Mem.* IV vi 13–14).

14. Robinson, *Plato's Earlier Dialectic*, p. 57.

15. For references see Sir W. D. Ross's *Aristotle* (4th ed., 1945), p. 40 n. 1, and Kapp, *Greek Foundations*, pp. 75–7.

16. See especially, for references and discussion, W. A. Heidel, *Hippocratic Medicine* (New York, Columbia University Press, 1941), pp. 71 ff.

17. E.g., H. Maier, *Sokrates, sein Werk und seine geschichtliche Stellung* (Tübingen, 1913), pp. 180 ff.

18. In his introduction to *Plato's Protagoras* (New York, Liberal Arts Press Inc., 1956), p. xxxviii. I disagree with Vlastos on several points in his account here of Socrates' method. But it is a most valuable and stimulating account (pp. xxvi–li).

19. Ibid. p. xxxvii.

20. Ibid.

21. Diogenes Laertius (VIII 57) says that Aristotle in his *Sophist* calls Zeno the inventor of dialectic. Richard Robinson (*Earlier Dialectic*, pp. 91–2) is right, I think, in taking Aristotle's remark to be a reference to Zeno's originality in inventing the *reductio ad absurdum* type of argument rather than in making question and answer an essential feature of his method. 'Undoubtedly', he says, 'Zeno's book was the first explicit and striking appearance of reduction to impossibility in the western world. No doubt it was reflection on this element in dialectic that led Aristotle in his dialogue to say that Zeno discovered dialectic, instead of the more accurate statement that Zeno discovered reduction to impossibility.'

22. For Plato's references to the eristical arguments of the Sophists see *Euthydemus* 272b and *passim*, *Lysis* 211b, 216a; *Meno* 75c–d, 80e, 81d; *Theaetetus* 154d; *Sophist* 225b–c.

23. Doubts have been raised about the ascription of a book of this title to Protagoras on the ground that 'eristic' was a term of such disparagement that no one is likely to have called himself an eristic, and hence that no one is likely to have written a book which implies by its title that its author is an expert in eristic (Gomperz, *Greek Thinkers* (5th ed., 1964), vol. i (trans. Magnus), pp. 590–1. Cf. Maier, *Sokrates*, pp. 200–1). It is true that in Plato eristic is disparagingly contrasted with dialectic. But I see no implausibility in assuming an earlier and less opprobrious use of the word.

24. H. Diels, *Die Fragmente der Vorsokratiker*, 5th and later editions (Berlin 1934–54), ed. W. Kranz, section 90. This work will subsequently be referred to as DK., followed by relevant section and passage numbers.

25. DK. 82 B 11.

26. See Aristotle, *Soph. El.* 175b.

27. *Theaet.* 188c–189b; *Soph.* 240d–241b, 260b–263d.

28. *Theaet.* 167a–b.

29. On these points see Plato, *Prot.* 317c, 349a.

30. At 275c the boy Cleinias is said to be quite accustomed to answer questions in argument. This is an indication of the popularity of question-and-answer argument in Athens at this time (about 420 B.C.). But Cleinias is so young that no inference can be made as to how long this type of argument had been popular.

31. See A. E. Taylor, *Plato, the Man and his Work* (5th ed., 1948), pp. 90–1.

32. *Journal of Philology*, vol. iv (1872), p. 299; quoted by E. S. Thompson in his excellent discussion of Eristic in his edition of the *Meno* (Macmillan, 1901), pp. 272–85.

33. *Journal of Philology*, vol. iv, p. 300.

34. Ibid. p. 298.

35. See also *Theaet.* 167d–168c.

36. As in the first of the *Dissoi Logoi* (*peri agatho kai kako*): DK.90.

37. See the remarks of Aristotle (*Rhet.* 1402a23 ff.), Cicero (*Brutus* 12, 46), and Seneca (*Ep.* 88, 43).

38. See the references in DK.80 A 24–8.

39. Plato, *Crat.* 384b, *Charm.* 163d, *Lach.* 197d, *Euthyd.* 277e, *Prot.* 337a–c, 339e–342a, 358a–e.

40. See Richard Robinson's excellent discussion of the meaning of 'dialectic', *Plato's Earlier Dialectic*, ch. vi.

41. For further references see Thompson's note on *Meno* 83d in *Meno* (Macmillan, 1901), p. 134.

42. On Protagoras see DK.80 A 14, 19, 21a; B 1. On Gorgias see DK.82 B 3.

43. Op. cit. p. 15.

44. For this, see especially Vlastos, *Plato's Protagoras*, pp. xxvi–vii.

45. Noted by Robinson, op. cit. p. 39.

46. In his *Plato: Gorgias* (Oxford, 1959), p. 314.

47. Cf. *Sophist* 230b–e, with Robinson's remarks on it (op. cit. pp. 12–13).

48. Robinson, op. cit. p. 111, with references.

49. Ibid. p. 113. Cf. Thompson's note on *Meno* 86e (op. cit. p. 146).

50. In his paper 'Back to the Pre-Socratics' (*Proceedings of the Aristotelian Society*, New Series, vol. lxi (1959), pp. 1–24); reprinted with an appendix in his *Conjectures and Refutations* (Routledge, 1963), pp. 136–65.

51. Sir David Ross, *Proceedings of the Classical Association*, vol. xxx, p. 21. He takes the references in Xenophon to be confirmation that 'the method of hypotheses' was 'a piece of Socratic technique'. 'And if it be said that Xenophon got it out of Plato we may well ask why Xenophon, when he left out so much that is in Plato (including the whole ideal theory) put this in.'

52. We noted in an earlier section, in discussing the importance attached by Socrates to general definition, how Socrates always leads the argument away from the particularity of a problem towards the general principles in terms of which the problem can be fully understood, and the solution of it found. E.g., at *Laches* 189e he says that, in order to understand what form of training or exercise is best for a young man, it is necessary to go back to a first principle in the form of a definition of virtue. Similarly Xenophon (*Mem.* IV vi 13–15) says that when anyone asserted something, 'without proof', of a particular thing or person (e.g. that this or that person was braver or a better citizen than another), Socrates used to 'lead back' the argument to a basic principle, assuming that if we can define what courage is, or what goodness is for a citizen, then we can

demonstrate that this person is braver or better than that. Xenophon calls the principle a 'hypothesis' in its sense of starting-point or basis for demonstration. It is Socrates' habit of searching analysis of all such principles which makes them in his eyes merely provisional 'hypotheses'.

53. Robinson (op. cit. pp. 97–8) notes a similar opposition between 'assuming' and 'positing' something at *Charmides* 172c.

54. *Apol.* 23c.

55. *Rep.* 539b.

56. *Meno* 80a–b.

57. *Apol.* 30e.

58. Compare with the *Protagoras*'s remarks the familiar passage in Plato's *Phaedrus* (274b–278b) where Plato argues for the superiority of the spoken word, especially as employed in the art of dialectic, over the written word.

59. Op. cit. p. 16.

60. Ibid.

61. See also *Ph.* 78d, *Rep.* 534d.

62. Op. cit. p. 8.

63. By Leonard Nelson in *Socratic Method and Critical Philosophy* (New Haven, Yale Univ. Press, 1949), p. 17.

64. *Plato's Protagoras*, pp. xxx–xxxi. The other following quotations from Vlastos are from these two pages.

65. See Dodds, op. cit. pp. 16–30, for an excellent discussion of the dating of the *Gorgias* and of the differences between the *Gorgias* and other early dialogues.

66. *Plato: Gorgias*, p. 341.

67. *E.E.* 1246b35–6.

68. Of dialogues earlier than the *Meno*, only the *Gorgias* shows signs of a change in Plato's attitude to Socrates' method, as we noted earlier. And it is surely not merely a coincidence that also in the *Gorgias* there first emerge positive convictions and distinctions which, from the *Meno* onwards, become part of Plato's metaphysical theory. For the details see Dodds, op. cit. pp. 20–1.

NOTES TO CHAPTER 2

1. So E. R. Dodds, who says of Callicles that, 'like Nietzsche', he 'transvalues' terms for such accepted virtues as justice, courage, and wisdom (*Plato: Gorgias* (Oxford, 1959), p. 15).

2. See especially *Gorgias* 452c ff., and *Philebus* 58a–b.

3. Plato, *Theaetetus* 166d–167d.

4. For Gorgias' scepticism, see DK.82 B 3.

5. Cf. K. R. Popper's remarks in *The Open Society and its Enemies*, vol. i, (4th ed., 1962), pp. 70–1. One cannot, of course, assume that Socrates' attitude towards Callicles' 'natural right' thesis in Plato's *Gorgias* is, without qualifica-

tion, the genuinely Socratic attitude. But what we can fairly attribute to Socrates as the main features of his rationalism in ethics allows us to accept Socrates' attitude towards Callicles in the *Gorgias* as broadly representative of his reaction to that type of sophistic doctrine.

6. This point deserves some emphasis in view of arguments that Socrates conceived moral knowledge as a skill or technique, a form of 'knowing how' rather than of 'knowing that'. See especially John Gould's *The Development of Plato's Ethics* (Cambridge, 1955), chs i and ii. For a criticism of Gould's thesis, see my review in *Philosophy*, vol. xxxi (1956), pp. 376–9, and the review by Gregory Vlastos in *Philosophical Review*, lxvi (1957), pp. 226–32. For a more detailed examination see J. M. Rist, *Eros and Psyche: Studies in Plato, Plotinus, and Origen* (1964), pp. 115–42.

7. The translation is B. Jowett's, *The Dialogues of Plato* (4th ed., Oxford, 1953), vol. i, pp. 178–86, except that at 355d I have used 'worthy' instead of 'has the value' and 'is worth' instead of 'is equivalent to'.

8. 352d7. See the similar language at 355a8, 358c1, and 358d4.

9. Socrates says that this is sufficient for the purpose of the demonstration he has to give in answer to the question raised earlier. The question raised earlier (353a) was the question of what the experience popularly called 'being overcome by pleasure' should properly be called, assuming the popular description to be false.

10. The ambiguity of the Greek verb *hamartanein* (to err) is to be noted here. In one sense it means to go wrong. Thus those who 'go wrong' in their choice of pleasures and pains get wrong their assessment of the amounts of pleasure and pain consequent on different possible courses of action. In another sense it means to do what is morally wrong. Socrates appears to take advantage of this ambiguity when he says (357d–e) that 'the erring act which is done without knowledge is done in ignorance'. Looking back to what has just been said about 'going wrong' in choosing pleasures and pains, the 'erring act' (the Greek passive participle of *hamartanein* is used here) is the 'miscalculated' act. Looking forward to the conclusion of the argument, the 'erring act' is the 'wrongly done' act. The ambiguity thus plays its part in the transition in the argument from miscalculation to wrongdoing and to the conclusion that morally wrong actions are 'miscalculated' actions.

11. *Amathia* is Plato's favourite term for moral 'ignorance' (see also *Apol.* 29b *Gorg.* 477b ff., *Rep.* 444a–e, *Tim.* 86b, *Soph.* 229c, *Laws* 689a–e). In using it, the positive sense of 'being mistaken' or 'falsely believing' is always uppermost in his mind.

12. Socrates formulates the popular view, at 355b, as the view that sometimes a person 'is unwilling' to do what he knows to be good because he is overcome by the pleasures of the moment. But it is true to say that in explicating his own view he does not introduce the notion of desire until 358c.

13. D. Gallop notes this ambiguity in his discussion of *Protagoras* 351b ff. in *Phronesis*, vol. ix (1964), pp. 117–29. He asserts (p. 128) that in this ambiguity

'the nerve of the Socratic Paradox is laid bare'. Cf. G. Santas's remarks in *Philosophical Review*, lxxv (1966), p. 17, n. 21.

14. To be compared with Socrates' language at 356b–c is Aristotle's language when describing the form of practical moral reasoning. At 1147a26–31 in the *Nicomachean Ethics* he says that there is a necessity belonging to the conclusion of the practical syllogism as well as to that of the scientific syllogism. The difference between the two is that in the case of the scientific syllogism 'the soul must necessarily affirm the conclusion', whereas in the case of the practical syllogism 'the soul must necessarily act immediately'. Thus 'if everything sweet ought to be tasted, and this here is a particular sweet thing, then the man who is able and is not prevented must necessarily at the same time do this' (i.e. taste this sweet thing). Here Aristotle speaks of what it is necessary (*anankê*) to do. But in an alternative formulation, in *De Motu Animalium* 701a7 ff., he uses for *anankê* the verbal adjective form used by Socrates in the *Protagoras*. He emphasises in this passage not only that a person *must* do what the major and minor premisses in conjunction prescribe (the condition being that what the major prescribes is in conformity with his desire – *orexis*), but that the conclusion of the syllogism *is* an action. Aristotle's use here of the verbal adjective has essentially the same force as I think Socrates' use has in *Protagoras* 356b–c.

15. Gallop in *Phronesis* (1964), p. 117.

16. Grote, in an interesting note in his *Plato and the other companions of Socrates* (1865), vol. ii, pp. 87–8, reviews the opinions of nineteenth-century German scholars who argued for the un-Socratic or un-Platonic character of the hedonism of the *Protagoras*. For more recent arguments see Vlastos's note in his introduction to Ostwald's translation of the *Protagoras* (Bobbs-Merrill, 1956), p. xl, and my review of Voigtländer's *Die Lust und das Gute bei Platon* in *Classical Review*, N.S., vol. xii (1962), pp. 38–40.

17. See Grote (op. cit. vol. ii, p. 78). He asserts that 'the substantial identity of Good with Pleasure, of Evil with Pain, was the doctrine of the historical Sokrates as declared in Xenophon's *Memorabilia*'. He appeals to *Mem.* I vi 8.

18. *Classical Quarterly*, vol. xxii (1928), p. 42.

19. This is the suggestion of Gregory Vlastos, *Plato's Protagoras*, p. xli. His suggestion is put forward as a solution to the puzzle of the discrepancy between Socrates' apparent declaration of hedonism in the *Protagoras* and 'the general temper or method of Socratic ethics'. He does not consider the puzzle within the *Protagoras* itself of Socrates' reservations at 357b. And his view is, not that Plato failed to make sufficiently explicit the distinction between the two theses, but that Socrates 'most likely' *confused* the two theses. 'It would be perfectly possible', he says, 'for Socrates to have failed to understand a matter which no one had as yet explained or even properly investigated.'

20. For Aristotle's discussion of Plato's stipulation, see *E.N.* III iv.

21. *In Remp.* ed. Kroll, ii 355; quoted by A. E. Taylor in his comments on *Timaeus* 87b4–6 (*A Commentary on Plato's Timaeus* (1928), p. 619).

22. Cf. Xenophon, *Mem.* III ix 4. And for the sense of *dunata* see Aristotle, *E.N.* 1111b20–6, 1112b24–7.

23. So Olympiodorus, commenting on *Gorgias* 509c (*In Plat. Gorg. Comm,* ed. Norvin, p. 175).

24. The *Gorgias*, though it considers wrongdoing to be punishable, at least has a remediable conception of punishment (477e–479e). This does not justify the inference that Plato is already thinking that the 'involuntary' nature of wrongdoing makes it non-blameworthy. But it is an interesting pointer to later developments in his views about this. Cf. Dodds, *Plato: Gorgias,* pp. 254–5.

25. Cf. Taylor, *A Commentary,* pp. 612–14. His argument that 'the determinist who speaks is not Plato, nor Socrates, but Timaeus' is quite implausible.

26. Taylor, *Plato, The Man and his Work* (5th ed., 1948), p. 235.

27. *Plato's Protagoras,* p. xliii.

28. *E.N.* 1142b33. The text here allows an alternative interpretation to the one I have given. Aristotle says that 'if it is characteristic of men of practical wisdom to have deliberated well, excellence in deliberation will be correctness in respect of what is conducive to the end of which practical wisdom (*phronêsis*) is the true apprehension'. It seems more natural to take 'the end' as the antecedent to the relative, rather than 'what is conducive to the end', but the latter is a possible interpretation. The problem of interpretation here does not, I think, have the importance sometimes attached to it. *Phronêsis,* in Aristotle's view, 'truly apprehends' both the means to the end and the end itself. *Phronêsis* does not, it should be added, *determine* what the end is. The end is determined by the agent's character. But it is a characteristic of *phronêsis,* belonging as it does only to those of good character, that it 'truly apprehends' the end.

29. 1246b36. Aristotle is here using *phronêsis* in the same sense of 'practical wisdom' as he gives to it in the passages of the *Nicomachean Ethics* we have referred to. This is the usual sense of *phronêsis* in Aristotle's ethical works. Sometimes he uses it in a general Platonic sense which allows it to be associated with *theōria,* 'speculative wisdom' rather than 'practical wisdom'. This usage is found in both the *Eudemian* and the *Nicomachean Ethics.* It cannot be made, as Jaeger tried to make it (*Aristotle,* English translation by R. Robinson (2nd ed., 1934), pp. 235 ff.), the basis of an argument about the order of composition of the two works. See *E.E.* 1214a33, 1215b3, 1216a20; *E.N.* 1096b24, 1153a21, cf. 1172b30.

30. Burnet argues that this was the contention of some of 'Plato's followers'. See his note in *The Ethics of Aristotle* (1900), p. 294.

31. The text of 1146b2 is obviously corrupt. But the later passage (1151a11 ff.) makes perfectly clear Aristotle's view.

32. See *Met.* 1025b–1026a.

33. *Met.* 993b20. Cf. *E.N.* 1094a3–5.

34. Compare the language used at *E.E.* 1216b11–15 in describing the aim of the theoretical sciences.

35. For a discussion of the difficulties both in text and argument, see H. Jackson in *Journal of Philology*, xxxii (1913), pp. 170 ff. Gauthier and Jolif, *L'Éthique à Nicomache* (Louvain, 1958), vol. ii, pp. 474–7, offer an interpretation of the passage.

36. For the meaning of technical knowledge (*technê*) and its scientific status see especially *Met.* 980b27 ff.

37. Aristotle's view is that theoretical knowledge is a higher and more valuable form of knowledge than practical knowledge. See *Met.* 1026a, 1064b; *E.N.* 1141a20 ff., 1145a6–11.

38. One would have expected Aristotle to say that a good disposition or excellence in the 'irrational element' (i.e. a disposition to put medicine to good uses) cannot convert ignorance of medicine to knowledge and thus enable the good aims to be realised. No doubt he means to imply that this is so.

39. *Plato's Earlier Dialectic* (2nd ed., 1953), p. 14. Robinson, like Aristotle, finds Socrates' contention unconvincing. 'To many persons the Socratic elenchus would seem a most unsuitable instrument for moral education. They would argue that such logic-chopping cannot be followed by most persons, does not command respect, and at best improves only the agility of the mind while leaving the character untouched. Socrates was certainly a unique reformer if he hoped to make men virtuous by logic.'

40. He is, however, anxious to insist that the theoretical arguments (*logoi*) which he uses to substantiate his definition of the good are not the ultimate criterion for its correctness. The arguments must be seen to be in harmony with 'the opinions of the wise', and, more fundamentally, with 'the facts of life'. If there is no such harmony, then the arguments are mere theory (*E.N.* 1179a16–22). Aristotle does nothing, however, to bring his theoretical arguments at *E.N.* x vii–viii to the test of agreement with 'the facts of life'. His remarks are an ineffectual attempt to dissociate his method of establishing a definition of the good from the sort of 'theorizing' in ethics for which he criticises Socrates.

41. Vlastos, op. cit. p. xliv, commenting on Socrates' thesis that virtue is knowledge.

42. For a discussion of the relation between the *Laches* and the *Protagoras* in respect of their analyses of courage, see A. J. Festugière in *Bulletin de correspondance hellénique*, lxxi (1946), pp. 179–86.

43. On Socrates' 'discovery of a new kind of courage', see Vlastos, op. cit. p. xlviii.

44. See also *E.N.* 1147a7–9.

NOTES TO CHAPTER 3

1. Zeller, *Die Philosophie der Griechen*, ii 1 (5th ed., 1922), p. 152, suggests, on the basis of this evidence, that Socrates appears to hold that there is no

absolute, but only a relative good, no standard for good and bad except advantage and disadvantage.

2. *Encyclopaedia Britannica*, 11th ed., vol. 25, p. 36.

3. Ibid.

4. *The Open Society and its Enemies*, vol. i (4th ed., 1962), p. 131.

5. Ibid. pp. 124–5.

6. Ibid. p. 126.

7. Ibid. p. 127. Popper's italics.

8. The distinction between 'what the state has' and 'the state itself' is meant to distinguish material prosperity and military power from the moral well-being of the state. Compare Plato's remarks at *Gorgias* 519a, where he complains of fifth-century statesmen that 'they have filled the state with harbours and docks and walls and revenues and trash of that kind, to the neglect of moderation and justice'.

9. See *Mem.* III vi–vii; IV i–ii.

10. Plato *Apol.* 39c–d.

11. Op. cit. p. 191.

12. Popper, op. cit. p. 194. 'Plato, his most gifted disciple, was soon to prove the least faithful. He betrayed Socrates, just as his uncles had done. . . . Plato tried to implicate Socrates in his grandiose attempt to construct the theory of the arrested society; and he had no difficulty in succeeding, for Socrates was dead.'

13. Popper, op. cit. p. 301.

14. Cf. Plato *Republic* 387d–e.

15. Plato *Crito* 49a–e. There are places in Xenophon's *Memorabilia* where Socrates appears to approve of the traditional virtue of benefiting friends and harming enemies (II iii 14; II vi 35). But I do not think, in view of their contexts, that they can be pressed as expressions of Socrates' serious views. See Burnet's note on *Crito* 49b10 (*Plato's Euthyphro, Apology of Socrates, and Crito* (Oxford, 1924), pp. 198–9).

16. Cf. Professor H. L. A. Hart's remarks ('Immorality and Treason', *The Listener*, 30 July 1959) in criticism of the view that the function of human law should be not merely to provide men with the opportunity for leading a good life, but to see that they actually *do* lead it.

17. Hackforth's translation (*Plato's Phaedo* (1955), pp. 124–6).

18. See DK.60 A 1–3, A 5, A 7.

19. I am thinking of the use, in the context of an argument for theism, of such words and phrases as *sophou tinos dēmiourgou kai philozōou technēmati* (I iv 7), *pronoia* and *pronoētikos* (I iv 6 and IV iii 7), *ho ton holon kosmon syntattōn* and *noēmatos anamartētōs hypēretounta* (IV iii 13). Compare with this sort of language the Latin of Cicero's account of Stoic theology at *D.N.D.* II 113 ff., and the Greek of Diogenes' summary of Zeno's views (Diogenes Laertius VII, 147–8).

20. K. Lincke, *Neue Jahrbücher für Klassische Altertum*, xvii (1906), pp. 673–91.

21. *Phaedo* 97c. For Anaxagoras' own statement on this see DK.59 B 12: 'And

whatever things were going to be, and whatever things existed that are not now, and all things that now exist and whatever shall exist – Mind arranged them all, including the revolution now followed by the stars, the sun and moon, and the air and the aether which are being separated off.'

22. DK.59 A 47.

23. DK.64 B 3.

24. DK.64 B 5.

25. Theophrastus, *De sensu*, 42.

26. Cic. *Tusc. Disp.* I 20, 46; noted by W. K. C. Guthrie in *A History of Greek Philosophy*, vol. ii (1962), p. 374, n. 2.

27. W. Jaeger, in *The Theology of the Early Greek Philosophers* (Oxford, 1947), p. 246, n. 91, argued that the *Philebus* passage 'proved' that at *Mem.* I iv 8 Xenophon is 'making his Socrates pronounce doctrines of pre-Socratic origin', since 'in the *Philebus* Socrates expressly names some earlier philosophers of nature as his source for this argument to which he subscribes'. Socrates does not in fact name any one when he refers at 28d,e to 'earlier philosophers'. And all he ascribes to them is the general thesis that mind (*nous*) is ruler over everything. When he says at 30d that the argument from human to cosmic intelligence gives support to that general thesis he implies that 'earlier philosophers' who subscribed to the general thesis did not have this particular argument. No doubt he is thinking of Anaxagoras, and possibly also of Diogenes, as the philosophers who maintained that mind is ruler over everything.

28. See DK.64 B 6.

29. A possible implicit reference is at *Phaedo* 96b, where Socrates mentions the theory that it is air that we think with as a theory he encountered in his early inquiries in natural science. The context of the reference shows that it is not considered to be a theory with any teleological implications.

30. See especially DK.59 A 41, with the remarks of G. S. Kirk and J. E. Raven, *The Presocratic Philosophers* (Cambridge, 1957), p. 375.

31. The most probable date for the *Supplices* is about 420 B.C. Possibly Euripides is adapting to his own purposes at 201–15 what he had heard from Socrates.

32. For the terminology see note 19 above. Cf. Jaeger's comments (op. cit. pp. 244–5, n. 76) on the use by Xenophon's Socrates at *Mem.* I iv 7 of the term *dēmiourgos*. Jaeger thinks that 'it is perfectly believable that this term had been used by previous philosophers who, like Diogenes, interpreted nature in this teleological way'.

33. See especially D. J. Furley, *The Early History of the Concept of Soul* (University of London, Institute of Classical Studies, Bulletin no. 3 (1956), pp. 1–18), with references there to the most important recent literature on the subject.

34. Ibid. p. 6.

35. E.g., Pindar, *Pythian* I 47; *Nemean* 9, 32: Aeschylus, *Persae* 840: Sophocles, *O.C.* 498; *Phil.* 1013; fr. 101: Euripides, *Hippolytus* 504, 526, 1006; Herodotus III 14, V 124; Thucydides II 40 3.

36. DK.22 B 45, 107, 117, 118.

37. See also Euripides, *Orestes* 1180, and Antiphon, *De Caede Herodis* 93.

38. DK.13 A 2.

39. In most important respects it is, of course, the theory of the Greek atomists which marks the culmination of this tradition of thought, and their views on the soul are perhaps, for that reason, worth mentioning here. Democritus associated the soul with life and also with sensation. As Aristotle says (*De An.* 403b25–8), sensation is one of the two chief characteristics in which that which has soul is thought to differ from that which has not. Democritus' view was that the soul is concerned with what is perceptible, whereas the mind (*nous*) is concerned with 'truth'. A condition of correctness of thought was, however, that the mixture of atoms constituting the soul should be a 'harmonious' one (DK.68 A 113, A 135, sec. 58). Democritus follows the general practice of pre-Socratic scientists in not allotting to the soul itself intellectual activities. Even at the end of the fifth century the idea of allotting intellectual activity to the soul was an unconventional one.

40. DK.58 D 1. The authorities for this are Aristoxenus and Iamblichus.

41. DK.14, 6a.

42. Aristotle *De An.* 404a, 407b with Plato *Phaedo* 86b–d.

43. Aristotle *De An.* 408a.

44. DK.31 B 115.

45. *Proceedings of the Classical Association*, vol. xxx (1933), p. 22.

46. In my account of Socrates' conception of the soul, as well as of his religious views, I have leaned rather heavily on Xenophon's *Memorabilia*. It might be argued that Xenophon is taking the essential parts of his own account of these matters from Plato, and especially from the *Phaedo*, and that his testimony therefore has no independent worth. But we have seen that in his account of Socrates' religious views Xenophon goes well beyond what he could have got from the *Phaedo*. And his remarks about the soul and the notion of 'caring for the soul' are made in contexts which distinguish his account quite clearly from any account which is simply a literal borrowing from the *Phaedo*. Even in the very fragmentary remains of the Socratic dialogues of Aeschines of Sphettus we find some reflection of Socrates' notion of 'caring for oneself' and of his religious views (*Aeschinis Socratici Reliquiae*, ed. Krauss: *Alcibiades*, fr. 1, lines 49–64).

Indexes

I. GENERAL INDEX

II. INDEX OF PASSAGES IN ARISTOTLE, PLATO AND XENOPHON

4   426DAL
BR
1\96 6432-70